# Modern Italy

*Modern Italy* is an introduction to contemporary Italian politics and to the development of public policy in Italy. The book provides an exhaustive account of how Italy's political institutions have developed since 1945, and of how they now function. By providing a clear description and a convincing explanation of political change in Italy, Paul Furlong places the current upheaval in Italian politics in its historical context, analysing the practical results of the policy-making process in key policy areas.

The book illuminates the Italian case by applying a comparative framework throughout. Contrary to received opinion, the author argues, Italian politics should not be treated as the exception to the European rule. Furlong shifts away from the traditional focus of Italian political studies – the machinations of party politics – to examine how Italy's constitutional and administrative structures have contributed to the climate of political instability.

**Paul Furlong** is Senior Lecturer in the Department of Political Science and International Studies at the University of Birmingham.

# Modern Italy

Representation and reform

Paul Furlong

London and New York

First published 1994
by Routledge
11 New Fetter Lane, London EC4P 4EE

Simultaneously published in the USA and Canada
by Routledge
29 West 35th Street, New York, NY 10001

© 1994 Paul Furlong

Typeset in Baskerville by Megaron, Cardiff, Wales

Printed and bound in Great Britain by T. J. Press (Padstow) Ltd, Padstow,
Cornwall

Printed on acid-free paper

*British Library Cataloguing in Publication Data*

A catalogue record for this book is available from the British Library

*Library of Congress Cataloguing in Publication Data has been applied for*

ISBN 0–415–01564–2     ISBN 0–415–01565–0(pbk)

# Contents

# Figures and Maps

**FIGURES**

The conflict/dependency/exchange model – Italian variant:

**MAPS**

# Tables

# Series editor's preface

The making and implementation of public policy is where government impacts most directly on the lives of individuals and policy choices dominate political debate. It is the 'business' of government. The academic study of public policy has become firmly established as an area of wide interest in the social sciences and a component of most politics degrees.

Viewing politics through the lens of public policy offers a distinctive interpretation of many aspects of the political process. The problems of representing popular preferences, filtering technical information, normative evaluation of options and delivery of services through a bureaucracy are all involved. Each country approaches these problems in distinctive ways but in each case the solutions, or failures, illuminate the distribution of power within the polity.

The intention of this series is to offer advanced studies of public policy-making in leading countries. The target is second- and third-year undergraduates and readers with a general interest in the country. Authors have been asked to address a common set of concerns, but to interpret them in the light of an overall assessment of the politics of the country concerned. Since each author is a recognised country specialist, the series embodies analyses of public policy, but also a portfolio of distinctive interpretations of national political systems.

Books in this series, therefore, operate at two levels. First, as free-standing national studies; second, as a basis for comparative studies. Each book takes an approach that considers the historical evolution of the state, the machinery of government, the form of economic policy and one or two policy case studies. This is intended to provide a minimum basis for comparability and a potential for study within courses on comparative politics or even comparative policy studies.

To launch the series with a study of Italian public policy-making is most appropriate. Italy is one of the most important and least researched countries of Europe and Paul Furlong's book can claim to be the only text to deal comprehensively with the complexities of policy-making in modern Italy. He has risen to the challenge with verve and creativity. His study is based on a deep knowledge of Italian politics. It contains perceptive analysis and original research and it gives the series a flying start. Dr Furlong's arguments about Italian pluralism, the problem of representation and the limits to Italian 'exceptionalism' offer illumination in a period of exceptional turmoil in Italian public life. His analysis of the policy framework and policies in practice will provide a foundation and, one hopes, an inspiration for further studies.

Stephen Wilks
Exeter

# Preface

When I first began this book, I had a clear idea of what was required, and I was confident it could be written quickly. I was disabused of these preconceptions rather painfully, as what had started life with pretensions to description and analysis of Italian public policy-making came up hard against my own inadequacies and the many empirical and theoretical gaps in the available research. But as I was drawn into the subject, I became increasingly dissatisfied with the conventional ways of understanding Italian politics, and this among other things gave me the intellectual momentum to proceed despite the difficulties. Conventional analyses have tended to treat Italy as an exception to our understanding of Western European politics. This partly reflects the generalised failure of comparative politics over recent years, and partly a pervasive if discreet sense of professional territoriality. There is a tendency for country specialists to acknowledge the worth of comparative frameworks, and in the next breath to plead that their specific interest does not fit the general model and has to be understood as a special case. I do not claim immunity from this, but I have attempted in this book to show how Italy does share common features and how common terms can reasonably be applied. At the same time, both the scope of the available material and loyalty to the specifics of the case require one to consider in detail the way in which Italy's recent history has affected its path through political and economic development.

The interactions between these dichotomies, between the common and the particular, the modern and the historical, are essential for proper political explanation. Those who are most interested in the general explanation may wish to pay particular attention to chapters 1, 7 and 10. These set out the terms and attempt to analyse policy-making in ways which associate Italy with other Western European countries. The remaining chapters provide the historical specificity, explain how the political institutions operate, and apply the terms and the models to some specific sectors. The work as a whole assumes no previous knowledge of Italian politics or history on the part of the reader, and should be accessible to second- or third-year English-speaking undergraduates. The analysis aims to explain Italian policy processes through the 1980s. More recent events are referred to in chapters 1 to 9 only when essential for the general argument. The work would be incomplete without some description of the party-political and governmental developments of the period 1990 to 1992, and these are described in the final chapter. Whenever possible, text notes refer to appropriate English-language works as well as to Italian and other sources. English place-names are given instead of Italian if they are in common use.

Any work of this kind involves its author in more debts than it is possible to acknowledge here. Some, however, must be singled out. The idea for the book came originally from the series editor, Stephen Wilks of the University of Exeter. He has borne the delays and rewritings with patience and good humour, and I am grateful to him for his help and encouragement. Though it may come as a surprise to them, some of my colleagues at Hull have stimulated me to work harder to get to the bottom of these matters, and wittingly or unwittingly have put in front of me ideas and arguments with which I no doubt should have been familiar but was not. In this respect I particularly want to thank Andrew Cox, Ed Page, and Noel O'Sullivan for their critical support. In Rome, very many people have helped – indeed the work would have been impossible without the generosity of friends there. It is a pleasure to be able to acknowledge especially, with affection and gratitude, the support of Fabio Parenti, and of Fulco Lanchester, Renato Sebastiani, Marinella Ferrarotto, Massimo Troisi and Antonio and Rachel Bartolino. I gained much from wide-ranging conversations with Paolo Sylos-Labini, whose belief in a better Italy has been a powerful antidote to prevailing cynicisms. Much of the research on Parliament on which chapter 6 is based was supported by a research fellowship from the Nuffield foundation, whose support is gratefully acknowledged. For their help particularly in the preparation of the maps, I also wish to thank Professor Mike Turner, of the Department of Economic and Social History, University of Hull, and Dr Rod Souter, Longcroft School, Beverley.

Finally, and most important, I want to thank my wife Wissit and my children for all their help. They have put up with the long and sometimes uncomfortable gestation of this book steadfastly and cheerfully, and have contributed more than can possibly be described. I certainly could not have done it without them. This book is for my family. It is a collective enterprise, not an individual one. I am responsible for the errors that remain.

Paul Furlong
University of Birmingham

# Key to Maps

| REGION | PROVINCE | CONSTITUENCY | REGION | PROVINCE | CONSTITUENCY |
|---|---|---|---|---|---|
| Piedmont | 1. Turin | I | Marche | 51. Pesaro | XVII |
| | 2. Vercelli | I | | 52. Ancona | XVII |
| | 3. Novara | I | | 53. Macerata | XVII |
| | 4. Cuneo | II | | 54. Ascoli Piceno | XVII |
| | 5. Asti | II | | | |
| | 6. Alessandria | II | Umbria | 55. Perugia | XVIII |
| | | | | 56. Terni | XVIII |
| Valle d'Aosta | 7. Valle d'Aosta | XXXI | Lazio | 57. Viterbo | XIX |
| | | | | 58. Rieti | XVIII |
| | | | | 59. Rome | XIX |
| Liguria | 8. Imperia | III | | 60. Latina | XIX |
| | 9. Savona | III | | 61. Frosinone | XIX |
| | 10. Genova | III | | | |
| | 11. La Spezia | III | Abruzzi | 62. Teramo | XX |
| | | | | 63. Pescara | XX |
| Lombardy | 12. Varese | V | | 64. L'Aquila | XX |
| | 13. Como | V | | 63. Chieti | XX |
| | 14. Sondrio | V | | | |
| | 15. Milan | IV | Molise | 66. Isernia | XXI |
| | 16. Bergamo | VI | | 67. Campobasso | XXI |
| | 17. Brescia | VI | | | |
| | 18. Pavia | IV | Campania | 68. Caserta | XXII |
| | 19. Cremona | VII | | 69. Benevento | XXIII |
| | 20. Mantova | VII | | 70. Naples | XXII |
| | | | | 71. Avellino | XXIII |
| Trentino – A.A. | 21. Bolzano | VIII | | 72. Salerno | XXIII |
| | 22. Trent | VIII | | | |
| | | | Puglia | 73. Foggia | XXIV |
| Veneto | 23. Belluno | XI | | 74. Bari | XXIV |
| | 24. Verona | IX | | 75. Taranto | XXV |
| | 25. Vicenza | IX | | 76. Brindisi | XXV |
| | 26. Treviso | X | | 77. Lecce | XXV |
| | 27. Padua | IX | | | |
| | 28. Venice | X | Basilicata | 78. Potenza | XXVI |
| | 29. Rovigo | IX | | 79. Matera | XXVI |
| | | | | | |
| Friuli V.G. | 30. Pordenone | XI | Calabria | 80. Cosenza | XXVII |
| | 31. Udine | XI | | 81. Catanzaro | XXVII |
| | 32. Gorizia | XI | | 82. Reggio Calabria | XXVII |
| | | | | | |
| Trieste | 33. Trieste | XXXII | Sicily | 83. Trapani | XXIX |
| | | | | 84. Palermo | XXIX |
| Emilia-Romagna | 34. Piacenza | XIII | | 85. Messina | XXVIII |
| | 35. Parma | XIII | | 86. Agrigento | XXIX |
| | 36. Reggio Emilia | XIII | | 87. Caltanisetta | XXIX |
| | 37. Modena | XIII | | 88. Enna | XXVIII |
| | 38. Bologna | XII | | 89. Catania | XXVIII |
| | 39. Ferrara | XII | | 90. Ragusa | XXVIII |
| | 40. Ravenna | XII | | 91. Siracusa | XXVIII |
| | 41. Forlì | XII | | | |
| | | | Sardinia | 92. Sassari | XXX |
| Tuscany | 42. Massa Canara | XV | | 93. Nuoro | XXX |
| | 43. Lucca | XV | | 94. Oristano | XXX |
| | 44. Pistoia | XIV | | 95. Cagliari | XXX |
| | 45. Florence | XIV | | | |
| | 46. Liverno | XV | | | |
| | 47. Pisa | XV | | | |
| | 48. Arezzo | XVI | | | |
| | 49. Siena | XVI | | | |
| | 50. Grosseto | XVI | | | |

Map 1 Italy – regions, 1992

*Map 2* Italy – provinces, 1992
*Note* Key on p. xiv

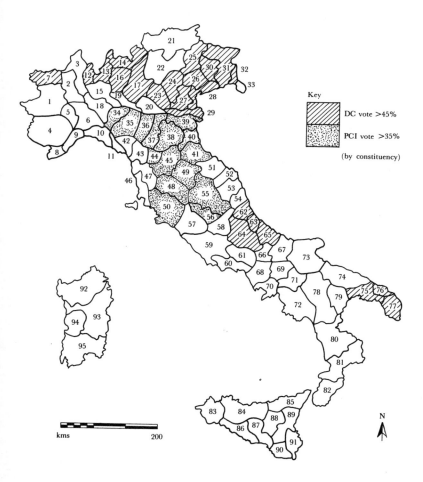

Key

DC vote >45%

PCI vote >35%

(by constituency)

N

kms                    200

*Map 3* 1963 elections – DC and PCI heartlands
   *Note* Key on p. xiv

# Chapter 1

# Introduction
## Issues and explanations in Italian policy

'When is the government going to fall, and is the system stable?'
Usually phrased more diplomatically, these tend to be the main
concerns of the foreign policy communities of the developed world,
not only about the world's problem cases but also, more privately,
about one another. Whatever is the case about other countries, it is
striking how much and how overtly these questions have dominated
studies of Italian politics, with rather more pertinence than might be so
for some of Italy's neighbours and for many beyond the foreign
policy communities. Underlying them is a quest for the holy grail of
Italian politics, the efficient secret which sustains the system in the
face of government instability and apparently endemic political
conflict.

This book does not pretend to be able to answer these dominant
questions directly. This is a study of how public policy is made in
Italy, and about the practical results of these processes in some key
policy areas. Nevertheless, the picture which it builds up may assist
readers in answering the dominant questions, and perhaps even in
questioning the terms of the questions. The structure of the work
assumes that the reader will not necessarily be familiar either with
modern Italian politics or with its historical and cultural background.
This chapter therefore begins by discussing the various ways in which
Italian politics is commonly analysed and then introduces the main
arguments of the book. The chapters which immediately follow
describe the historical development of the Italian state, its constitutional and administrative structure, and the operations of the
political parties. The second section of the book provides an explanatory framework and develops the arguments with particular reference
to specific areas of policy.

## EXPLANATIONS OF ITALIAN POLITICS – AN OVERVIEW

Italian political studies have been characterised for some time by a broad consensus about certain hypotheses, or perhaps better about certain overall impressions. There is a striking degree of agreement on several generalisations: political parties are central to the political system, public opinion holds politicians in low esteem, public administration is widely regarded as inefficient and difficult to reform, and the Italian economy, broadly speaking and with appropriate qualifications, is rather more successful than might be expected from the above description. It is the parties which constitute the new political Italy, and the new politics is held to be a constraint on the newer economics. Is this a satisfactory way of looking at the problem, and how else can we analyse the relationship between the two?

Because the political parties tend to be regarded as necessary evils, the interaction between the political sphere and the buoyant civil society has tended to be viewed in almost wholly negative terms, and has been dominated by the current explanations of the way the parties develop and interact. The term 'civil society' in this context refers to the groups and institutions, including the local organisations of political parties, which organise and articulate societal interests and values. It is used to identify the ways in which societies structure their interests and ideas prior to and distinct from state organisations. The term therefore enables us to identify political activity without necessarily including any reference to the state but without treating society as a collection of atomised individuals.[1]

From the 1960s until the mid-1980s, the most popular explanations attributed the ailments of the Italian political system typically to 'political lag'.[2] This term referred to the persistence of anachronistic political processes in a modern economy – the anachronisms being the extremist political parties, the influence of organised religion, and the inefficiency of the traditional state structures. In this view, politics in Italy is constrained, slow to respond to socio-economic change, because of the shape of the party-political system laid down in the late 1940s, because of the reliance on clientelism, and because of the difficulties the parties have in reforming the state structures. One formulation of this, which emphasises the continuities with the previous regimes, argues that the compromise and clientelism of the old Liberal state (1860–1922) adapted to the demands of mass politics by developing a more modern but still stultifying and wasteful policy immobilism. Immobilism in this context is the term used to refer to the incapacity of the Liberal state to respond to changing international and domestic pressures because of extensive reciprocal veto powers within the restricted governing elites. Clientelism refers to the use of state resources of various kinds to develop relatively long-term personal electoral support.

The state can only circumvent the new immobilism, runs the conventional argument, by allowing sub-governments to form. Sub-governments therefore represent in this argument the dynamic modern organisation given a tacit or even explicit leave to direct development in specific sectors or regions – examples would be the *Cassa* for southern development, *Federconsorzi* and *Coldiretti* for agriculture, IRI and ENI in the heavy industrial sector supporting the non-profitable infrastructure and labour market requirements of manufacturing industry. Some of these cases will be discussed in detail in the later chapters. Another example would be the state-supported pension and health insurance schemes, dominated by INAM, the fund for private employees.

The political lag approach is not necessarily misleading, but suffers from the limitation that it places the burden of explanation on the parties and treats them almost as independent variables, responding to societal changes in specific ways but unaffected by their own changing relationship with the state. It also treats clientelism and immobilism as unfortunate empirical phenomena not as functional parts of the system, and neglects the independent scope of the institutions themselves. The idea that in some way clientelism and modern economic development might be interdependent through the political system cannot be readily accommodated in an explanation which begins by ascribing wholly negative effects to the one and generally positive consequences to the other.

It also became clear that the term immobilism was insufficiently precise to explain the full range of policy, particularly since it seemed to suggest misleadingly a complete lack of major change. But there certainly has been change. For example, in the four sectors. referred to above, the *Cassa* and *Federconsorzi* have been dissolved, and INAM's functions have been radically reformed. Only the state participation system retains significant independent authority (after some privatisation). But while as we shall see the debate over party politics gave way to a more complex analysis of the voter–party relationship, the 'political lag' view impressed itself on the elites as a more continuous explanation for the repeated failures of the policy side of the political system.

In the 1970s, the first major efforts at studying how policy actually worked concentrated on the national and local uses of power by the parties – the concern being to identify the means by which the political parties could (to use one of the fashionable terms of the period) 'occupy the state'.[3] When the Communists supported the governing coalition in 1976, there was a widespread expectation that the new alliance could develop new uses for the instruments of office. The failure of that experience, the reversion to a five-party coalition in 1979 and the recession of the early 1980s reinforced interest in institutional reform, again within the context of the failure of the political system to keep pace with the needs of the economy.

The 1980s were characterised by an unprecedented degree of concern for institutional reform. This failed to produce lasting agreement over how to cope with new or radically altered con-formations of interest intermediation in society at large. Underlying the disagreement over particular policy there was consensus at least about the need for major institutional reform, but the prescriptions differ over principle. The debates on the issue of institutional reform are revealing for their assumptions at least, if not for their empirical basis. That they issued eventually into the almost desperate search for reform in the 1990s makes them even more pertinent.

Underlying them are three differing views of how the system works. The most popular view among the political elites themselves, more of a bundle of serious anxieties than a problem with an explanation, uses the term 'ungovernability' to refer to the difficulties of the political system.[4] Implicitly this view acknowledges both the importance of the parties and the difficulty of reforming them. It turns attention towards the dysfunctions of the institutions, particularly of Parliament. Though there are some extended and more academic versions of the argument, the ungovernability syndrome is most influentially described in the pages of the newspapers close to the DC (the Christian Democrats) and the other governing parties. Here particular emphasis is placed on the capacity of irresponsible parliamentary opposition to dilute or to negate the efforts of beleaguered governments. The main concern of the DC, reflected in part in the agenda of the reform debate, is to restore their own control over the position of Prime Minister and if possible to enhance the stability of the office, but without funda-mentally altering the way in which policy is made; this strategy would seek to increase the capacity of the DC to integrate a wider range of interests and to give civil society a secure capable interlocutor in government.

An influential part of the radical right shares the concern over 'ungovernability', and places considerable emphasis on institutional reform, with the aim of enhancing the executive arm at the expense of all organised political groupings – hence their concern has been to promote the reform of Parliamentary procedure and rather more generically the reform of Public Administration. Some of their leaders such as the industrialist Carlo De Benedetti identified 'corporative pressures' at the root of the difficulties.[5] Another version of this is to describe the existing system as 'consociational.' These phrases are code for 'clientelist practice', but they also cover what the Right take to be excessive involvement of the trade unions in policy-making – the activities of the unions are thus unsympathetically associated by the Right with party-based patronage. The success of Italy's economy in recovering from the recession of the early 1980s (when Italy managed growth rates of over 3 per cent per year from 1985 to 1989) is used by them as evidence of what Italy's potential could be if only its government matched the efficiency and drive of the private sector. A variant of this, associated with the DC leader Mario Segni, concentrates on the need for electoral reform with the explicit aim of reducing the number of parties and producing strong governments.

An indication of the influence of the ungovernability argument in the early 1980s was the establishment of the Bozzi Commission, a joint commission of both chambers of Parliament to investigate the institutional deficiencies of the system and to make proposals for reform. There was sufficient concern for the high-powered membership to spend twelve months in deliberation. But it was symptomatic of the lack of pressure to reach agreement that when the Bozzi Commission reported in January 1985 there were six separate minority reports dissenting in whole or in part from the conclusions, written by the six groups representing non-governmental parties, including a substantial minority report by the Communist group, which criticised the majority report for concentrating exclusively on the rapidity and certainty of decision-making in Parliament.[6] Even within the majority report there was a wide variety of proposals added by individual members and small groups, including nine different reforms of the electoral system. There was finally a degree of agreement over electoral reform favouring the introduction of a system rather similar to the West German, but the Commission report was unable to do more than pass this on to Parliament as worthy of further debate. Despite this effort, typical of the style of Parliamentary proposals, to include the entire range of available opinion, there were obvious disagreements of principle, limited but sharp. In the event, the Bozzi Commission split into two separate positions, not three, since the DC adopted without undue resistance a view representing an uneven compromise with the radical Right. The majority view of the Commission emphasised the need to concentrate power in the hands of the executive by increasing the authority of the Prime Minister within the Cabinet, and by giving the government greater control over the Parliamentary timetable and procedures. This had the support of all the governing parties, including the Socialists. It would not be unduly cynical to argue that this apparent unity among the governing parties was strongly conditioned by scepticism about the capacity of any government to make such reforms work under existing constitutional and political arrangements. The majority report of the Bozzi Commission stands as an example of the verbal activism and hollow intentions of Italy's governing elites. But also it indicated the success of Italy's industrial and financial managers in supplanting the Catholic populist rhetoric of the DC with a more radical free-market vision, not yet however translated into political practice.

The failure of the Bozzi Commission was followed by a shift of emphasis from institutional reform to full-blooded constitutional reform, concentrating on the balance of power between Head of State, Prime Minister and Parliament. This was rendered more urgent by the increasing strength of radical separatist parties in the wealthy regions of the North and by the unprecedented activist inclinations of the Head of State, Francesco Cossiga (1985–1992). After the 1992 elections, the success of the separatist groups known as the Leagues destroyed the fragile consensus on institutional reform without however providing an alternative. These developments are discussed in more detail in the final chapter.

The alternative to this was represented by the PCI (the Italian Communist Party) and the Independent Left, with support on particular issues from the Radicals and the far Left group Proletarian Democracy. In 1991, the Communists and the Independent Left became the PDS (Democratic Party of the Left), while the other groups splintered into new and unstable formations. The Left emerged from this metamorphosis significantly weaker in electoral support and political authority. For the Left the institutional problem is not stability or efficiency but defective representation, of which Parliamentary recalcitrance and governmental instability are merely symptoms. Gianfranco Pasquino, a political scientist at the University of Bologna and from 1983 to 1992 a Senator for the Independent Left, has argued consistently over a long period that the problem is the incapacity of the system to accomodate change, particularly societal change.[7] This perspective emphasises the entrenched nature of the party hegemony, and suggests that the result of the permanence in office of one party is to weaken the institutions, to keep decision-making informal yet stable, and to ensure that pressure groups, associations, organised interests of whatever sort in civil society only achieve influence in so far as their activities are mediated through the political parties.

A sub-theme in this argument is the failure of the parties to represent the range of interests and opinions in society. For the immediate post-war period this means the interests associated with the Left and particularly with the Communists. After 1968 the groups most clearly excluded were firstly the new social movements which emerged out of the upheavals of the period, such as the civil liberties groups, grassroots trade union organisations, and unemployed workers groups, and then regional and environmental groups. In the 1980s the repeated success of the regional protest groups in the North, such as the *Liga Veneta* and the *Liga Lombarda*, bore witness to the extent to which relatively prosperous areas and social groups were frustrated at the inequities and inefficiencies of central government organisations, particularly those associated with tax collection and economic development.

The Communists have argued that in the debate on ungovernability the objective of the DC is to identify itself once more as central to the functioning of the political system; hence, according to the Communists, the emphasis on governmental stability, on techniques for enhancing the strength of the majority and on encouraging the survival of the five-party coalition formula. The PCI and its successor the PDS interpreted this not only as an attack on themselves but also as an attempt to redress the balance of the political system, which since 1968 had become more open and more pluralistic, however insufficiently.[8] The PCI proposals, in opposition to this, stressed the perceived need to bring the parties closer to the people through electoral reform, through devolution, and through administrative decentralisation. The underlying purpose to these reforms would be not to treat the legislature as an opponent of the executive, but rather to enhance the power of both within their respective spheres, particularly by strengthening the non-legislative powers of one of the chambers, the Senate, in the area of scrutiny and redress. To the criticism that this would all rest on the effective removal of the block on communist participation and would re-introduce 'consociational methods', the PCI reply was that they sought not a privileged position for themselves but a more participatory democracy without a priori exclusions. There is a problem of government–interest-group relations, according to the Left, and it results from the arbitrary character of these relations and from the government's vulnerability to what they refer to as 'particularistic pressures'. This phrase is the Left's code for clientelism, which enables them to imply that the underlying issue is the representativeness of the favoured groups. It is clear from their recent policy statements that the PDS do not oppose a more structured organisation of interest-group access, so long as the structures are not used to favour interests reliant on the governing parties.

The third view, associated with La Palombara, argues that the problems are over-stated, and that Italy's various political and economic elites have a *modus vivendi* which enables them to get the best out of the apparently intractable problems of ideological division and wasteful incompetent bureaucracy.[9] The sub-theme to this argument brings it closer to the first argument, some of whose premises it implicitly adopts; it is easy to move from the La Palombara view to an emphasis on the mature capitalist socio-economic system held back by political deficiencies. The La Palombara view also echoes the ambiguous self-assessment of Italy's traditional political leaders: Giulio Andreotti, a senior DC notable, is often quoted as describing the Christian Democrats as 'condemned to govern', a phrase redolent with the anxieties, the fatalisms and the pragmatism of those who believe themselves to be carrying a burden imposed on them by the constraints of history.[10] The burden has its compensations, certainly, but is no less of a constraint to practical action despite them. In this view, much of the Italian political system is regarded as given, more or less unalterable in its fundamentals. The political parties are not so much the creators of the problem as its victims, and together with the economic elites should have their achievements recognised in context.

Few if any of the studies associated with these arguments have paid particular attention to the question of how the parties actually affect policy, though virtually all accept implicitly or explicitly that Italy is characterised by party government, and that the numerical dominance of the parties throughout the system determines in some specific and direct way the actual outcomes of the decisions. These assumptions may lead to the further supposition that for all significant purposes the universe of 'what happens in policy' is made up of what the governing parties actually want, what they have some preference for or are prepared to compromise on for the sake of reaching agreement with one another; other actors may be held therefore to be of lesser significance – the bureaucracy with its sectoral elites, the interest groups associated with particular parties; institutional mechanisms and internal rules are also downgraded. Until recently, research in Italian politics has had only a limited and tangential theoretical bearing on public policy-making. When it was theoretical in orientation it was mainly concerned with other sectors, or its empirical reference to policy-making was not reinforced by theoretical concerns.[11] In this sense the idea of the political lag, whatever form it was held to have taken, has covered the absence of a clear detailed explanation for why the political system has failed to provide acceptable levels of equity, uniformity or managerial efficiency.

## PARTIES AND POLICY – CRISES OF REPRESENTATION

The specific assumptions which underlie this work are threefold. Firstly, the division between economic and social development on the one hand and political development on the other, while it is a helpful analytical device in some contexts, should not be taken in too radical a sense. The difficulties of the system are not merely institutional, and should be understood as involving the processes of economic and social development. The interaction between civil society and the state though flawed in many ways is intense, and is highly pluralistic in form. In other terms, the notion of dualism, which occurs so readily in the Italian context, should not be allowed to mask the interdependence of sectors which may appear to be radically diverse.

Secondly, many of the problems can be found, sometimes with different terminology, at earlier points in Italian history. Italy's difficulties are not to be associated solely with the processes of political development post-war. On the contrary, there are strong elements of continuity with past regimes. As chapters 2 and 3 describe, the institutions which Italy now lives with are inherited to a very great extent from the Liberal and Fascist regimes. The conventions and the formal rules which they follow are not the creation of the post-war period alone. Even the constitution which established the new Republic after the war is the product of the experience and the practices of the past.

Thirdly, if the core of the problem lies in the way in which the parties operate, it must follow that among other things the crises which the system seems to undergo periodically are crises of the parties. A straightforward way of synthesising these three assumptions of socio-economic determination, historical continuity and party centrality is to describe the system in terms of the central function of representation, and the associated functions of decision, participation and legitimation. Representation serves several purposes. Through the electoral process, it provides a normative criterion, a source of authority to guide other parts of the process – in particular, coalition formation, cabinet decision-making, and legislative deliberation. Secondly, through political participation, it enables parties to translate the heterogeneous intentions and interests of the mass electorate into the specific realities of government action. It obliges governments to identify and give expression to public interests in the face of sectoral concerns. Finally, through its association with the basic values of society, it is the mould by means of which the exercise of power is stamped with an acceptable imprint. It legitimises the actions of the state, a function which is of particular importance within a state system characterised by a categorical separation of the state from civil society.[12]

At the general level, representation is exercised in several ways: through the electoral process, which is intended to establish the relative weights of balance of parties; through the individual activities of elected members in Parliament and in the state sector; and through the routine interaction of interest groups with the state structures. The opening up of civil society, a major change in the post-war system, throws representation into the forefront of Italian politics. Because of the way Italy has developed, representation is arguably the most important single problem facing the Italian political system today, underlying not only issues such as bureaucratic reform and judicial authority but also the pressing problems of the content and scope of economic policy.

Both the method of decision-making and the substance of the decisions are threatened by the representation issue. In most west European democracies, the political parties form the main link between the apparatus of the state and the organisation of civil society. In Italy, these functions are exercised in specific ways. The parties determine which routes issues are to follow in the intricate paths which make up the formal and informal modes of Italian policy-making. It is the governing parties who exercise discretion over access to public resources, whether these are material, moral, legal, or hierarchical. It is they who control the gates between the formal and the informal, who mediate between the rigidity of the bureaucracy and the dynamism of an active and expanding economy, who maintain and develop the conventions by which the political system operates. In public, the system may appear dominated by rigid conventions and fixed political positions, but the internal weaknesses of the governing parties require them to moderate in private their public inflexibility. Hence informal politics (meaning less publicised, perhaps actually covert politics) develops by convention. Its function is primarily to allow formally excluded groups a minimum degree of access: the level of the minimum is set by the need to ensure the routine management of policy while maintaining the established balance of forces. The contrast and the interaction between the formal and the informal, between the public and the private, between legal norms and practical short-cuts, between the modern and the traditional, give shape and meaning to the entire policy-making process. Representation in this context entails a complex process of exchange between conflicting groups mediated by the political parties, who use public resources as currency to contain and to reduce societal conflict. Contrasts of method and ethics permeate the way politics works and serve an important function, that of stabilising and enforcing the rules for the distribution of public spoils in conditions of fragmented and conflictual social organisation. The contrasts, the dichotomies, the abrupt barriers between categories, are needed above all to maintain the conventional pecking order among parties and among groups, by enforcing a priori the disparity of treatment to be expected for favoured interests and by legitimising sanctions against excessive opportunism on the part of those most favoured. The notion of 'public interest' is absent from this discourse, for the representation is directed at the distribution of spoils to particular interests, not at the identification and implementation of collective policy for the collectivity as a whole.

The various meanings attached to the concept of representation are associated with different ways of regulating the relationship between society, its elected representatives and the state structures. One of the commonest notions of representation uses Parliament to link the elector, the representative and the national interest directly. The individual representative is held to speak for the best interests of the collectivity as a whole. This interpretation therefore gives priority to decision-making and to the exercise of authority, above the functions of participation and legitimation. In its clearest form, this has two important implications: first, that the deputy or member is elected on the basis of the electorate's perceptions of judgemental capacity and, second, that the Assembly or Parliament as an entity represents the public interest in some higher and possibly transcendent sense.[13] A variant of this, sometimes regarded as a pluralist or communitarian approach, is that the elected representative individually does no more than speak for the best interests of his or her local community, rather than of the collectivity as a whole. Parliament in a system of this kind would be an amalgam of many different local views, a summation whose whole is definitely not greater than the sum of its parts. To say that a Parliamentarian represented the Nation in this form of representation would be misleading, since it would be Parliament as a whole which represented the Nation or collectivity, and not its individual members. The Nation, and the state in this view, are not superior to the communities which make them up. This view, the communitarian idea of representation, is implicit in many pluralist versions of liberal democracy, but is not one that finds favour in Italian constitutional doctrine.[14]

The Italian constitution does however seem quite partial to the more orthodox 'national representation' view, particularly in Article 67, which states 'Every member of Parliament represents the Nation and carries out his duties without being bound by mandate'. Associated with this view is the notion that Parliament is in some sense central to the Italian political system. 'Centrality' here appears to be a metaphor used to suggest that Parliament is a rather special institution, because of particular rights which its members enjoy and because it has a formal pre-eminence in the making of law. This is discussed in more detail in chapter 5. It implies that Parliament has an essential role in the making of law and that its members act with full independence in carrying this out. But the formal centrality of Parliament is weakened by the deliberate erection of institutions which have limited countervailing power in the sphere of legislation. In particular, regional assemblies and popular referenda compete to some extent with Parliament in the exercise of this function. The constitutional model is of a competitive pluralism between free-standing institutions of state, each of which can constrain but not overwhelm the others. This is a pluralism founded on the sovereignty of the people expressed in constitutional form, giving Parliament the determinant role in making future legislation. This implies that Parliamentarians are responsible only to their own best judgement, not to a majority in the constituency and not to any interest or associational group. In this sense, and limited by other constitutional provisions and by political practice, the national role attributed to Parliament encourages individualistic representation on the part of its elected members.

However, the individualistic view of the Deputies' and Senators' roles is also subject to competition. As the system has developed, Parliament and government have attempted to restrict the formal pluralism, primarily through the pervasive control exercised by the political parties. An alternative notion of representation is that it is not Parliament which is central but the parties, and this implies a rather different approach, prioritising participation instead of authority. This second view of representation describes the elected representative as standing for the preferences of his or her electors. In this case the representatives owe the electors not their best judgement, but their proximity to the preferences of the electors in their constituencies.[15] In practice, this implies some form of organised politics to enable the candidates to gather the views of the electorate and to respond to them. In principle, this ties the elected representative directly to the electors, and may in its radical forms allow the electors to recall representatives who fail to express the views of the constituency. Such radical instruments of popular democracy are not explicitly condoned by the Italian constitution or by its political practice, as indeed is the case with virtually all West European liberal democracies. But most modern systems implicitly accept some form of mandate and some form of direct accountability on the basis of constituency preference. The Italian constitution recognises the role of political parties in two separate places, in Article 18 on general freedom of association and in Article 49 on association in political parties for democratic purposes. Parliamentary regulations do not recognise the existence of political parties as such, though they give an important role to the Parliamentary groups, particularly since the reform of the regulations in 1971. The chapters which follow argue that the mass parties are a major and positive innovation in post-war Italian politics. They successfully integrated into their ranks, in one way or another, the occupational groups emerging in the process of rapid social and economic transformation in the first two decades after 1945. The problem of representation which Italy now faces is one which results from the specific way in which the internal and external constraints imposed a rigid political framework on party-based representation, from which it has been unable to escape. A consequence is that neither of the two forms of representation, individualist or the party-based, is able to function effectively or uniformly over the whole territory and over all classes. Also, these two different kinds of representation are associated with different types of voting in the electorate: the earlier Liberal view encourages individualistic representation, whereas the more modern party-based representation encourages voting on the basis of perceived affiliation to societal groups represented by the parties. The post-war formulation clearly establishes a constitutional status for political parties and sits very uneasily with the Liberal formulation.[16]

A logical extension of the party-based form of representation is representation based on interest groups. Interest groups are not subject to territorially-based electoral scrutiny, and in Italy as elsewhere may reflect no more than the preferences of their most active or concerned members. Because of their flexibility, their capacity for functional adaptation, the way they work in Italy is a crucial indicator of the practice of policy-making. The written constitution has little to say about interest groups as such, but there is a striking contrast between on the one hand the traditional role which convention allots to societal associations and on the other hand the requirements entailed by the post-war objectives of the political parties. As chapter 3 argues, the ethos of the traditional bureaucracy is explicitly opposed to particularistic interest, and identifies its own role as impartial and impermeable. The rigidity of its development prevented the integration of interest groups into the formal structures of the Liberal state. Its consultative procedures drew on only a small section of the available associations. Its priorities tended to discourage it from adapting draft legislation to meet many societal demands which otherwise might have been regarded as legitimate. Its recruitment policies denied it access to the full range of talents available. The practice of the traditional bureaucracy therefore denied the validity of pluralistic liberal democratic models of representation, and left the direction of the process of modernisation to the non-state powers. The Fascist experiment with corporatism responded to the failure of the Liberal state by attempting to replace its structures with a new organic vision of the state based on compulsory integration and an intense transformative strategy. The corporatist model associated with Fascism attempted to impose a monopoly of interest-group representation in licensed organisations. These were marshalled in a strict hierarchy under the National Fascist Party, finding their outlet through the Chamber of Fasces and Corporations which eventually replaced the Chamber of Deputies. The associational structures failed to develop any substantial life of their own.[17]

After the war the major political parties quickly perceived the dangers of the associational vacuum, and attempted to fill it to their own advantage by encouraging the development of occupational and social organisations tied closely to party structures, particularly in the sphere of trade union activity and in the agricultural sector. In terms of the idea of representation involved, this is clearly a party-dominated pluralism, but the non-governing parties have full representation only in the legislature. Their relationship with the executive is unstable and ambiguous both inside and outside Parliament. Also, the state itself does not figure as a strategic co-ordinator, still less as a director of policy for the overall national interest. Its authority is subsumed by the power of the individual parties in some sectors and by the power of vested interests in others. Though it is pluralism of a sort, it is uncertain, unbalanced, and deficient in the core structures which pluralists presuppose to make the system work.

An aspect of these methods of representation is that they relate in different ways to what the representatives decide on behalf of the collectivity – or more broadly to what is sometimes called the output side of politics. The development of this way of thinking about politics occurs in its modern form with eighteenth-century writers such as Rousseau, and is usually regarded as one of the major historical changes in the way politics operates. It presupposes that the appropriate questions to ask about politics are not questions such as 'By what authority does X govern?' but rather questions such as 'How well (according to specified criteria) does X govern?'. This concern with representation as a determinant of output is related to the development of representative democracies in the place of autocratic systems of rule, which relied on tradition, on transcendent notions of authority or on conquest.

There is however another much-neglected form of electoral relationship, clientelism, to which I have already referred, which has little concern for questions either about interests or about preferences. The traditional clientelism of the Liberal period encouraged the development of personalised relations between the voter and the representative based on exchange of resources. Clientelism usually bears little direct relationship to broad policy or to strategic objectives. On the contrary, it requires the voter not to consider such matters, and in its traditional guise presupposes forms of societal organisation which militate strongly against the development of such a policy-based relationship. The reason for its neglect in this context is that it is not conventional to regard it as a form of representation at all.[18] It is a mistake however to consign clientelism to the other disciplines, as if it were some quaint residue from earlier types of political community. The Italian example indicates clearly that clientelism can modernise itself and that it can develop sophisticated and complex forms of social aggregation. Probably the only way to make sense of it in terms of democratic theory would be to describe it as a crude form of mandate, in which voters require the politicians only to render particular services and on all other matters to use their own judgement. But this would be misleading, because though the relationship is certainly based on exchange, it is not usually a specific exchange. Even where it is so, the implied individual contract between the two is given weight and substance by the network of similar relations of which it is part and by the stability of the relationship. The implied contract, in other words, should not normally be regarded as a one-off, my vote for this job or this pension only. Patron and clients have long-term if narrow interests in each other's welfare, and clientelism should be seen as a set of such relationships rather than as a series of specific exchanges.

A further difficulty with the narrow quasi-contractual view of clientelism is that in modern politics it is often difficult for either participant in the contract to know for sure whether the other side of the bargain has been kept. The client may not be able to tell whether the patron has been effective. Even where a specific benefit has been obtained, such as a job, a pension or a licence, a client may have tried several levers and may not know whose influence (if anyone's) was ultimately decisive. This problem can be overcome if the patron is part (preferably a leader) of a cohesive faction operating with internal discipline. But clientelism feeds on personal competition between politicians. Though the hierarchical organisation of the state apparatus encourages the hierarchical organisation of patronage, clientelist factions are highly personalised and are notoriously difficult to keep together. Clientelism encourages the competitive pursuit of clients' interests by separate patrons.

On the other hand, secret ballots and the extension of suffrage would usually be regarded as making it very difficult for the modern patron to check on the voting behaviour of all his or her prospective clients. Evidence from Italian election campaigns suggests that clientelist campaigning differs from other campaigning mainly in the directness of its appeal to the short-term material interest of relatively specific and well-identified groups of voters. Personal canvassing for votes is forbidden in the Communist Party and in the smaller left-wing parties, but it is widespread in all the governing parties. Particular personalised techniques of mobilisation may also be present, which may involve 'treating' the voter with gifts or with very specific material promises. Though the ballot is secret, survey evidence suggests that in some areas, particularly in the south, there is a widespread belief that the patron does have means of identifying how individuals in relevant groups have voted.[19] The persistence of this belief helps explain the capacity of clientelism to survive the formal regularity of electoral procedure and the increasing influence of national factors in election campaigns. Until recently there has been little evidence of widespread electoral malpractice, but local elections in Sicily in 1991 were followed by extensive police investigations and a considerable number of prosecutions. After the 1992 elections, the Amato government proposed new legislation as part of its anti-mafia drive which was aimed at curbing 'treating' or electoral bribery.

The preference voting system does give some scope for technical manipulation by means of which a well-organised faction of candidates can identify voting within certain electoral groups, but there is little hard evidence as to how widespread such practices actually are. Until its reform in 1991, in the Italian electoral system the voter had the opportunity to vote both for a party and for individual candidates on that party's list. This second type of vote, the preference vote, is as we have seen a throwback to earlier Liberal notions of representation. Though intended to strengthen the individual candidate against the party organisation, one of its effects was to encourage the accumulation of personal votes on a large scale. It was by no means unusual for senior faction leaders in the DC to get over 100,000 preference votes in Parliamentary elections, and on occasions the most influential have received over 200,000.[20] Not all of these can be described as clientele votes – in many cases they are obviously associated with the general reputation of the politician concerned. Nevertheless, the preference vote does provide an important instrument by which the relative standing of individual politicians in the same party in the same constituency can be measured. The influence exercised in securing the election of particular candidates to Parliament can be used in other electoral processes within the party and in local government, and to aid members of the same faction or other allies. The preference vote is the embodiment of personalised representation in the Christian Democrat organisation, in local government, and in national government. It constitutes a crucial part of the process of accumulation of office for politicians and for their factions.

In May 1991, a national referendum was held on the preference vote system. More than 90 per cent of those voting were in favour of the repeal of the multiple preference. Of the major parties, only the socialists did not support the repeal, arguing that the referendum was not relevant to the substantial constitutional reforms needed. The reduction of the number of preference votes to one per voter reduces but does not eliminate the scope for personal competition between candidates on the same list. It is likely therefore to enhance the power of the party organisations at regional and local level. Its effects on the system of patronage are likely to be long-term rather than immediate, and in this sense the socialists were undoubtedly correct in arguing that more and different reforms were required to make the system genuinely representative.

## RELEVANT COMPARATIVE FACTORS

The critical question which follows directly from these observations is how to locate the assumptions, terminology and current explanations into the more general framework associated with policy studies in Western Europe. In the current state of research, it would be impractical to attempt to provide in this sense a complete explanatory map of the way public policy works in Italy. What we can try to do is to outline some of the key features of the map, first from a comparative analytical perspective, and secondly identifying the particular historical variations which differentiate explanation in the case of Italy. The historical variations will be detailed in the chapters which follow and fitted into the general framework in chapter 7. Here the concern is to introduce the terminology and the general explanations.

The idea of political lag, of government in a state of stall, or of a political system whose development had been arrested, provided evocative descriptions which could be adapted by groups of widely differing political persuasions. But for a variety of reasons it cannot provide an overall explanation. Most immediately, as was argued above, it places excessive emphasis on one particular factor, namely the parties, and implicitly lacks a complete view of the role of the other actors. Though the idea of a highly pluralist system unbalanced in the course of development is suggestive, the critical explanatory details are generally lacking. As a result, it is difficult to place Italy within a comparative framework. Secondly, the idea of arrested development may over-emphasise the lack of change, when what differentiates the Italian case may be precisely the kind of change which actually has taken place not just in society but also in government.

Until recently, either neglect or segregation were Italy's lot in comparative studies of public policy. The Heidenheimer Heclo and Adams (1975) cross-national survey has very little reference to Italy, while the Flora and Heidenheimer work (1981) pursues the other convention of treating Italy as a special case.[21] This treatment was established by economists and political scientists in the early post-war, struggling with the analysis of Italy's underdevelopment and instability.[22] The policy aspects were rarely studied at any depth in Italy itself, but the 1980s have seen a distinct shift in favour of empirical work on the policy side, and this has altered the tenor of the policy debate in Italy considerably, both academic and political.[23]

What is beginning to emerge from the new academic interest in the subject is a considerable degree of consensus that Italy may be a special case, but only in the sense that in our present state of knowledge all countries have some nationally specific features which require modification to the current comparative frameworks. What any comparative framework has to do initially is to apply the same questions to different cases. The 'political lag' argument identifies arrested development as the problem. This places Italy outside the normally accepted comparative frameworks, since by definition this is not a question to be put about other advanced industrial countries. The emerging studies of public policy in Italy begin by identifying a problem which Italy shares with other similar countries: that is, the size, complexity and rate of growth of government spending, with particular reference to its objectives and instruments. This is a particularly apt question for Italian public policy, since it brings directly into discussion the issue of the public sector deficit (dealt with in chapter 8). The second assumption generally made is the entirely reasonable one that in some sense Italy has to be regarded as a pluralist political system. This is for two main reasons. Firstly, in constitutional and legal terms, Italy has many of the formal and practical features associated with pluralist liberal democracies. Second, one of the key assumptions of pluralist analysis is that there should be no presupposition about the continuous and pervasive predominance in decision-making of any one single group. This implies that all actors are able to exercise some power, and all are in some way dependent on others. Hence the term 'power dependence' is frequently applied to such models.

These are reasonable assumptions to make about Italy in view of the existing state of research about decision-making, which has clearly suggested a system which is highly permeable to a variety of specific interests. The qualifications to be made in the Italian case would have to relate to the permanence in office of the largest single party (the Christian Democrats), and to the constraints on non-governmental parties. But they are also concerned with the extent to which the bureaucracy, to the exclusion of others, consolidates relationships with specific closely knit groups of professional interests, referred to here as policy communities, or maintains more distant relations with looser associations referred to as issue networks. A further factor is the way in which clientelism superimposes a particular structure on other forms of decision-making. These weaknesses are concentrated on the exercise of authority, on the decision-making elements in the process of representation, rather than on the functions of participation and solidarity, although these are also affected. These terms are explained in more detail below.

The presuppositions of pluralist analysis are that there are several factors to be considered in identifying the specific conformation of decision-making.[24] Simplifying for the purpose of argument, the 'power dependence' framework referred to above identifies these factors as follows:

1 Differentials in *resources* giving organisations comparative advantages.
2 Processes of *exchange* in which the comparative advantages are traded off against one another.
3 Discrete *objectives* of organisations determining the flow, direction and size of transaction in the exchange of resources.
4 *Value-systems* of organisations (particularly of the dominant coalition) determining periodic decisions over choice of partners.
5 *Strategies* employed by dominant coalitions to regulate the process of exchange within accepted rules.

This model does not presuppose that all actors start off with equal resources; on the contrary, it recognises that resources are not only scarce but also unevenly distributed. Objectives on the other hand are more closely related to one another in scope and substance, and the mismatch between objectives and resources necessarily creates a situation of power-dependency. The extent of this dependence varies not only between countries but also between sectors within countries. In any developed polity, it may be assumed that the likelihood of finding any single organisation or actor able to act from a position of complete independence is extremely low. One of the reasons for this is that the relevant resources are diverse in character. Financial, legal, informational, political, and hierarchical resources are not uniformly available, and in different societies the distribution may be characterised by more or less concentration in fewer or more hands.

Also, while the organisations may have some degree of freedom over objectives and over strategies, they tend to have less control over the informal rules which set the 'approximate limits within which discretionary behaviour may take place.'[25] Such informal rules constitute an essential part of how modern bureaucratic organisation works: they serve to guide organisations in spheres of action where no clear formal framework applies, and to help organisations achieve practical results where positive action may otherwise be stifled by the excessive rigidity of formal procedures. Because these informal rules relate to the discretion enjoyed by organisations, they tend to deal with the maintenance of boundaries between organisations, the conditions under which discretion may be used, and the safeguards to prevent abuse of the discretion.

The central function identified by this model is the exchange of resources. The power-dependence framework argues that within the plurality of competing actors there may be assumed to be a dominant coalition, which retains significant discretion over entry and exit to the community and which uses specific strategies within the known 'rules of the game' to regulate the process of exchange. In this context a resource is any tradeable good, and in organisations will often be a form of authority, a right to decide, the functions of an office, the political authority of an elected leader, as well as the more obvious financial rewards. The right to determine the material working conditions of others may be a critical resource in the context of the growth of government employment, including benefits associated with professional status, with career development and with job satisfaction. The control of resources, or the lack of them, interacts with objectives and strategies. Within the public sector, the relative job security and the insulation of professionals from external influences give administrators a complex view of what their proper objectives are; this also has to operate within the responsibility they owe to elected politicians.

The 'power-dependence' framework does not presuppose any specific set of relationships for a given political system. The strategies adopted to direct the process of exchange and to maintain the relationships on the part of public organisations depend on the degree of plurality within the system, and on the extent to which the process of exchange is tilted towards domination by particular kinds of organisation or by none (see Table 1.1).

At one extreme, where a close relationship of interdependence and solidarity is established between administrators and interest-groups in a particular sector, we have a 'policy community', clearly

*Table 1.1* Form of regulation of group interests

| dominant structure | decision-making process | form of obligation | favoured strategy | group mode |
|---|---|---|---|---|
| state | direction | hierarchy | separation | pressure group |
| market | negotiation/ exchange | contract | bargaining | issue network |
| community | cooperation | solidarity | incorporation | policy community |

differentiated from those it regards as outsiders, characterised by a high degree of internal cohesion, and acting so as to defend and promote a collective sectoral interest.[26] A straightforward definition of the term is provided by Richardson and Jordan:

> that part of a political system that, by virtue of its functional responsibilities, its vested interests, and its specialised knowledge, acquires a dominant voice in determining government decision in a specific field of public activity.[27]

The policy community then can be viewed as a sectoral elite, controlling collective action within a particular issue area. At the other end of the spectrum, where relationships are more confrontational, we have the open, single-issue participatory and relatively short-lived pressure-group, and in the centre of the spectrum the issue network characterised by the predominance of the exchange relationship. The 'policy community' characterisation has proved particularly useful in the Anglo-American context, where it helps to explain extensive state involvement in individual sectors without overall reference to the controversial model of neo-corporatism.[28]

Terms such as network and community are metaphors, or shortened images used to refer to interpretations; they do not constitute a theory and do not even entail a specific explanation, though clearly they predispose the researcher to identify interaction among multiple groups and to position such interaction along continuums relating to what Meisel referred to as 'consciousness, cohesion and conspiracy'.[29] The power-dependence which underlies the metaphor is assumed to be asymmetrical: central government in modern industrial societies has a degree of structural control which can be assumed to enable it to influence the informal rules in its favour and to restrict the range of options available to non-central-government actors, whether these are public sector or not. These metaphors should not predispose us to adopt sophisticated general theories of the state, to argue for corporatism, neo-corporatism or other such grand designs. On the contrary, they direct our attention to a more microscopic view of the policy process and encourage us from the beginning to view the public policy process as a series of articulated interactions between discrete segmented actors.

This chapter has presented some of the current explanations of Italian politics and has argued that they identify Italy as suffering from arrested or at least delayed development, caused by the failure of the state to match the complexity and flexibility of a modern industrialised society. The study which follows emphasises both historical continuity and the weight of modern socio-economic factors in explaining why the state is the way it is. It also attempts to explain the interaction of the various components of the political system in terms which might make Italy broadly comparable to other West European countries – in terms of resources, objectives, exchange, values and strategies. The interaction between these makes for an explanation which is perhaps inevitably complex, but the complexity itself is part of the answer to the basic questions put at the beginning of this chapter.

## NOTES

1 On the concept of 'civil society', see Bobbio, N., *Stato, governo, società* (Torino, Einaudi, 1985); in English, 'Gramsci and the concept of civil society', pp.139–161 in Bobbio, N., *Which socialism – Marxism, Socialism and Democracy* (intro. and ed. by Bellamy, R., London, Polity Press, 1987). The discussion by Antonio Gramsci, on which much of the modern usage is based, can be found in Gramsci, A., *Quaderni del Carcere* (Edizione critica dell'Istituto Gramsci, a cura di Valentino Gerratana, Torino, Giulio Einaudi Editore, 4 volumes, 1975); an edited English version is Hoare, Q., and Nowell Smith, G., (eds.), *Selections from the Prison Notebooks* (London, Lawrence and Wishart, 1971)

2 Zariski, R., *Italy – the politics of uneven development* (Hinsdale Illinois, Dryden Press, 1972) ch. 11; similar arguments are in Bibes, G., *Le système politique italien* (Paris, P.U.F., 1974), and Sartori, G., *Teoria dei partiti e caso italiano* (Milano, Sugarco edizioni, 1982).

3 Orfei, R., *L'occupazione dello stato – democristiani e potere 1945–1975* (Milano, Longanesi, 1976); also Tamburrano, G., *L'Iceberg democristiano* (Milano, Sugarco edizioni, 1975); Caciagli, M., *Democrazia Cristiana e potere nel Mezzogiorno: il sistèma democristiano a Catania* (Firenze, Guaraldi, 1977).

4 An non-Italian version of this can be found in Spotts, F. and Weiser, T., *Italy – a difficult democracy* (Cambridge, Cambridge University Press, 1986).

5 Turani, G., 'Nuova mappa del capitalismo' pp. 164-169 in *L'Espresso*, 30 June 1985; Lane, D., 'How FIAT managed to get out of a corner by putting the foot down', p. 27 in the *Guardian*, 8 April 1987; Carli, G.,

*Pensieri di un ex governatore* (Pordenone, Edizioni Studio Tesi, 1988). On the objectives of Carli and Ciampi, see Wyles, J., 'Ringmasters in control', *Financial Times Survey* – Italian Banking Finance and Investment, 22 November 1989.

6  Camera dei Deputati – Senato della Repubblica, *Relazione della Commissione Parlamentare per le riforme istituzionali* (2 vols, Roma, 29 gennaio 1985). Referred to hereafter as Bozzi 1985.

7  See particularly Pasquino, G., *Degenerazioni dei partiti e riforme istituzionali* (Bari, Laterza, 1982); same author, 'The debate on institutional reform' pp.117–133 in Leonardi, R. and Nanetti, R., *Italian Politics: a review* (London, Frances Pinter, 1986); same author, 'That obscure object of desire: a new electoral law for Italy' pp.280–294 in *West European Politics* vol.12 no.3 July 1989. Extensive versions of this case can be found in Lange, P. and Tarrow, S.G. (eds), *Italy in transition: conflict and consensus* (London, Frank Cass, 1980). Much of this argument derives from the analyses of Pizzorno, A., *I soggetti del pluralismo* (Bologna, Il Mulino, 1980).

8  Bozzi 1985, vol.2, pp.603–625. Also Barbera, A. *et al.*, *Il Parlamento tra crisi e riforma* (Milano, Franco Angeli, 1985); Barcellona, P. *et al.*, *Riforme istituzionali e riforme della politica* (Roma, Claudio Salemi ed./ Sezione formazione e scuole di partito del PCI, 1983).

9  La Palombara, J., *Democracy, Italian style* (New Haven, Conn., Yale U.P., 1987).

10  On Andreotti, see Orfei, R., *Andreotti* (Milano, Feltrinelli, 1975); Andreotti, G., *Intervista su De Gasperi* (Bari, Laterza, 1977).

11  For the theory, see particularly Farneti, P., *The Italian party system 1945–1980* (London, Frances Pinter, 1985); a good example of the empirical material is Tozzi, S., *Pressioni e Veicoli* (Milano, Giuffrè, 1975).

12  For an introduction to the theory of representation in general, see Pennock, R., and Chapman, J. (eds), *Nomos X – Representation* (New York, Atherton Press, 1968); Pitkin, H.F., *The concept of representation* (Berkeley, University of California Press, 1967); Birch, A.H., *Representative and Responsible Government*, Part 1 (London, Allen and Unwin, 1972).

13  The notion of representation as judgemental is usually regarded as derived from the eighteenth century liberal theories of individual rights – see Montesquieu, *The spirit of the laws* (trans. Cohler, A. *et al.*, Cambridge University Press, 1989); Locke, J., *The second treatise on government* (Oxford, Basil Blackwell, 1966); see also Mill, J.S., *Utilitarianism, liberty and representative government* (London, Dent, 1910).

14  Edmund Burke, *On government, politics and society* (ed. B.W. Hill, London, Fontana, 1975); de Tocqueville, A., *Democracy in America* (New York, Harper and Row, 1966).

15  The best-known critic of this preference-based representation is perhaps Schumpeter, J., *Capitalism, Socialism and Democracy* (London, Allen and Unwin, 1943).

16  Cheli, E., *Costituzione e sviluppo delle istituzione in Italia* (Bologna, Il Mulino, 1978).

17  On Fascist views of representation, see De Felice, R., *Interpretations of Fascism*, (Cambridge, Mass., Harvard University Press, 1977); same author, *Fascism – an informal introduction to its theory and practice* (Ann Arbor, Michigan U.P., 1976); Lyttelton, A., *Italian Fascisms from Pareto to Gentile*

(London, Jonathan Cape, 1973); Kitchen, M., *Fascism* (London, Macmillan, 1976)

18  Among the wealth of anthropological material on clientelism, see Weingrod, A., 'Patrons patronage and political parties' pp.377–401 in *Contemporary Studies in Society and History*, July 1968; Graziani, L., 'Patron–client relations in southern Italy,' *European Journal of Political Research* vol.1, 1973 pp.3–34; Tarrow, S.G., *Peasant Communism in Southern Italy* (New Haven, Conn., Yale U.P., 1967); Powell, J.D., 'Peasant society and clientelist politics,' pp. 411ff. in *American Political Science Review*, vol.64, 1970.

19  For discussion of this evidence, see Allum, P.A., *Politics and society in post-war Naples* (Cambridge, Cambridge University Press, 1973) pp.153–191; Walston, J., *The mafia and clientelism* (London, Routledge, 1987) pp.40–91.

20  In the 1983 Parliamentary Elections, two DC leaders got over 200,000 preference votes (Giulio Andreotti 206,944 in Rome, and Ciriaco De Mita 203,252 in Benevento Avellino). A further 16 deputies got over 100,000 preference votes. Only one of these was in a constituency north of Rome.

21  Heidenheimer, A.J., Heclo, H., and Adams, C.T., *Comparative public policy – the politics of social choice in Europe and America* (London, Macmillan, 1983, 2nd edn); Flora, P., and Heidenheimer, A.J., *The development of welfare states in Europe and America* (London, Transaction Books, 1981); Flora, P. (ed.) *Growth to limits – the Western European welfare states since World War II* (5 vols, Berlin, Walter de Gruyter, 1986).

22  Neufeld, M.F., *Italy – a school for awakening countries* (Ithaca, NY, Cornell U.P., 1961); Lutz, V., *Italy – a study in economic development* (London, George Allen and Unwin, 1962); Hildebrande, G., *Growth and structure in the economy of modern Italy* (Cambridge, Mass., Harvard U.P., 1965). A critical view of this approach is Pinto, D. (ed.), *Contemporary Italian sociology – a reader* (Cambridge, Cambridge U.P., 1981)

23  See particularly Ferrera, M., 'Italy' pp. 385–482 in Flora, 1986, vol.2; Cassese, S., *Il sistèma amministrativo italiano* (Bologna, Il Mulino, 1983); Morisi, M., *Parlamento e politiche pubbliche* (Roma, Edizioni Lavoro, 1988).

24  In the now vast literature, see particularly Rhodes, R.A.W., *Power dependence, policy communities and intergovernmental networks*, Essex Papers in Politics and Government no. 35, September 1985; Benson, J.K., 'Networks and policy sectors: a framework for extending interorganisational analysis' in Rogers, D. and Whitten, D. (eds), *Interorganisational coordination* (Iowa, Iowa State University Press, 1982); for a general introduction to the debate, Dunleavy, P., *Democracy, bureaucracy and public choice* (London, Harvester/Wheatsheaf, 1991).

25  Truman, D., *The governmental process* (New York, Alfred Knopf, 1951) pp.343–344.

26  On policy communities, see Benson 1982; also Rhodes, R.A.W., *The national world of local government* (London, George Allen and Unwin, 1986); Wilks, S. and Wright, M., *Comparative government–industry relations* (Oxford, Clarendon Press, 1987).

27  Richardson, J. and Jordan, G., *Governing under pressure – the policy process in a post-parliamentary democracy* (Oxford, Martin Robertson, 1979).

28  The literature on neo-corporatism, which threatened at one stage to swamp the field, has now receded somewhat before the pluralist fightback.

See particularly the work which arguably set the debate going, Schmitter P. and Lehmbruch, G., *Trends towards corporatist intermediation* (London, Sage, 1979).

29 Introduction to Meisel, J.H., *The myth of the ruling class* (Ann Arbor, Michigan U.P., 1962).

# Part I

# The policy framework

# Chapter 2

# The Italian political tradition
# The historical and cultural context

## CIVIL SOCIETY IN THE LIBERAL PERIOD

The unification of Italy in 1860 brought together a collection of small states sharing a common written language and some aspirations to a common national identity, but little else.[1] None of the component parts of the new kingdom of Italy had any consistent tradition of democratic participation. There were wide disparities in levels of economic development and in the scope of political authority. In particular, the leading northern and central areas of Piedmont, Lombardy and Emilia-Romagna differed from one another widely in terms of prevailing political institutions, though all had relatively advanced economies with emerging industries and considerable external trade. Piedmont had had a constitutional monarchy under the kingdom of Savoy since 1848 and a relatively settled institutional structure for some time before then. Lombardy had been fought over by the French and the Habsburgs and had only sporadic recent experience of non-absolutist rule, while the central regions were accustomed to (if not content with) the ineffective authoritarianism prevalent in the Papal States. The South of Italy and the islands of Sardinia and Sicily were much less developed economically and politically, and communications between them and the rest of the country were poor. In the circumstances, the extent to which the political elites could have achieved either a more rapid progress towards liberal democracy or a more balanced and sustainable economic growth is a matter for conjecture. It is clear however that the main concerns of the ruling groups initially were not the development of parliamentary representation but rather the maintenance of internal order and the consolidation of Italy as a European power economically and politically.

The new Italy was not the result of mass revolt in any modern sense, but, influential as the Piedmontese politicians were, it was not entirely their creation either. Unification was the result of elite diplomacy, of military exploits, of widespread simultaneous popular revolt, and not least of an extraordinary expedition led by a radical adventurer. In April 1859 war broke out in Northern Italy between Piedmont and Austria over Piedmontese aggression in Lombardy. This was followed by a string of Piedmontese military successes in Northern Italy, backed by the French, who however stopped short of supporting the full-scale unification of the country, seeking instead a confederation including the Papal States. In Central Italy, popular uprisings led to the voluntary annexation of large areas of Papal territory. The South remained outside these processes. But in May 1860 Giuseppe Garibaldi launched an armed revolt in Sicily with a small group of followers. He was financed and armed partly by the Piedmontese, but the success of his expedition surprised and dismayed not only his direct adversaries, the Bourbon monarchy of the South, but also in different ways the future political leaders of united Italy. Behind Garibaldi was the endemic potential for violent anarchic protest in the South and, almost everywhere, fragmented but substantial middle-class support for a united Italy, which later developed into the Radical and Republican parties in opposition to the ruling elites. Garibaldi's greatest success arguably was to compel Cavour, the Prime Minister of Piedmont, and the Piedmont conservatives to take further military action, if only to prevent the revolt sweeping away others as well as the feudal remnants immediately facing Garibaldi.[2] How likely or possible this eventuality was does not concern us here: the point is rather that the Liberal state, which lasted from 1860 to 1922, came into being in a decidedly illiberal manner and for much of its life could not or would not extend the political benefits of liberalism to the majority of the population.

The problem of political participation which in a certain sense it bequeathed to its successors is not predominantly a numerical one. It was not that the various political elites have paid no attention to electoral law: on the contrary the franchise has been a subject of continued interest to them, though actual changes in recent years have been rare. Under the Liberal state the electoral law was that inherited from the Piedmontese state, based like much else on the *Statuto Albertino* adopted in Piedmont in 1848. Initially this law admitted as electors only males over 25 years of age who were literate and who paid a property tax of 40 lire per year. This was complicated by a great number of direct qualifications and exemptions, and by rules allowing for transfer of tax qualification. The law was modified in 1860, 1866, 1882 and 1889; extensive male suffrage was introduced in 1912, excluding in effect only illiterate males aged between 21 and 30 who had not completed military service. This final barrier was removed in 1918. Women had to wait for the vote in parliamentary elections until after the Second World War. For the elections of 1861, the electorate amounted to 1.9 per cent of the entire population, and only about 57 per cent of electors actually voted – a turnout of approximately 240,000 in a population of over 26 million. Even the relatively radical reform of 1882 which lowered the age and tax requirements produced an electorate of under 7 per cent of the population. The complexity of the law made the system open to manipulation by those who understood it and who had the opportunity to apply it, particularly prefects and other local agents of central government.[3]

The development of electoral law is a good example of the priorities, modes of operations and unintended consequences of the policies of the Italian state. The priority for the Liberal state was the maintenance of political power in the hands of those considered certain to be responsible and patriotic; the instruments were local officials and notables applying a complex restrictive law; the results included long-term disaffection in the population as a whole and cynical manipulation for short-term ends. Other mildly spectacular examples of the Liberal logic were the tax laws and the laws on military conscription, but as well as these there was an arsenal of regulations, licences, registers and the inevitable exemptions covering a wide range of commercial and cultural activities, unevenly administered and widely resented. The state attempted to maintain central control over key policy areas such as public order, education and public works. But whether in these areas or when imposing regulatory functions in other areas on its local agents and on local government, the state usually lacked the apparatus to manage effectively. For political reasons it could not grant its agents the resources or the freedom to work efficiently. On the contrary, the scope and style of policy were determined by the priority given to legality and to formal consistency above efficiency and competent management.

This incongruence between the grand aims of freedom, progress and nationhood, and the stark inadequacy of the human instruments is one of the paradoxes of the Liberal state; but perhaps the contradiction lies in the nature of the enterprise. Forcing people to be free at the point of a bayonet is likely to be a lengthy task at the best of times, and the Liberal state had many short-term problems which took priority. In short, the establishment of liberty through progress, reason, civilisation and patriotism suffered continuous postponement.

The immediate issues facing the Liberal state and necessitating the curtailment of its radical ambitions were usually referred to as the Vatican question and the Southern question. These problems threatened the legitimacy and organisation of the state, and the expedients developed to resolve them in the short-term had high long-term costs. Gramsci's discussion of this is categorical: the Vatican question and the Southern question, he argued, were typical and specific Italian forms of the peasant agrarian question – a problem for the Socialists, because historically they were excluded from and had neglected the peasantry, but also a problem for the state, because of the opposition of interests between the rural peasant masses of the *Mezzogiorno* (the mainland South and the islands) and the city-dwellers of the more developed North. For the Liberal state, says Gramsci, these problems could be solved by:

> two series of measures: police measures involving the complete repression of every mass movement, with the periodic massacre of peasants; political–police measures: personal favours to the intellectual or *paglietta* class, in the form of employment in the public administration, unhindered pillage of local government, ecclesiastical legislation applied less rigidly than elsewhere, leaving the clergy considerable financial resources, etc.; that is, the incorporation by personal relationship of the most active southern members into the state personnel, with particular privileges, bureaucratic, judicial, etc.[4]

The most important group excluded from the Liberals' crabwise march into the future was the Catholic clergy and laity, but as Gramsci implies the exclusion was mitigated in several ways. In response to the expropriation of the Papal States, Pope Pius IX (1846–1878) refused to come to terms with the new state and forbade Catholics to participate directly or indirectly in political life. As in other cases, the Church's stance can be explained partly as the convergence of ideological and material interests. The Papacy sought the return of its lands and restoration of its temporal sovereignty from the Liberal State, but it also opposed liberalism as an atheistic and anti-clerical doctrine. These two strands found expression in numerous Papal pronouncements of the period, of which the best known were the Papal Bull *Non Expedit* published in 1874 for the parliamentary elections of that year, and the collection of declarations of anathema published in

1864 and known as the 'Syllabus of Errors'. The Popes maintained these self-denying ordinances with a stubbornness which was either saintly or obtuse, depending on one's point of view, until the development of wider suffrage, the changing international position of Catholicism, and the increased threat of Socialism caused the Church to modify its politics in practice.[5]

Though the propaganda battle between Church and state at the national level was incessant and sometimes bitter, local realities were more confused. The rupture between them certainly obstructed the development of a national parliamentary party based on Catholic conservatism until very much later, and deprived the state of large numbers of potential political activists. It stimulated the development of Liberal policies in competition with the Church, in particular in education. The establishment of a state-controlled system of schooling contributed to the spread of the Italian language and national culture among those fortunate enough to have access to state education. The land expropriations released onto the market large tracts of Church estates, mainly in the South. These formed an important economic resource for the urban professionals and entrepreneurs who were the backbone of the cadre of notables – Gramsci's *paglietta* class in the quotation above. From a more positive perspective for the Catholics, *Non Expedit* did not apply to local elections, and Catholic aristocrats and professionals were active in local politics particularly in the northeast, the Veneto region.

A particular theme pursued by the religious intransigents of the time was the separation of the Liberal state from the real wishes and interests of the people as a whole: the Liberal politicians were held to represent only the formal structures, the *paese legale*, but it was the Church that knew and expressed the values of the authentic Italy, the *paese reale*. This theme, the difference between the 'legal country' and the 'real country', has resurfaced constantly since the late nineteenth century, not only from religious propagandists but from many others also who considered themselves genuinely in touch with the people while excluded from the central authorities of the state.

With national political outlets blocked, Catholic laity and local clergy developed widespread and effective social organisations in traditional charitable welfare fields and in economic activity, in the form of producer co-operatives in agriculture and in the provision of credit and insurance. The organisation of these activities under the *Opera dei Congressi* and later under Catholic Action ensured that the Church retained a strong presence in social and political affairs at the local level; this survived through Fascism and was to be an invaluable support for Catholics both in recruitment of members and in mobilisation of votes later. It also affected the way the welfare state developed, sometimes in competition with the Church, sometimes sharing responsibility with the clergy, sometimes leaving entire sectors, particularly in agriculture, to the clerical organisations which were first in the field. Some of those involved in the Christian Social organisations came into conflict with Church authorities for their connection with the Modernist movement, which was condemned by Pope Pius X in 1907. But by this time the Church hierarchy had swung decisively towards the development of active social policy, a change of direction usually associated with *Rerum Novarum*, the first major Papal encyclical on the subject, published in 1891 by the predecessor of Pius X, Pope Leo XIII. Though informal arrangements had worked in previous parliamentary elections, the first explicit agreement between Catholic conservatives and Liberals came in 1913 with the Gentilone Pact, which secured the election of Catholic deputies in some constituencies but only with the approval of the local hierarchy. Notwithstanding the brief and unhappy experience of the Popular Party after 1918, the unhindered and enthusiastic commitment of Catholics to political life did not come about until after Fascism.

The Southern problem was intimately connected with the religious difficulties of the regime, but it was the expression also of the social and economic diversity of the territory and the incapacity of the political elites to integrate the rural peasantry.[6] The unification had been followed by a wave of social unrest and violent public disorder, particularly in the South, which continued to pose major problems for the new regime. In many parts of the South the new state faced the problem of establishing legal, comprehensive and authoritative structures virtually for the first time, where previously the established political authority had been associated with arbitrary coercion, inequitable taxation and distant spendthrift aristocracies. The persistence of sporadic severe banditry, rioting, land occupations and disorganised civil disobedience required virtually a permanent military presence in the South; among its other consequences this gave particular character to the Italian army, whose officers tended to regard themselves as a separate caste representing the embodiment of state authority and national unity.[7]

The fact that military matters and foreign affairs were policy areas over which the King managed to retain considerable influence also encouraged the insulation of the military from the political elites. The scope for foreign policy was limited by the gravity of Italy's internal difficulties, but this did not alleviate the frustration of the armed forces at the narrowness of their role. It is scarcely surprising that Italy's foreign policy was characterised by occasional opportunist military adventures in North Africa mitigated by long periods of simmering domestic discontent at the nation's forced inactivity. The exclusive and transcendent status was particularly claimed by the militarised police, the *Carabinieri*, pretensions that were to persist through the Fascist period and into the post-war Republic. The internal divisions among the military, the lack of political support, the failure to provide them with adequate resources, and the persistent unpopularity and arbitrariness of conscription were the major reasons why the potentially destabilising military ethic did not have a greater effect on the course of Italian political history. The same factors also contributed to the lack of success in the use of coercion to resolve the problem of lawlessness in the South.

Brigandage, banditry and lawlessness in the *Mezzogiorno* continued until severe repression together with improved opportunities for emigration worked an efficient scissors movement on the population. Political and occupational associations which might articulate popular discontent more effectively were better established in the North and Centre, but found themselves subject to constant surveillance and the threat of disbandment at times of particular social tension. This applied not only to the anarchists and socialists but also to the Catholic movement and even to the Republicans on occasions. But the *Mezzogiorno* appeared to the Northern liberals much like a foreign country, to which different solutions applied. Sending in the army was one solution they did not shirk, but another response to the conditions was to establish an alliance with those forces of the old regime which survived – the landed aristocracy, and by practical necessity the Church; eventually the Southern professional bourgeoisie also had to be accommodated.

In parliamentary terms, this link between the Northern liberal groups and the Southern conservative rural interests was known as the *blocco agrario*. This loose grouping was central to governmental stability and was an effective obstacle to major reform either of the central structures of the state or of the fragmented and inefficient agricultural sector. The *blocco agrario* was a complex and inconsistent set of alliances. Its cohesion, development and final demise were arguably crucial to the career of the Liberal state and in a more indirect way to the future pattern of political development in Italy. This was the result of its occupation of the central institutions of the state, not of any particular strength in civil society. Indeed, its almost obsessive exclusivity was a serious disadvantage in view of the need to mobilise the population around new national objectives. This was therefore an alliance which on its own could never fully control the state or encompass civil society. In its incapacity to unify and direct the new state, it veered between outright repression of the majority, accommodation of the few acceptable emerging groups and delegation of powers where its strategic interests required this. Pacification of the countryside demanded the presence of troops to quell the outbreaks of banditry and revolt.

Despite the colourful rhetoric of some of the Southern bishops and the willingness of some Liberals to believe the worst of the clergy, the Church did not in fact foment rebellion, still less try to organise it. Throughout the country as a whole, the Church's propensity to encourage passivity among the peasant population was a crucial long-term support for the regime. The electoral system functioned through the widespread use of patronage by local notables, but in many areas, particularly in the South, the Church provided the only welfare and educational resources and could justifiably be regarded as a substitute for an ineffective and poorly organised legal authority. Thus the Papal policy of *Non Expedit* did not entirely block the development of a political role for Catholics. In the North and Centre, the social organisation of Catholics maintained the Church's support in a hostile political environment, and set up structures which in time would develop into powerful sources of political recruitment and electoral support. In the *Mezzogiorno*, the more conservative cast of the hierarchy ensured practical moral support for the new regime in the absence of any widespread Catholic lay movement to integrate the rural population in a more positive way. It seems fair to say, therefore, that the pattern established for the relationship between civil society and state was that of a modest state structure using more or less autonomous agents, including the Church and the military, to control large areas and sectors which a more effective legal authority might have taken direct responsibility for. The development of social and political organisations in civil society was distorted by the two-fold strategy of the liberal elites, which either incorporated the most active and dynamic elements through individual patronage or excluded and attempted to stifle those groups whose demands challenged the established distribution of resources.

# THE INSTITUTIONS OF THE LIBERAL STATE

The institutional structures which evolved during the Liberal state, exclusive, fragmented and distant from society, developed their own mechanisms and modes of operation. The *Statuto Albertino* of 1848 was the basis of the legal system and the source of the Constitutional framework; in deference to the prevailing notions of executive responsibility the Statute was a flexible constitution which could be overridden by ordinary law. According to the Statute, executive authority rested with the monarch, who appointed the government and to whom the ministers were responsible. Legislative authority was to be exercised jointly 'by the King and the two Chambers'. There was no Constitutional Court, and only very limited judicial redress against executive action through the Council of State. In principle there was no clear legal basis for parliamentary votes of confidence to establish or dismiss the government, but this practice rapidly developed. With such a restricted suffrage, the dominant political party remained the Liberals, a classic arrangement of notables with no party discipline or formal organisation. The deputy was held to represent the nation and was bound by no mandate from the electorate. The ethos and organisation of Parliament placed great emphasis on the material and ideological independence of the elected representative, and its regulations recognised no internal formal groupings until 1919.[8]

The formation of governments and their maintenance in office therefore depended on the individual skills and political resources of Prime Ministers and their supporters. There were no government programmes as such, and Prime Ministers could not rely on stable majorities in Parliament to sustain them or to guarantee passage of government legislation. On the contrary, the broad church of the Liberal Party nourished factions and personal rivalry. The lack of acceptable organised opposition meant that there was no electoral sanction against deputies using government instability to further their own ministerial careers. The dominant grouping within the Liberals, as we have seen, was the *blocco agrario*, which took power from the Piedmont-dominated Right in 1876; but it was a heterogeneous collection united initially by generic support for greater government spending rather than by specific objectives. Prime Ministers could not rely on the majority grouping to provide consistent support, but often had to cobble majorities together for individual bills through persuasion and through enhanced encouragement amounting to patronage. The patronage would usually be in the form of help in building up local support for the deputy; this support could range from appointed local office for the deputy, to public works in the constituency and to the promise of prefectoral assistance at elections. Known as transformism, this highly unstable method of maintaining governments in office through temporary majorities usually encouraged a piecemeal approach to policy and militated strongly against radical reforms. The only Prime Minister able to transcend the system was arguably also its most successful exponent, Giovanni Giolitti, who held office intermittently from 1900 to 1913 and then again less successfully after 1919.[9] Giolitti presided over the introduction of major reforms of the Civil Service and of the state pensions system. But within this policy framework the more general pattern was that important areas of policy tended to lose priority to immediate demands relating to the maintenance of public order and the disbursement of the spoils of office.

This pattern should not be understood to imply that elected local government flourished with significant powers of discretion and control of its own finance. This was a centralised state determined to put executive authority above the representation of local interests. Whether it did or did not exert its authority successfully, the effect on the distribution of political power was profound. Throughout the Liberal period local government had little formal autonomy and was dominated by notables who had other levers as well as local office. There are many significant similarities between the Italian Liberal state and the French Third Republic both in the development of party politics and in the structure of state administration. The importance of the local notables is one of these. But in Italy, the power of the notables was not based on the *cumule des mandats*, as was the case in France. Though many Italian deputies and senators also held local office in a variety of sectors, these were the spoils of success rather than the immediate means of achieving it. The local notable relied on informal networks and procedures, on secure personal contact with prefects and magistrates, on his status as an educated professional, on his access to or control over the important local economic resources such as employment or land, and preferably on a pre-established link with a major politician in the local large urban centre or in Rome. All of these would assist in the development of a personal clientele without which electoral success was inconceivable.

The link between voter and deputy in this system was not based on representation of opinion or interest. Traditional clientelism is an instrumental form of elite–mass linkage not necessarily consistent with liberal principles or democratic practice. As practised, particularly in the South, it had important political consequences. It was (and is) typically a personal relationship between the patron and the client, in which the client implicitly barters his or her vote and perhaps other services in return for the protection and assistance of the patron. Often the client will barter not only the personal vote but also the votes of the extended family, which of course give extra leverage. The patron–client link is non-ideological and strictly instrumental; implicitly it places the patron in a position of superiority, enhanced by the unspecific, uncertain and open-ended nature of the deal struck, which obliges the client to seek favours from the patron in tacit acknowledgement of the inequality between them. Clientelism militates strongly against the development of class-based parties or of parties based on opinion. It is also a peculiarly stable mode of political representation. The stability rests on the perceived capacity of the patron to deliver his part of the implied contract and to enforce the client to do likewise. Once the relationship is demonstrated to have worked, it is likely to be strongly in the immediate interests of both participants to maintain it in being. It also impedes the client from pursuing other political options if they would threaten the existence of the relationship. The client is thus kept in a subservient dyadic position of dependence, from which he or she can only escape by risking the loss of assured benefits in favour of less certain advantages, which are furthermore likely to be of long-term value whereas the need is for immediate support.

After 1889 and particularly after the riots and repression of 1897 and 1898 more modern political organisations based on Catholic and Socialist support began to pose a threat to the Liberal methods. But these were not a dominant force until after the First World War; clientelistic representation proved itself a hardy and adaptable beast. Mass political organisation associated with class or issue-based representation really took effect in Italy only after 1918, and even then did not entirely replace the old forms but rather laid a new system on top of the old. For the first fifty years of its existence, with all the economic and social development of the time, with all the ideals of the neutral civil service, the rule of law, the extension of communication and the benefits of modern nationhood, the Liberal state spoke to its subjects through patronage and through its obverse, which is exclusion and in this case repression. The participants and actors in the apparatuses of power were the literate, property-owning males of the established landed interests, the emerging industrial and commercial sectors in the North and Centre, and the expanding urban professional classes everywhere.

## LIBERAL PRACTICE

The education system had a key role in maintaining the fragile superiority of the political elites. State-run education was badly-funded, and illiteracy remained a serious problem until after the Second World War.[10] This was to a certain extent a matter of deliberate policy; the Casati Law of 1861 introduced new educational objectives to meet the requirements of the new state and particularly to nurture a common identity, but the new objectives were incongruent with the Malthusian principles which inspired some of the detailed provisions. The importance of providing a skilled labour force for the processes of modernisation was recognised, but it was widely believed among the political elites that advanced employment opportunities were bound to be less numerous than the potential supply of recruits. These views were supported by fashionable intellectual theories associated with positivism, which encouraged among other things the belief that some social classes were unavoidably inferior in intellect and morals.[11] The cause of social stability, in this sector as in others, would not be served by hasty expansion of the benefits of liberalism. University education and to a lesser extent secondary education were available only to those with consistent private financial support; universities were relatively numerous but tended to be small and lacked resources. Their output was a privileged elite of graduates whose title of *dottore* brought social status and some prospect of secure employment in the public sector, particularly for the graduates in law, who formed the largest single group. But the supply of graduates in some subjects was excessive even despite the financial and social constraints on education; whereas the doctors, architects, and engineers could find employment in the expanding economy or, failing that, through emigration, graduates trained in law found opportunities were more restricted. The study of law in practice covered a wide variety of subjects including economics, history and philosophy, which helps explain both its sustained domination of university organisation and the restricted development of these subjects under the Liberal regime. Its growing popularity among prospective students particularly in the South resulted in part from its importance as a qualification for employment in public administration. After the turn of the century there was constant pressure on the state to expand its recruitment to meet the increased numbers coming out of the university law faculties.[12]

Some of the effects of this on the state structure are considered in chapter 4. One of the wider social and economic consequences was to reinforce the division between North and South, since opportunities to study more modern subjects in technical institutes or universities were much more limited in the *Mezzogiorno*. This problem in turn is related to the division which had already begun to emerge between the predominantly Northern private industrialists, export-oriented, often small-scale, innovative, producing finished goods or supplying to finishing manufacturers, and the more geographically diversified state-protected sector concentrated on heavy industry or agricultural production.

Italian industrial development was characterised from the last decade of the nineteenth century by a progressively greater interdependence of the financial system and the emerging industrial producers.[13] In contemporary debates, much importance was attached to the primary sector of industry, heavy engineering and iron and steel production. But in practice Italian economic development when it finally began to take off in the 1890s seems to have been led by the traditional textile sector together with consumer goods and new intermediate industrial production. The state's involvement in economic development was limited in ambition and in its instruments. Though economic success was a critical issue, it was not considered something the state could or should have a direct role in. Nevertheless, because of the weakness of the capital markets and the political effectiveness of the *blocco agrario*, the state did develop regulatory and supplementary roles. Selective protectionist policies were adopted from 1888 onwards, and the state was instrumental in establishing a major steel works at Terni in 1876, but the state had little hand in providing finance, and where it was a customer (as in railways and shipbuilding) had perforce to rely on foreign suppliers, mainly British and German. It was the Germans also who were involved in the development of the financial sector. A major banking scandal and crisis in 1893 resulted in the collapse of two large domestic banks; though there was a growing network of local savings banks and small credit institutions, the capital market remained weak at the national level, and required outside intervention to sustain the economic take-off and to replace the institutions that had failed.

The void was filled mainly by German financiers, who were involved in establishing and developing the two largest national banks of the period, namely *Banca Commerciale Italiana* (known as Comit) and *Credito Italiano*. The German pattern was for banks to be involved as managers as well as financiers, and routinely to take an interest in production and marketing operations. In a similar fashion, the new

Italian banks also were mixed banks: they were directly committed to the economic expansion not only through long-term loans but also through share-holdings in publicly quoted companies. Their financial interest in Italy's economic growth was therefore considerable, though on the whole the bankers tended not to have the same immediate involvement as their associates had in Germany. This was an institutional response to the needs of Italian industry in the medium term, but it did not resolve the problems of the domestic capital market, hampered by a narrow share-holding base and unreliable regulatory mechanisms.

Some of the weaknesses were recognised and met when at the beginning of the First World War the government established the Consortium for Industrial Securities with the precise purpose of enabling Italian industry to respond to urgent military supply needs. From this point on, the state developed increasingly close relations with industry and particularly with industrial entrepreneurs in the primary sector, working through negotiation and credit support rather than through ownership and prescription.[14] The political consequences of this were to encourage still further the growth of privileged sectors within the economy and to accentuate the imbalance in effective access to political decision-making. This incremental growth of the state's role legitimised governmental involvement and resulted in the creation of institutions which eventually developed into a much wider intervention.

The divisions we have described between technical and classical, between North and South and between private and semi-public sector overlapped only to a certain extent, but independently they remained as constant features of Italian politics through different regimes, and contributed greatly to the fragmentation of the ruling elites.

## THE LEGACY OF THE FASCIST PERIOD

The rapidity of Mussolini's rise to the office of Prime Minister in 1922 and the ease with which he consolidated his position were closely associated with the decay of the Liberal system of government and with its incapacity to respond to the emerging mass parties.[15] The Fascists were also aided by the willingness of the large Liberal industrial and agricultural interests to look beyond their traditional representatives in support of their developing sectoral interests. Italian Fascism should be seen therefore not as a relatively simple anti-modern reaction to Socialist and Catholic organisation but rather as a complex movement supported also by groups seeking alternative routes to modernisation.

The take-over of power thus owed much to the political passivity and limited responses of the Liberal governing elites, but consolidation of Fascist authority still required compromises with a wide span of the existing interests. It was not only a few conservatives in the Armed Forces and in the Court who were willing to believe that Fascism represented a strictly temporary means of controlling urban and rural unrest. If this was a misunderstanding of the strength of the state structures and of the need for alternative organisations, they were not alone in their error. The Liberal elites, particularly the modern industrialists of the North and the senior civil servants, unpractised at integrating new groups and interests, were themselves ingested by the Fascist regime and had an important impact on the practical development of policy. Indeed, with the enormous and notorious gap between the Fascist rhetoric and its capacity to implement its policies, the persistence and further development of the existing structures was subject to serious threat only in relatively few policy areas, mainly those related to public order and political participation. In other areas, Mussolini did not sweep away the old but either built on it, as in social welfare, or attempted to bypass it, as in industrial policy.

The Fascist period was not one of complete stagnation either in civil society or in the institutions of state, though the success of its alternative approach to modernisation was strictly limited. Political participation was restricted to the National Fascist Party and to its subsidiary organisations – the Fascist Trade Union Organisation, the youth movements, the agricultural support associations, and the welfare societies. One effect of this was to diminish the range of acceptable political opinions still further, and to remove from public circulation progressive liberal voices such as *Giustizia e Libertà*, as well as the socialist and Communist parties and their peripheral organisations. Bombastic, arrogant, intolerant and anti-Semitic it certainly was, but the Italian Fascist regime stopped short of the excesses of the German Nazis. Its treatment of dissenters and minorities was harsh and vindictive, but inconsistent. Many senior members of the dissident parties and groups were imprisoned after 1926, but were eventually released and went into exile, to return after 1943. Only the Communist Party retained any substantial underground network, and though never a direct threat to the regime this was to be of major importance during the Resistance movement.

Relations with the Church were a case apart. Fascism, unlike Liberalism, sought to mobilise the entire people, to remodel mass values. The Church's solid organisational structure and popular following made it essential for the regime to come to an accommodation with the ecclesiastical authorities, and this was achieved at a formal level through the Lateran Pacts of 1929. The Pacts resolved the territorial dispute by establishing the sovereign state of the Vatican City, making very large financial compensation to the Church for the loss of the Papal states, and granting the Church legal privileges in Italy. The privileges were mainly in tax exemption and in educational and welfare services, but they included the right of the Church to administer matrimonial law and thus blocked any moves for the introduction of divorce. We have seen that in the North and Centre the Church had been in effect an alternative state to the Liberal regime, and in the South a substitute state. This ambivalent relationship rested on the potentially universalistic demands of the Papacy – its claim to the rights to teach all nations and to speak with divine authority on the moral aspects of all human activities. These remained after the Lateran Pacts, and could not be resolved by an agreement which, being very much a work of secular diplomacy, gave rise to differing interpretations on matters of principle. But the Pacts did remove the historical and legal barriers to the integration of Catholicism into Italian politics, while allowing the Church to keep Fascism at arm's length.

One area where the Fascist regime made considerable lasting changes was state involvement in the economy. It was in this period that the intimate and direct links between the state and major economic enterprises largely replaced the haphazard regulatory mechanisms of the Liberals. As in other areas, however, the new institutions and procedures retained the legal framework of the previous period; also, because they were introduced incrementally in response to a succession of crises they were far from all-encompassing, and tended to leave some of the key structures intact.

In the 1920s and early 1930s the structural weaknesses associated with the path of Italian economic development together with worsening international conditions resulted in radical changes in the structure of the economy and in the propensities of the state to get involved. One of the structural weaknesses was the capital market. In view of the volatility of the careers of some of Italy's best-known industrial concerns, it was hardly surprising that the relatively high rate of saving in the Italian economy did not benefit the stock market directly. Italian savers have tended to favour highly liquid claims on banks and government bonds, rather than risk the speculative gains of the equity market. The initial dependence on foreign capital and the restricted geographical and sectoral nature of industrial expansion certainly contributed as well. These factors stimulated the activities of the larger banks in developing long-term commitments in industrial companies, and when the manufacturing concerns ran into difficulties, the banks were also threatened. The political support given by the industrial proprietors to the Fascists as well as their own policies of autarky entailed an active policy of intervention. During the 1920s this embroiled the state increasingly in the ownership not only of the banks but also of their manufacturing subsidiaries. The first of the major post-war salvages was untypical because it occurred under the Liberal state and involved the banking subsidiary of a manufacturing company: in 1921, through the Consortium for Industrial Securities, the state took a majority share-holding in the Ansaldo engineering firm of Genoa, in return for loans to bail out its troubled banking subsidiary, *Banca Italiana di Sconto*. In 1922, the new Fascist government established a special department of the Treasury known as the Autonomous Section, to take over the functions of the Consortium (referred to on p. 41). In 1926 this was expanded yet again to become the Liquidation Institute, supposedly with the aim of soaking up the excess liquidity generated by salvage operations by returning the assets to the private sector. These efforts were largely unsuccessful, and the post-1929 depression in Italy therefore fell upon a state and an economy already equipped with structures and experience attuned to state intervention, even though the institutions which finally emerged were a major development from the Liquidation Institute.

The specific mechanisms by which the process occurred need not detain us here. The three major mixed banks, namely *Banca Commerciale Italiana, Credito Italiano*, and *Banco di Roma*, all became increasingly exposed financially as a result of the worsening domestic and international economic conditions. Short-term support was given them by the Bank of Italy to avoid embroiling the entire financial system in the crisis, and perhaps the regime itself. When the loans proved impossible to repay in the long-term they were consolidated in the form of share-holdings in the industrial enterprises hitherto owned by *Comit, Credito Italiano* and *Banco di Roma*. The procedure has been described by Kindleberger as 'expediency elevated into principle'.[16]

The principle was that from then on long-term credit particularly to industry was to be insulated from short-term deposit-takers. Industrial credit was to be provided by special credit institutes, and a major step in the establishment of such a sector was taken with the setting up of the *Istituto Mobiliare Italiano* (IMI) in 1931; it was in 1933 that its now better-known relative the *Istituto per la Ricostruzione Industriale* (IRI) was established, initially to administer the return of the ailing industrial companies to the private sector. This objective rapidly showed itself to be unattainable in the prevailing economic climate, and IRI was soon set on its career as the major force for public direction of industrial development. In 1934 IRI took control of the three banks whose difficulties had been the immediate stimulus to the development. In 1937 it was given permanent legal status, by which time it had already established several financial subsidiaries as sectoral holding companies, namely STET for telecommunications, FINMARE for shipping and Finsider for steel.

The verbal activism of the Fascists extended to social welfare also. In response to the unemployment induced by the depression of the 1930s, the mainly voluntary social insurance schemes introduced under Liberalism were made statutory and increased in scope to cover more of the population. Typically, this was done at first through the creation of several large sectoral agencies, administratively independent of the state, which were to collect compulsory contributions and manage the provision of services and transfer payments. In this way were created the welfare bureaucracies of the post-war – not just INPS, INAIL and INAM, but a host of smaller agencies for specific categories also. Despite these developments, recent research has suggested that the provision of welfare in the Fascist period fell far short of the statutory obligations, partly because it was entrusted to the Fascist Party to co-ordinate at the local level.[17] There is also some evidence that a share of the insurance funds maintained by statutory contributions was diverted from welfare to finance industrial policy and to aid the Abyssinian war effort.

Some have interpreted these institutional developments as a practical demonstration of the modernising radicalism of the Fascists. Gregor has argued that the form and scope of the extension of state control in the 1930s represented a victory for the Fascists over the pillars of the old Liberal regime, the industrial entrepreneurs of the North-west and Centre, who in the 1920s had been still able to withstand the reforming drive of the PNF. In this view, the industrial policies of Italian Fascism were the practical implementation of its strategy of economic nationalism, and were part of a set of reforms extending government control over wide areas of economic and social activity. An implication of this is that Fascism, or at least its Italian variant, would have to be interpreted as part of a continuous historical process in so far as it could be described as 'modernising'.[18] A further aspect is the extent to which Fascism actually succeeded in mobilising the support of the population around Fascist values – the extent to which, in other words, it induced long-term social and cultural change in the way it claimed to seek. If the answer is in the affirmative, the post-war Italian Republic that inherited the material and cultural conditions passed on from Fascism might have to be understood not as a radical break with Fascism but as a dangerous, unstable, or in some sense ambiguous democracy, and this has in fact been suggested by several authors.

We do not have the scope here to analyse these problems of historiography more fully, but clearly they represent a central theme in how we understand contemporary Italy. Is Fascism to be understood as a phase, as an interlude, or as a separate epoch? If it was a phase, we would have to regard it as a rationalising and in some sense positive phenomenon, occurring in response to specific Italian problems of political and economic development, fundamentally continuous with earlier and later regimes, and passing on to the post-war Republic its own contribution to the solution of problems of retarded economic and political development; if an interlude, Fascism is an aberration, a period of stagnation or even regression, which made no positive contribution to the post-war Republic; and if an epoch, then it is to be understood in its own terms as an attempt to apply particular values and to achieve specific temporary goals, unrepeatable and presumably unjudgeable, neither rational nor irrational. A major problem with the argument of historians such as Gregor is that the extent of the rationalisation supposed to have taken place is doubtful. Gramsci's comment at the time was that the establishment of IRI represented 'not so much a step forward as recognition of weakness'.[19] It may of course be necessary to recognise a weakness in order to make progress beyond it. But the haphazard and reactive nature of the processes of which the establishment of IRI was part suggests that if there was any rationalisation it was not to be found in the perspicacity of a supposed dynamic and enlightened *Duce*, and the outcomes were hardly conducive to sustained capitalist development, unless the term 'capitalist' is given extremely broad connotations.

The idea therefore that Fascism rationalised Italian economic and social structure must be treated with considerable caution. IRI and some other institutions survived the regime and the war, and found themselves important roles in post-war Italy, but these roles covered enduring weaknesses in market structures, and may even have perpetuated them. There is some ground for arguing that these solutions had a degree of political continuity with the more tentative and surreptitious intervention of the Liberal period. They confirmed the separation of the innovative Liberal industrialists from the state-supported sector, and compensated for the weakness of the capital market without remedying it. The political effect of Fascism was to weaken still further the already tenuous links between organised social activity and the state. This may seem surprising in view of the great efforts made by the Fascists at political organisation and political propaganda; what their efforts achieved was the forcible enrolling of large proportions of particular sectors of the population (notably industrial workers and male urban adolescents) in Fascist-controlled organisations, without however persuading these or many other groups of the overwhelming superiority of Fascist values. Despite its claims to the contrary, the regime survived on popular apathy rather than on mass enthusiasm, and by repressing dissent rather than by stimulating political participation.

The legacy of Fascism from this perspective was the consolidation and extension of the state's activity in a variety of policy sectors, the almost complete repression of party-political development, and the isolation of non-Fascist cultural and social organisation from any direct influence in the political sphere. The post-1943 rebuilding reacted against much of this, but with varying degrees of success. Fascism can only be understood as a phase in capitalist development if it is appreciated that whatever it did to resolve structural weaknesses in Italian economic development was not a necessary route but one of several alternatives. As a political and social phenomenon its costs were high, and in political terms it is best seen as a harsh interlude in which the extension of participation was subordinated to the interests of highly limited sectoral restructuring.

## CONCLUSION

In a chapter which deals with the political tradition, it is perhaps inevitable that attention has been concentrated on those factors in Italian politics which provide continuity. In the next chapters, I go on to consider the modern and dynamic aspects of Italian policy processes, in particular the impact of the Constitution and the different approaches of the political parties. Here I have argued that some fundamental problems can be traced to political structures laid down during earlier regimes.

Public administration and the structures of the state in general were established and have developed in political systems which relied on a narrow base of political support and which had limited priorities. These related primarily to the maintenance of public order, to the consolidation of unitary political authority, and to the integration of Italy into the prevailing alliances as an equal and active partner. The price for the attainment of these objectives, it was argued at the beginning of this chapter, was a structure of government which concentrated formal decision-making at the centre and restricted access to it. With the development of mass politics and the pressures for modernisation over a considerable number of years, the responses of the state have tended to build on to existing structures, sometimes through highly informal structures and processes, rather than to sweep away what has gone before. This formal rigidity and practical flexibility illuminate the problems to which we referred earlier. The incongruences between the real Italy and the legal Italy, between the mass parties and the elitist bureaucracy, the lack of overall political direction, the existence of sectors of independent authority, all still appear in educated political comment. The political theorist Giovanni Mosca described such sectoral elites in late nineteenth century Italy in what is now a classic work of political theory.[20] The state then as now allowed some organisations in detached policy-areas to operate with wide autonomy. Liberal politicians knew well what was meant by 'the Vatican question' and 'the Southern question' which can still be found exercising policy-makers. The themes of violence in politics, of the political uses of welfare, of the legitimate representation of local interests through notables, all these have a resonance which pre-dates 1945.

But we should not be misled into believing that all is as it was before. Italy is now a modern industrialised country, the fifth largest in the industrialised West. It has over forty years of sustained liberal democracy behind it, and an extraordinary record of social and economic development. Many of its products are household names throughout the West; its civil engineering and its modern architecture provide models of how to combine innovative flair with practical demands. In textiles, in car manufacturing, in food-associated industries, and other areas, Italy is a world-leader. Clearly, the nineteenth-century terms do not mean now what they meant then. Having suggested the original context for the old meanings, we can now move on to consider their modern applications, and to try to explain how they are part of Italy now, successes as well as problems.

## NOTES

1 On the process of unification, see Mack Smith, D., *Italy – a modern history* (Ann Arbor, Michigan U.P., 1969); Procacci, G., *History of the Italian people* (Harmondsworth, Penguin, 1968); for an influential 'insider' view, Croce, B., *A History of Italy 1871–1915* (Oxford, Clarendon Press, 1929); but see also Gramsci, A., 1971, pp. 52–120.

2 See Mack Smith, D., *Cavour* (London, Methuen, 1985).

3 Caracciolo, A., *Il Parlamento nella formazione del Regno d'Italia* (Milano, Giuffre, 1960); Negri, G., 'La Camera dei Deputati dallo Statuto Albertino alla Costituente Repubblicana,' pp. 119–135 in *Bollettino di informazioni costituzionali e parlamentari*, settembre 1983.

4 Gramsci, 1971, p. 94.

5 On Church–state relations in the Liberal period, see Jemolo, A.C., *Chiesa e stato in Italia dall'unificazione a Giovanni XXIII* (Torino, Einaudi Editore, 1974); see also Candeloro, G., *Il movimento cattolico in Italia* (Roma, Editori Riuniti, 1974, 3rd edn.).

6 There are plentiful sources on the 'southern question' in English as well as in Italian. For an introduction to the problems, see Allum, P.A., 1973, chapters 1 and 2; Gramsci, A., *La quistione meridionale* (Roma, Editori Riuniti, 1974, 3rd edn.); English translation in Gramsci, A., *Political writings 1921–1926* (London, Lawrence and Wishart, 1976); Salvemini, G., *Stato e chiesa in Italia* (Opere II, vol. III, Conti E. (ed.), Milano, Feltrinelli editore, 1969); Salvadori, M., *Il mito del buongoverno* (Torino, Einaudi, 1960); Sereni, E., *Il mezzogiorno all'opposizione* (Torino, Einaudi, 1948); Hobsbawm, E.J., *Primitive rebels* (Manchester, Manchester University Press, 1974).

7 On the structure and roles of the military, see Davis, J., *Conflict and control – law and order in nineteenth-century Italy* (London, Methuen, 1988); Whittam, J., *The politics of the Italian Army* (London, Croom Helm, 1977); on the *Carabinieri*, Collin, R., 'The police in Italy,' in Roach, J. and Thomaneck, J. (eds), *The police and public order in Western Europe* (London, Croom Helm, 1985); Bova, S. and Rochat, G., 'Le forze armati in Italia', pp. 463–486 in Farneti, P. (ed.), *Il sistema politico italiano* (Bologna, Il Mulino, 1973). On the role of the military in western society, see Harries-Jenkins, G., 'Armed forces in European society,' in Archer, M. and Giner, S., *Contemporary Europe* (London, Routledge, 1978); Feit, S., *The Armed Bureaucrats* (Boston, Houghton Mifflin, 1978); Huntington, S., *The soldier and the state* (Cambridge, Mass., Bellknap Press, 1957).

8 Caracciolo, A., 1960; Manzella, A., *Il Parlamento* (Bologna, Il Mulino, 1977) chapter 5; Carocci, G., *Il Parlamento nella stòria d'Italia* (Bari, Laterza, 1964); Anderson, E.N. and Anderson P.R., *Political institutions and social change in continental Europe in the nineteenth century* (Berkeley, University of California Press, 1967).

9 Mack Smith, D., 1969; Seton Watson, C., *Italy from liberalism to fascism* (London, Methuen, 1967); Salomone, A.W., *Italy in the Giolittian era – Italian democracy in the making 1900–1914* (Philadelphia, University of Pennsylvania Press, 1960).

10  See Ruffolo, G., 'The Italian educational crisis', pp. 24–74 in *Review of Economic Conditions in Italy*, January 1975; Clark, M., *Modern Italy 1870–1980* (London, Longman, 1984) Chs 7 and 8.

11  On the influence of Italian positivism, particularly its relationship to Liberal idealism, see Bellamy, R., *Modern Italian social theory* (London, Polity Press, 1987) Ch.1; on the intellectual background, Stuart Hughes, H., *Consciousness and society* (New York, Knopf Press, 1958).

12  Malintoppi, A., 'Italy: Universities adrift', pp. 103–124 in Daalder, H. and Shils, E. (eds), *Universities, politicians and bureaucrats – Europe and the United States* (Cambridge, Cambridge U.P., 1982); Cassese, S., *Il sistèma amministrativo italiano* (Bologna, Il Mulino, 1983) Chs 4 and 5; Cassese, S., *Questione amministrativa e questione meridionale* (Milano, Giuffré, 1977); Cendalli Pignatelli, A., 'Italy: the development of a late developing state', pp. 163–199 in Rose, R. (ed.), *Public employment in Western Europe* (Cambridge, Cambridge U.P., 1985). On the problem during and after Fascism, see Mignella Calvosa, F., 'Stato e burocrazia in Italia: un'analisi storico-sociale (1923–1975)', pp. 158–197 in *Revue Internationale de Sociologie*, vol. 14, 1978.

13  On Italian economic development in the nineteenth century, a useful survey is Cafagna, L., 'Italy 1830–1914' pp. 279–328 in Cipolla, C.M. (ed.), *The Fontana Economic History of Europe*, vol. 3 pt 1, 'The emergence of industrial societies' (Glasgow, Fontana/Collins, 1973); see also Caracciolo, A. (ed.), *La formazione dell'Italia industriale* (Bari, Laterza, 1969); Gerschenkron, A., 'Notes on the rate of industrial growth in Italy', pp. 360–375 in *Journal of Economic History*, vol. 15 1955; Romeo, R., *Breve storia della grande industria in Italia* (Milano, La Nuova/Cappelli, 1961). I discuss the long-term problems of the finance sector in more detail in Furlong, P.F., 'State, finance and industry in Italy', pp. 142–171 in Cox, A.W. (ed.), *The state, finance and industry* (Brighton, Harvester Press, 1986).

14  Cafagna., L., 1973, pp. 320–321; Gerschenkron, A., *Economic backwardness in historical perspective* (Cambridge, Mass., Harvard University Press, 1962); Kindleberger, C.P., 'Banking and industry between the two wars,' pp. 7–28 in *Journal of European Economic History*, vol. 13 no. 2, Fall 1984.

15  The bibliography on the rise of Fascism in Italy is now extremely extensive. See particularly Mack Smith, D., *Mussolini* (London, Weidenfeld and Nicholson, 1981); De Felice, 1977; and Webster, R.A., *The Cross and the Fasces: Christian Democracy and Fascism in Italy* (Stanford, Calif., Stanford U.P., 1960).

16  Kindleberger 1984, p. 10.

17  Fargion, V., 'L'Assistenza Publica in Italia dall'unità al fascismo', pp. 25–70 in *Rivista Trimestrale di Scienza dell'Amministrazione*, vol. 2 1983; Ascoli, U. (ed.), *Welfare state all'italiana* (Bari, Laterza, 1984); Ferrera, M., *Il Welfare State in Italia* (Bologna, Il Mulino, 1984) pp. 27–37.

18  For the 'modernising' argument, see particularly Gregor, A.J., *Italian fascism and developmental dictatorship* (Princeton, Princeton NJ, University Press, 1979); per contra, Castronovo, V., 'Il potere economico e il fascismo', pp. 47–88 in Quazza, G. (ed.), *Fascismo e società Italiana* (Torino, Einaudi, 1973); Mason, T., 'Italy and modernisation' pp. 127–147 in *History Workshop Journal* vol. 25 Spring 1986.

19 Gramsci, A., *Quaderni del Carcere* (a cura di Valentino Gerratana, Torino, Einaudi, 1975) vol. III p. 1749.
20 Mosca, G., *The ruling class* (ed. A. Livingston, New York, McGraw-Hill, 1939); also Meisel, J.H., 1962.

# Chapter 3

# The constitutional framework

## THE FOUNDING OF THE REPUBLIC AND THE NEW PARTIES

In this chapter we see how the policy process was structured by the hectic and difficult reconstruction after the war. In particular, the distribution of basic political resources, the objectives and the strategies were moulded by international and national constraints and sanctioned by a long and highly pluralist constitution. Not least, the conventional norms controlling the rules of exchange of resources were fixed into a relatively rigid pattern which ensured the dependence of most of the actors on a particularly uncertain source of authority, namely the Christian Democrats. The process of reconstruction, in which a new politics emerged and was fixed into the Constitution, is of particular importance not just because it represents the relatively radical aspirations of the period and transmits them to later generations, or because it shows how difficult it is to wipe away past practices and institutions. What this reconstruction passed on to the future operators was an awkward compromise, which is both byzantine where it was detailed and ambiguous where it was not. It was a compromise between the past, represented by the old mainly pre-Fascist institutions of state, the future, represented by the radical idealist hopes of the Constituent Assembly, and the present, in the shape of the international and domestic constraints on freedom of action for the new political classes. The constitutional compromise has shown a perhaps surprising intractability in the face of great changes in international and domestic conditions. This intractability is in itself a drawback; worse still, the compromise has been revealed to be flawed and unsound, and now seems to hold back future development. The process of reconstruction is therefore of more than antiquarian interest, and had a profound effect on the contemporary political system. Its effect on policy-making is particularly important, since as I describe later in this chapter and in chapter 4, in the Italian legal tradition the Constitution provides the highest expression of law, within which all state activity must take place. The Constitution therefore expresses the principles, values and methods of the new state and attempts to provide a formal framework for political development.

The reconstruction of the Italian state after the collapse of the Fascist regime was lengthy and difficult, even by comparison with the other major European countries who faced similar problems of rebuilding from the devastation of war. Mussolini was defeated in the Grand Council and removed from office by King Victor Emmanuel III on 25 July 1943. Italy was occupied by two opposing armies for about 20 months thereafter, and did not have a national government with significant independent powers over the whole territory until 21 June 1945. But it was not until almost a year after that (2 June 1946) that national elections were held for the Constituent Assembly, and then almost a further two years before the first parliamentary elections took place. In the period between the fall of Fascism in July 1943 and the elections for the first legislature on 18 April 1948, Italy changed sides to good effect in the war, gained two political parties with mass support, lost a monarch by popular referendum, and both gained and lost the Soviet Union as an ally. This long interval of regime collapse, occupation, provisional government, reconstruction and drafting of the new constitution meant that there was every opportunity for the parties and interest groups to reorganise and to stake their claim to a role in the new republic. Within the limits of their political resources, the major parties did this with a relatively clear eye on the long-term and on the need to consolidate their own position. The rigidity of the post-war settlement reflects the success of the post-war generation in entrenching themselves into the institutions of state.

The long-term objective of the new government immediately after the fall of Fascism was to prepare for a 'return to the Statute'. The decree-law of 2 August 1943 dissolved the Fascist legislature, the 30th since unification, and required elections for a new Chamber of Deputies, which would be the 31st of the Liberal state, to be held within four months of the end of the war. The 'return to the Statute' implied the reassertion of the powers of the King as Head of State and Head of the executive. It also implied the abolition of the Fascist Lower House, and the reinstatement of the limited powers and rights of the Chamber of Deputies envisaged in the *Statuto Albertino*. This pious hope of the Liberal elites, that they could treat Fascism as an interlude and pick up their role from 1922, was swept aside by those who were actually determining events, namely the Allies, the Resistance and the new political parties. On 25 June 1944, after consultation with the Committee of National Liberation and with the agreement of the Allies, a decree of the Lieutenant-General acting as head of the Executive made new dispositions for the future conduct of the Italian government during the period of hostilities and after. Article One of the decree required elections for a Constituent Assembly to be held by universal suffrage as soon as practical after the end of the war. The link with the old Liberal regime was broken. Italy was to have a new Constitution based on popular sovereignty for the first time.[1]

Very rapidly in the interregnum from August 1943 to June 1945 a variety of political groups emerged, claiming the right to participate in the temporary government formed by the Committee of National Liberation under the control of the Allies. Some, like the *Partito Repubblicano Italiano*, the *Partito d'Azione* and the *Partito Democratico del Lavoro*, were energetic, well-qualified, but restricted clubs of intellectuals and concerned professionals. Others, such as the *Blocco Nazionale della Libertà*, which arrived later, were heterogeneous collections of former or aspiring local notables. If it had been left to these, the new arrangements might in the end have been little different from the old Liberal state with the addition of universal suffrage, despite the radical enthusiasms of the PRI and the Pd'A. The weight of the old regime was still strong in local politics and in public administration, and the Church hierarchy was demonstrating a distinct willingness to consider authoritarian versions of liberal democratic rule.[2] Schematically, we can say that the old regime was represented by local interest-groups, by religious authority and by the remaining apparatus of government, including the judiciary.

The crucial new factors were threefold: the experience of the resistance movement, the physical and moral presence of the Allies, particularly the United States, and the emergence of two mass-based political groupings. In their institutional aspirations for the new system, most of the resistance groups favoured a break with the old.[3] They supported wide suffrage and accountability, extensive civil liberties and, in different ways, radical reforms in the cause of social justice. However, they shared with the old order one crucial characteristic, which was that they were divided internally and from one another by deep ideological and regional differences. The resistance movement was restricted entirely to the North and Centre, and inevitably operated in dispersed, fragmented and clandestine groups, many having only loose links with the mass political parties. Even the PCI had difficulty controlling its local units, and there was sometimes bitter rivalry between groups with differing political allegiances fighting in neighbouring areas. With great difficulty, the resistance groups set up the CLNAI, the Committees of National Liberation for Northern Italy; these were dominated by the Communists and Socialists, and were used by them not only or even primarily to co-ordinate the partisan fighting but also to ensure that, in the administrative chaos as the Germans were finally defeated, provisional authority could be adopted by reliable groups. The CLNAI gave a strong radical impetus to the process of reconstruction, and they often found themselves in political conflict with the CLN in Southern Italy.

The presence of the Allies was a further complicating factor. Italy was not a military or political priority for them, and their preferences were not always clear or consistent. Though present in some force in the Italian peninsula, the senior British diplomats and military staff (with some notable exceptions) had little regard for or understanding of the complexity of Italian politics, and the view from London generally favoured the strengthening of the monarchy and relatively strict peace settlement terms. The US representatives usually showed a greater degree of understanding. Some American senior officers and State Department officials were surprised and appalled at the poverty and deprivation they witnessed in the South, and were willing to give limited tacit support to relatively radical reform programmes involving government aid and land distribution. One such was the Gullo reform programme of 1944, sponsored by the Communist minister of agriculture; the lack of success of this ambitious effort now seems mainly attributable to internal opposition which as in other cases was able to conceal its responsibility behind Allied reticence.[4] But there was serious Allied concern at the possibility of further political and social instability which might allow the Communists to gain the upper hand. The prospect of a Communist takeover in such a strategically significant area was not to be entertained: the issue which divided the American foreign policy community was how best to avert it. There were those who favoured the line adopted initially by the British. A penal peace settlement and an authoritarian democratic constitution would satisfy the conservative opinions in the State Department and in the interested public, but this would require continuing US involvement and would almost certainly lead to serious unrest in the short term. The alternative was to find an ally within the emerging system and to encourage rather than to direct developments.

The great success of the Christian Democrats was to claim the role of ally for themselves and to sustain it beyond the immediate problems of reconstruction. American involvement was direct and positive until the end of the war, but thereafter limited itself to close and usually informal diplomatic contacts together with substantial financial support for appropriate political groups. On appropriate occasions American interest was forcefully expressed at the highest levels, and this served to determine basic political trends at crucial points in the process of reconstruction. US aid channelled through the Marshall programme gave positive and material indication of American commitment, as well as being of great symbolic significance, though Italy was not always able to make proper use of the support. The State Department presented the US relationship with Italy as an 'alliance for progress', a kind phrase which glossed over the evident inequality of the relationship and the complexity of its objectives.[5] What the DC gave was the security of attachment to liberal democratic forms free of Communist influence, together with the apparent certainty that without them matters would be considerably more troublesome and demanding of US involvement. The DC could not appear to be too strong, as this might suggest it had no need of US support. The conundrum, which the DC resolved in practice very successfully for many years, was to appear both essential for Italy's recovery and vulnerable to domestic upheaval. In view of the DC's use of its tenure of power, there might appear some validity in the argument recently advanced by historians that the State Department's 'alliance for progress' was 'only the latest marriage of convenience' for Italy's governing elites. If this was a marriage of convenience, it proved itself considerably more enduring and closer than such arrangements are conventionally expected to be. It did, however, reflect the historic reliance of the political elites on external forces to provide economic, military and moral support, or alternatively to provide justification for domestic strategy.

But the development which most clearly marked out the new from the old was the spectacular growth of party politics. The Christian Democrats on the one hand and the Communists and Socialists on the other recruited new members very rapidly after 1943. These new mass parties, associated to a greater or lesser extent with the Resistance, were strongly based on social organisations controlled and operated either by the Church or by the Communists once they were able to work freely after the war. The main support for the Christian Democrats came from *Azione Cattolica* (Catholic Action); indeed, in many areas the DC was no more (and no less) than the political wing of Catholic Action, though it had to be formally distinct from it.[6] Catholic Action had survived through the Fascist regime as the lay social and cultural arm of the Catholic church, and in accordance with the Lateran Pacts it was prohibited from political activity. But many of its national office-holders, such as Fanfani, Moro and Andreotti, passed straight into senior positions in the new DC, and at the local level Catholic Action provided a substantial proportion of political activists through the *Comitati Civici* (Civic Committees). The DC could also count on the active support of local clergy, whose influence on choice of candidates was often considerable. This new breed of Italian political group, a single Catholic Party for all Catholics, became the home for other smaller groups on the right who were more concerned with conservatism than with Catholicism. An avowedly inter-class party, the DC was internally divided: as well as some lay Southern conservatives, its recruits covered the entire spectrum of Catholic political opinion including Catholic integralists, liberal Catholics, Catholic trade unionists, and even for a brief period a few brave souls who dared to describe themselves as Catholic Socialists.

The new party found itself under constant pressure from the Vatican to pursue more identifiably Catholic policies, particularly in regard to the Communists. The DC's electorate was mainly Catholic, and its policies were necessarily constrained by the influence of the Bishops and the Vatican.[7] Pope Pius XII paid close attention to the detail of Italian domestic politics throughout his reign and particularly from 1943 on. The primary interest for the Church was to maintain the privileges embodied in the Lateran Pacts. But its traditional approach was to present itself as committed to no particular political system, and the world of party politics was not familiar to it. Both of these had to change for the Church to be politically effective. The opposition of the Papacy to Communism was on grounds both of principle and of practice. In the Papal view, Communism was by definition atheistic and therefore intolerable to Catholic doctrine. A major impulse in the same direction seems to have come from the Pope's grave concern over the threat of Communism in general and the treatment of Russian and Eastern European Catholics in particular. The prospect of a large indigenous Communist Party achieving governmental influence in post-war Italy, even of Rome itself in the hands of a PCI administration, was a major factor in persuading the Pope to give his support to the notion of a single Catholic Party, which all Catholics would be enjoined to support. It was therefore concern over both national and international threats that moved the Pope to commit Catholic laity wherever he could to the struggle against Communism, and the opportunities for this deployment in Italy appeared to be highly encouraging.

Inspired more by the relatively marginal tradition of Catholic pacificism than by the Church's conventional neutrality, some radical voices in the DC favoured Italy's neutrality, but the strategic importance of Italy, the presence of Allied troops and the weight of US aid in the Marshall Plan made Italy's support for NATO difficult to argue against. The Pope's explicit support for NATO was expressed in an exchange of letters with President Truman in 1949. His involvement with political developments in Western Europe was detailed, and was inevitably closer in Italy than elsewhere. He expected to be able to influence DC policy directly, and would have liked to use his authority with the electorate to push the DC to adopt Papal policy, particularly on coalition strategy.

De Gasperi's priorities were rather to establish the DC as the dominant centre party, able to appeal to a wide spectrum of voters and committed to the historical role of establishing a firm base for liberal democracy in Italy.[8] It was therefore important to him not to allow relatively extreme right-wing parties to siphon off traditionalist elements in the Catholic vote, but this was counterbalanced by the strategic imperative not to become over-dependent on restricted political groupings. De Gasperi was also concerned about the brooding presence of the owners of large-scale industry in the North, about whose political commitment he was known to express some doubts. The core of De Gasperi's strategy was to maintain this balancing act by widening the appeal of the DC and by seeking broad-based alliances with other parties of the centre-Right and centre-Left. Under De Gasperi, the avowedly agnostic, explicitly non-Catholic or Liberal – lay influence within the party was always minimal, though this was not De Gasperi's original declared intention. Nevertheless, the success of the DC was to integrate Catholics into Italian politics for the first time, to do so without equivocation, and to do so as the largest single party, the party without which no Government could be formed. For at least the first twenty years of the Republic, the stable core of the DC's electorate was made up of Catholics, but the term covered wide variations in levels of religious practice, in regional religious tradition and in the political application of religious belief. The DC therefore could never be said to have a strong positive sense of purpose, and this was part of the price it paid for its success in establishing itself at the heart of Italian politics. To recycle an old metaphor, the DC's politics are those of the chameleon, its colouring taken from its surroundings, particularly from its allies. Though one of its initial priorities was to achieve independence from the Church, this was an organisational not an ideological imperative. Thus the DC's complement to Church organisation (and eventual replacement for it) was not a modified set of policies for a different electorate, but a new way of reaching the same people. The new method and the new structure amounted to the use of state resources on a large scale, as a modern form of patronage, whose origins can be found in the land reforms of 1949, and the establishment of the fund for the South in 1950. Both of these were strongly supported by Fanfani, Minister of Agriculture at the time, who was one of the first to identify and to develop the use of the public sector for the purposes of mass patronage. The development of the public sector also helped to counterbalance the influence of the big private sector industrialists. Thus despite its internal inconsistencies the DC was able to put its imprint on post-war Italy through the vigour and ambition of its Catholic elites and through its organisational flexibility.

Like the DC, the PCI was a new party with antecedents. The PCI expanded its membership from 1942 onwards and by 1945 had over one million members.[9] Its clandestine tradition in the cities of the North during Fascism and its involvement in the Resistance movement had given a distinct Italian character to its organisation and strategy, though the origins of the Party tied it firmly to Moscow through the Third International and the Comintern. The national and independent aspects of its development were skilfully used by the post-war leader Palmiro Togliatti to ensure that the PCI played a full part in the reconstruction. This strategy, dubbed at the time 'the Italian road to Socialism', required the PCI to make significant compromises in the conduct of the interim governments, in return for which they had ministerial office at Cabinet level and influential posts in the Constituent Assembly. The PCI, a Leninist vanguard party in origins, had strong political links with the Soviet Union, and despite the uniqueness 'the Italian road' retained many of the characteristics of conventional Communist Parties. Its organisation was run on the principle of democratic centralism, its internal discipline was rigorous, it developed the cell structure typical of the vanguard party, and, not least, its revolutionary rhetoric continually belied its claims to be fully committed to the emerging liberal democracy. The PCI strength lay partly in the coherence and determination of its senior figures and of its core of disciplined activists, but also in its rapid assumption of control of the Trade Union movement CGIL and of the workers' cooperatives, particularly in the provinces of Emilia-Romagna and Tuscany. Its strategy was based on the assumption that the collaboration between East and West agreed at Yalta in 1944 would be sustained, at least sufficiently to allow the Communists to remain in government coalitions in Western Europe.

Thus the new party system was determined by the emergence of two mass parties, both having mass support in the trade unions and in social organisations and both able to build up administrative experience in local government. The two groups were divided internally, but despite the divisions both demonstrated the capacity to organise activists and to mobilise voters on a mass scale in a way that the Liberal state and the Fascist regime had not been able to countenance. But the key to the reconstruction is that the system was born under the sign of the Cold War, and one of the mass parties was on the wrong side of the front line. The participation of the Communists and socialists in the interim governments was increasingly difficult for the Vatican and for the United States to tolerate, and Communist use of the trade unions for political purposes (in particular through the use of strike action) was seen by the DC as a continual source of provocation.

After August 1943, the immediate assumption of many politicians seems to have been that the largest party on the left would once again be the socialists, and in fact they did win more votes than the PCI at the 1946 Constituent Assembly elections. The initial strategy of the PSI was to work closely with the Communists in government. When the genuine respective strengths of the two parties began to emerge, together with the costs of such an alliance, the Popular Front strategy became more difficult for the PSI to sustain. In June 1947, the PSI split and a new social-democratic party (PSLI, renamed later PSDI) was formed under the leadership of the veteran Giuseppe Saragat. This split and the exclusion of the PSI and PCI from the tripartite government in May 1947 mark the establishment of the ground rules for coalition formation which have dominated Italian politics since then.

The initial replacement for the tripartite coalition disbanded in May 1947 was a centre-Right formula in which the DC was supported by the three minor lay parties – the Liberal Party (PLI), the Republican Party (PRI) and the Social Democrats. In the first parliamentary elections, held on 18–19 April 1948, the DC fought a vigorous anti-Communist campaign, supported by the wholehearted efforts of the Church to mobilise Catholic voters in what was portrayed as a new Christian crusade against the Popular Front formed by the PCI and PSI. The DC won 48.4 per cent of the votes, a total never achieved since. Because of imbalances in the constituency boundaries, its share of the seats in the Chamber of Deputies was actually 304 out of 574, easily an overall majority.

Despite this, the DC leader De Gasperi chose to form a coalition with the three minor parties. This served two purposes: the coalition reduced De Gasperi's dependence on the integralist pro-clerical elements within his own party, and it enabled De Gasperi to claim (as he in fact did in his opening speech to the new Chamber) that all those outside the coalition were in some sense ambiguous in their commitment to the forms and principles sanctioned by the Constitution. In that sense the convention was immediately established that governing coalitions were to be formed with the maximum available numbers, where availability was determined more by alleged loyalty to the Constitution than by policy agreement. The question of government formation and its impact on policy processes is considered in more detail in chapter 5. Though the precise mechanisms by which governments fall and take up office are undoubtedly significant in policy terms, those mechanisms occur within a relatively rigid set of conventions, largely laid down in the early years of the Republic and not radically modified since then. There remained the principle of exclusion of the PCI (and presumably all parties identified as to the left of the Communists). Indeed, in the political jargon so beloved of the Italian political classes this principle was eventually graced with a Latin reference, surely symbolic of its totem-like venerability: the ban on government posts for the second largest party in the country was commonly referred to as the *conventio ad excludendum* – the agreement on what is to be excluded.[10] The principle of maximum available numbers has certainly been attenuated, and now competes with more pragmatic policy considerations. The notion remains that coalition formulae should serve three purposes – to widen support so as to prevent over-dependence on specific groups, to penalise with the stigma of unreliability those who are repeatedly left out, and to reward loyalty with the material privileges of office.

## THE CONSTITUENT ASSEMBLY

As we have seen, the elections of 2 June 1946 marked the end of the six-party coalition governments in which the strengths of the individual parties were unknown, and the beginning of 'political real time' based on domination by three mass parties (DC, PSI and PCI). The Constituent Assembly which resulted from these elections was intended to finish its work within six months. Giving an early demonstration of what was to become an institutional habit in Italian politics, the Assembly missed the deadline in spectacular fashion and did not in fact finish until December 1947, twelve months late.[11]

The most important reason for the delay, as indeed for much of the apparently endemic dilatoriness of future deliberations, was the need to ensure that all the political groups had their say. The proceedings of the Constituent Assembly reflected the spirit of national unity and solidarity of all the anti-Fascist forces; in this they differed markedly from what was happening in the world outside the old parliamentary palaces, where divisions between the Christian Democrats and Communists threatened the pluralism and solidarity of the interim governments and of the resistance, and eventually destroyed them.

In view of the delicacy and magnitude of the task facing it, the Assembly delegated wide powers to a special Committee established to draft a text for its consideration. Respect for the plurality of views present in the Assembly required that all 11 groups should be represented, and the Committee therefore had a large and unwieldy membership of 75 deputies. This in turn formed three sub-committees charged with drafting separate sections of the Constitution. Though the sub-committee members were intended to be technical experts, they were also party-political representatives, and their work was a complex mixture of legal technicalities and party compromise. Already the authority of the Assembly had been diluted by the length of time before it could be elected and by the contentious decision to hold a referendum on the issue of the monarchy, which the Left thought should have been decided in the Assembly. It was further constrained by the difficulty of its relationship with the provisional governments, and by the generally low level of public interest in its proceedings. Thus the Constitution could be said to have been written in three parts by separate groups of lawyers representing party political positions, deliberating largely without public attention or pressure, respecting the need to listen to one another's views and willing to spend a considerable time doing so. After limited editing, the full draft document then went to the Assembly at the beginning of March 1947, where it was subject to intense and sometimes passionate debate in which all the party political positions were given a thorough airing. The details of the draft from the '75' were generally approved with only technical amendments; the only issues which underwent radical amendment were State – Church relations, regional government, the Constitutional Court and the role of the Senate. There was no substantial support for the Constitution to be submitted to popular referendum, and it was ratified with the support of all the CLN parties on 28 December 1947.

The Governments of the day kept themselves formally separate from the proceedings, and their difficulties had little direct impact on the positions adopted by the parties on most individual clauses of the Constitution. After their exclusion from governmental office the PCI claimed to be fully a party of the Republic in the constitutional sense, even when the parties of the centre-Right cast doubt on their democratic legitimacy. This divergence between the Constitutional accord including the PCI and the institutional practice excluding them represents the fault line in Italian politics. After the exclusion of the PCI and PSI in May 1947 there were in effect two separate majorities functioning on different occasions in the same Assembly – the Constitutional majority made up of the parties who had worked together in the Committee of National Liberation (CLN) on the one hand, and on the other hand the government majority, a more restricted group made up of the DC and its allies. The notion of two (or more) separate majorities has continued in attenuated form throughout the post-war period. The final debate on the text of the Constitution was characterised by genuine efforts on almost all sides to emphasise the unity of purpose of the Assembly. But the depth of the differences within and between the parties could not be suppressed entirely. They were revealed in a last-ditch effort by the Christian Democrat member Giorgio La Pira to insert a preamble with a strongly religious tone at the beginning of the document. Despite the protests even of his own party, he insisted in persevering with what he regarded as his religious duty, thus disturbing the unanimity of the proceedings and forcing a vote which embarrassed his own party and which angered the lay parties.[12] The episode was symptomatic of the difficulties to come. Though for the most part it maintained the unity and indeed some of the radicalism of the resistance period, in its constitutional labours the Assembly established a pattern for organising its work which the ordinary Parliaments followed to a considerable extent: practical lack of accountability to public opinion, utter disrespect for deadlines, use of detailed legal technicalities to mask fundamental disagreements, the priority of seeking as wide an agreement as possible, and not least the vulnerability of Assembly debates to the wilfulness (or independence) of backbench deputies.

## THE CONSTITUTION – PRINCIPLES AND DEVELOPMENT

The Constitution of the Republic[13] is the product of the overriding concern of the parties to prevent a return to Fascism; like perhaps De Gaulle and Debré at the end of the French Fourth Republic in 1958, the framers of the Italian Constitution were again fighting battles originally fought (and lost) decades previously. In the case of Italy, the decision to have a rigid constitution followed the common diagnosis of Fascism: its success in achieving power was seen as essentially a revolt of the independent small property-owning middle-classes, mainly urban and provincial, aided by the breakdown of legality (responsibility for which was variously attributed); Mussolini achieved office through procedures of purely specious legal validity, and then was able to exploit the lack of constitutional impediments to overthrow the Liberal state from within. Once in power, the Fascist regime conducted itself with gross disrespect for formal legal procedures and for substantial human rights, and its success was partly determined by the lack of clear distinctions between law and politics in a variety of sectors – the formation of governments, for example, but also regulation of the judiciary, powers of the police, and scope of individual liberties. Hence a written constitution was seen as one way of preventing a return to Fascism, since it would put rigid obstacles in the way of any dictatorial usurpation of power, obstacles which could be circumvented only by complete overthrow of the constitutional framework.

In case there should be any doubt about the political sensitivities of the traditional property-owning sectors, 30 seats in the Assembly elections were won by the southern right-wing populist group *L'Uomo Qualunque* (literally 'the common man' or 'the man in the street'). Also, though the Constitution bans the re-founding of the National Fascist Party (article 139, clause 12), this did not stop the early appearance of many of its middle-ranking members in a new Party, the MSI (Italian Social Movement), which won only 5 seats in the 1948 elections but which quickly established its neo-Fascist identity and has been the fourth largest party for most of the post-war Republic.

To serve the purpose of putting the legal framework beyond the reach of politicians, the Constitution had to be not only written but also rigid. Unlike the *Statuto Albertino*, this constitution cannot be modified by ordinary law. It can only be amended by constitutional laws passed by special majorities in extraordinary procedures of the legislature. On the whole, Parliament has tended to respect the inviolability of the Constitution, perhaps even showing the text undue respect where experience has revealed its internal inconsistencies and inadequacies. Another way in which the Constitution was placed outside political debate was by protecting it with a constitutional court established for this purpose, having special membership and not being part of the ordinary judicial procedure.[14] While the need for a constitution was widely accepted, the provision of a separate court for it was not. Those who most strongly supported the notion of a constitutional court were, perhaps not surprisingly, the proponents also of the 'guarantee' functions of the Constitution. According to this view, strongly supported by the PRI and the Pd'A, the purpose of the Constitution was to prescribe the general framework and fundamental values of the Republic and to guarantee their observance; the alternative view was that of the Communists, according to whom the Constitution ought to lay down norms which would be used in policy-making and which would be relatively specific. This distinction reflected divergences of substance about what the Constitution ought to say both on the political structures and on the content of policy. As the largest single party, the DC had the greatest weight, but the Assembly found them lacking in any clear independent vision of the future Republic. The DC did however know what it disliked and that was, on principle, most of the proposals put forward by the PCI. The need for a semblance of unanimity and the impulse of the Resistance competed with the tactical demands of emerging party politics. The Constitution which results gives something to everybody, at the cost not only of brevity but also of internal consistency. Napoleon said that constitutions should be brief and obscure, but experience teaches that such qualities are difficult to achieve, and the Italian Constituent Assembly did not even try. The respected jurist Piero Calamandrei later referred to the text of the Constitution as 'that old aunt, a bit eccentric and a bit of a visionary', a phrase which suggests rather more fondness than respect.[15]

But in the view of *Azionisti* such as Calamandrei, the Constitution could and should have been very different. In this view, a constitution should be characterised by a high degree of rigidity and generality. It should have the precise function of prescribing general principles, and should guarantee these by placing them above the law and by giving them a special court to protect them. The general principles to be observed could be subsumed under the terms 'Legality, Democracy and Pluralism'. In the most categorical version of this argument, these principles are to be derived from the liberal democratic model of government which is adopted as part of the post-war compromise.

Strongly inflenced by the views of the Austrian jurist Hans Kelsen, the *Azionisti* put forward an idealist view of law-making, in which the Constitution (and its court) represented the abstract and general pinnacle of a coherent hierarchical system of norms, all derivable from the constitutional principles and the constitutional model. Thus, this argument derives the progressive character of the Constitution mainly from the content of its generic statements of value and principle, rather than from specific prescription as to structures, calendars, numbers of members, and precise policy objectives. In this view, ably and coherently presented by the small PRI and Pd'A groups, the scope of the Constitution was potentially all-embracing, but the level of activity of the constitutional court would progressively diminish as the preponderance of Fascist legislation was removed by a legislature committed to constitutional values. The mode of policy-making to be derived from this would be rational, organic, and highly integrated.

The PCI did not accept the standard analysis of the Fascist period. For PCI theoreticians, the success of Mussolini's regime was a due to a deficiency of democracy rather than to a failure of legality.[16] The Communists were therefore decidedly equivocal about the scope of the Constitution. They favoured a constitution which would be clearly committed to specific radical egalitarian values and which should leave their implementation to a political system dominated by a single-chamber legislature. The temporary continuation of Liberal and Fascist norms, particularly the Penal Code and the Code of Penal Procedure, was accepted only as the means of ensuring a peaceful and stable transitional period. To the legislature should fall the task of guaranteeing the progressive implementation of the Constitution and the transformation of Italian politics into a radical democratic participatory system. A crucial point of difference with the progressive Liberal view was that the Communists wanted all major policy-making channelled through the legislature and not through pluralist competing centres such as the constitutional court. Almost above all else, the PCI objected to the legislature being checked by non-elected powers. In this sense, the PCI saw themselves as the new Jacobins, who would guide Italy through the democratic revolution it had failed to have in the nineteenth century. In direct opposition to the *Azionisti*, the PCI opposed the idea of the Constitution as a general guarantee and sought to write into it relatively precise policy commitments which would bind future governments to radical social policy. In this area, the position adopted by the PCI leaders was a particular though important application of the 'Italian road to socialism'. This strategy required the PCI to work from within the liberal democratic system to achieve what were known as 'non-reformist reforms' – reforms which would undermine the domination and ideological control of the owners of capital.

In the face of these relatively well-developed notions of the function of the Constitution, the DC could call on the assistance of several expert jurists, such as Costantino Mortati and Egidio Tosato, who distinguished themselves in detailed drafting work in the Committee of 75. DC politicians frequently engaged in generic appeals to Catholic social doctrine, but this was curiously lacking in direct applicability to many of the issues faced by the drafters of the Constitution. De Gasperi's early views on constitutional structure had been represented in *Idee ricostruttive* (1943).[17] This put forward the traditional Catholic view, rejecting both capitalism and socialism, describing the state–society relationship in organic terms, and proposing a federal system for the post-war state. De Gasperi's proposals, though not worked out in any detail, were consonant with Catholic social doctrine since the time of *Rerum Novarum* in favouring the maximum possible degree of economic freedom for individuals, to be exercised within the framework of public and private social responsibility.

Generally, modern Catholic social doctrine has opposed absolutist views of the state and has sought the deconcentration of political power. The DC favoured explicit guarantees for civil liberties and a pluralistic power structure. Progressive Catholic thinkers such as Jacques Maritain had already articulated clear views on the need for the dispersion of economic and political power within liberal democratic structures. In 1943, De Gasperi had been thinking of some rather different solutions, to the extent that he proposed a second chamber which should be based on 'economic suffrage' and which should be 'the instrument of proportion and direction' of the economy. These quasi-corporatist proposals were unacceptable to the large industrial interests and to the progressive lay parties. Another reason for their lack of impact was that they smacked very much of Fascist forms of state control, though they owed their origins at least as much to the Papal support for Catholic corporatism expressed in the encyclical of Pope Pius XI *Quadragesimo Anno* (1931). Paradoxically, this source did not stand in their favour even in tactical terms, since by the time of the Constituent Assembly it was becoming important for De Gasperi to diminish his party's ideological reliance on papal orthodoxy. The economic second chamber, probably the most radical and certainly the most distinctive element in the DC's original proposals, did not survive beyond the Committee of 75. A vestige of it may be seen in the CNEL, the consultative third chamber which despite one or two forays into sensitive areas such as administrative reform has been largely without influence and indeed without history.

The Constitution itself bears clear marks of all three of these major ideological influences – the lay progressive group, the Communists and the Christian Democrats. It combines the lofty principles and guarantee functions of the *Azionisti* with some of the radical social engineering sought by the PCI and with the 'guided pluralism' favoured by the DC.[18] Overall, it might be said that what the Constitution lacks in coherence it makes up for in ambition. On central issues such as sovereignty, the spirit of the Constitution is Jacobin, but not unambiguously so. Sovereignty is exercised by the people 'within the forms and limits of the Constitution', which means this is a representative democracy, in which the central function of legislation is the prerogative of Parliament, exercised within the framework of established constitutional law. Above all else, Italy is a *stato di diritto*, a state founded on law. All political will, in other words, must be expressed through law or through norms having legal status, and the supreme instrument of this is Parliament.

But this apparently categorical position is qualified, so that the centrality of Parliament is mitigated in several ways. Firstly, two separate structures or offices exist which guarantee the proper functioning and continuity of the constitutional system. These are the Presidency of the Republic and the constitutional court. The President has few direct executive responsibilities, and the power of the office (whose scope is still largely untested) is usually held to lie in the functions related to government formation, dissolution of Parliament, and counter-signature of all laws. He (or she, though all have so far been males) chairs the Supreme Council of Magistrates and the Supreme Council of Defence. All these functions are to be exercised within the terms of the Constitution. Since most of the activities within the President's ambit originate from Parliament or the Council of Ministers, it is widely accepted that the President has the reserve function of ensuring that the actions of the major political institutions are constitutional, in the sense that they are within the constitutional competence of the legislature and executive, and that they observe the proper procedures. He or she exercises this function by powers of supervision, imparting advice and persuasion, rather than by wielding repeatedly the powers to send laws back without signature or to dissolve Parliament. In general, then, the President of the Republic protects and guarantees the constitutional framework, its powers and its relationships, and in this way is a limitation on the major institutions.

The guarantee function of the constitutional court refers specifically to the laws and norms which make up the routine activity of the state; but the court also has the reserve function of deciding in disputes of competence between state institutions, and is given the function of court of impeachment in cases involving the President of the Republic, the Prime Minister and ministers. The relationship between the President of the Republic and the constitutional court is one of overlapping competence, rather than strict separation. If there is a distinction between them in the Constitution, it is that the President represents the state, while the constitutional court represents the supremacy of law. Both depend on and limit the powers of the formally sovereign Parliament through their competence over interpretation of the Constitution.

These two are the heavyweights of the constitutional text. The second way in which popular sovereignty expressed through Parliament is constrained by the Constitution is more prosaic and more routine. By establishing several different 'constitutional organs' the Constitution implicitly supports the idea of the limited separation of powers. Indeed, in modern Italian jurisprudence this is usually argued to follow from the supremacy of law in the Italian tradition. Powers vested in institutions are separate in that the institutions have a degree of autonomy and self-regulation, but this is limited by the overlapping character of their functions and the direct competition between them. Quite deliberately, the Constituent Assembly (or rather, its drafting committee) established several other procedures or structures which can claim in some way to exercise the function of popular representation. The most obvious of these, which has emerged in recent years as a regular recourse, is the use of popular referendums. These may be called at the request of 500,000 electors or five regional councils, and can only concern the repeal of all or part of an ordinary law. Constitutional status is also given to the system of regional government, a reform particularly sought by the Christian Democrats in the Assembly, with specific functions protected by the Constitution and with directly elected assemblies having legislative power within the terms of the Constitution. Popular sovereignty beyond Parliament is also understood to be protected not only by the form of words in Article 1 but also by the variety of guarantees provided for forms of political association – there is a constitutional right for citizens to join political parties, citizens may present petitions to Parliament which have to be considered, and fundamental civil liberties are specifically covered – the right to trade union representation, to free association, to religious freedom and to freedom of speech. This is a constitution in which the sovereignty of popular representation in Parliament is hedged about by the recognition of the guarantee function of other powers and by the establishment of competing forms of representation. Finally, it should be observed that in many cases the Constitution leaves the implementation of its wishes to ordinary legislation, merely prescribing that such legislation shall be made. This applies explicitly, for example, to the clauses on freedom of the press, on trade union recognition, and on minority religions. It also applies implicitly to the statements of principle, such as the famous (or in some quarters notorious) Article 3 clause 2, which declares:

> It is the task [*compito*] of the Republic to remove all social and economic obstacles which by limiting in practice the liberty and equality of citizens impede the full development of the human person and the effective participation of all workers in the political economic and social organisation of the country.

Much of the organisation of the state itself, such as the structure of the public administration and the reform of the Prime Minister's office, was left to ordinary legislation, and this we discuss in the next chapter. It may seem that much space here has been devoted to consideration of what are after all matters of jurisprudence rather than of political practice. It must therefore be observed that the relationship between these two is extremely close in Italian policy-making – not in the simplistic sense that law defines entirely the realm of practice, but in the sense that interpretations of legality are the stuff of routine policy-making, and in the sense that interpretations of the Constitution are still the battleground of much political debate over forty years after its promulgation.

We have seen that during the period of the Constituent Assembly the governmental coalition of national unity broke down and was replaced by a much more restrictive formula. But the Constitution to a very considerable extent reflects the period of national unity, not the later divisions. It remains a potent symbol of anti-Fascism, but many of its programmatic norms (those norms which required the political will of future governments in their support) had to wait years and in some cases decades before they were acted on, and some are still awaiting implementation in law. It was seven years before the constitutional court was established, twenty years before the referendum law was approved and twenty-two years before the first elections for the ordinary regions. We discuss some of the specific cases later, but the general reasons can be briefly alluded to here. Some of the difficulties were inherent in the document itself. Merely to apply the Constitution to the existing legal codes required extensive revision of the codes, a work which is still not finished over forty years later. Major legislative reforms were required particularly in the sectors of associational activity and civil liberties, and the central functions of public administration such as the Prime Minister's office also needed the application of the programmatic norms. Neither Parliament nor public administration were equipped to deal with these problems immediately, whereas the priorities of economic reconstruction were immediate and apparently more amenable. Also, it was quickly realised that the vagueness of some of the text and its internal contradictions (for example, on the status of women) were likely to impede agreement on implementation.

But there were other reasons why the implementation of the Constitution limped badly. The pluralism favoured by the DC and others in the Assembly came to appear to many within its ranks as an unwelcome and possibly dangerous diminution of the powers of central government; the threat of Fascism which so exercised the Assembly was quickly replaced by the threat, apparent or real, of a mass Communist Party with considerable strength in local government and in the trade union movement. Instead of being an opportunity for guided progress, the Constitution became, as the DC leader Scelba described it, 'a snare-constitution', to be treated with extreme circumspection. The DC as the party of apparently permanent government not surprisingly came to the conclusion that they had to proceed with extreme caution, lest they should seriously weaken the state by diffusing its power excessively. The central function of government remained the control of the executive based on an assured majority in Parliament; it was this that came to be seen by the governing parties as the key to stability, not the democratic pluralism of the more radical readings of the Constitution. Control of the narrow institutional majority became the most important resource. The stability of the institutional exchanges between factions rested on the dominant role exercised by the DC in determining the allocation of ministerial responsibilities. This in turn rested on the unwavering electoral support for the DC and the categorical ban on their nearest rivals. Resources and objectives determined strategies within rules set by the DC, in accordance with processes of exchange which rendered the standard political processes increasingly irrelevant.

In reaction to this, the Communists, who had initially been tepid in their enthusiasm for the main thrust of the Constitution, came to appreciate its hidden qualities and found themselves able to become the leading supporters of its implementation. All of this had major effects not just on the formalities of administration but also on the practicalities of political organisation, since it allowed one group of parties to occupy the state indefinitely, and to identify the state apparatus as substitutes for their own bureaucracies. In terms of the initial discussion of the structural weaknesses of the political system and particularly of the separation of state from civil society, the reconstruction gave the opportunity to resolve this division, to fuse together, as it were, civil society and political society and to enable the two to develop together into a mass participatory liberal democracy. That this did not happen, that particular parties came to dominate the state exclusively, is not the direct responsibility of the Constitution, but it does suggest that a constitution is the instrument of future generations to abuse as they see fit, at least as much as it is the instrument of the original legislators.

## NOTES

1 For the social and political developments of the 1943–48 period, see Ginsborg, P., *A history of contemporary Italy – society and politics 1943–1988*, (London, Penguin, 1990) chapters 1–4; Harper, J.L., *America and the reconstruction of Italy, 1945–1948* (Cambridge, Cambridge U.P., 1986); Di Nolfo, E., 'The United States and Italian Communism 1942–1946: World War Two to the Cold War', pp. 74–94 in *Journal of Italian History*, vol. 1 no. 1 Spring 1978; Katz, R., *The fall of the House of Savoy* (New York, Macmillan, 1971); Delzell, C., 'The Italian anti-fascist resistance in retrospect: three decades of historiography', pp. 66–96 in *Journal of Modern History*, vol. 47 no. 1 March 1975.
2 Poggi, G., 'The church in Italian politics 1945–1950', pp. 133–155 in Woolf, S.J., *The rebirth of Italy* (London, Longman, 1972); Magister, S., *La politica vaticana e l'Italia 1943–1978* (Roma, Editori Riuniti, 1979); Settembrini, D., *La chiesa nella politica italiana* (Milano, Rizzoli, 1977). See also Falconi, C., *La chiesa e le organizzazioni cattoliche in Italia 1945–1955* (Torino, Einaudi, 1956).
3 On the resistance movement, see Battaglia, R., *Storia della resistenza italiana* (Torino, Einaudi, 1964); Ellwood, D., *Italy 1943–1945* (Leicester, Leicester U.P., 1985); Mafai, M., *L'uomo che sognava la lotta armata* (Milano, Feltrinelli, 1984); Quazza, G., *Resistenza e storia d'Italia* (Milano, Feltrinelli, 1976); Bocca, G., *Storia dell'Italia partigiana* (Bari, Laterza, 1977).

4  On the Gullo reforms, see Ginsborg, P., 'The Communist party and the agrarian question in southern Italy 1943–1948', pp. 81–101 in *History Workshop Journal*, no. 17 1984.

5  Harper, J.L., 1986, pp. 166–167.

6  The development of the DC in the immediate post-war is analysed from differing perspectives in Baget-Bozzo, G., *Il partito cristiano al potere, la DC di De Gasperi e di Dossetti* (Firenze, Vallecchi, 1974); Scoppola, P., *La proposta politica di De Gasperi* (Bologna, Il Mulino, 1977); Chiarante, G., 'A proposito della questione democristiana: democrazia, valori cristiani, società borghese', pp. 27–42 in *Critica Marxista*, vol. 15, 1975.

7  See Baget-Bozzo, G., 1974; also Furlong, P.F., *The Italian Christian Democrats – from Catholic movement to Conservative Party* (Hull Papers in Politics no. 25, University of Hull 1983)

8  Catti De Gasperi, M.R., *De Gasperi, uomo solo* (Milano, Mondadori, 1965); Settembrini, D., 1977. More generally, Leonardi, R. and Wertman, D.A., *Italian christian democracy: the politics of dominance* (London, Macmillan, 1989) ch. 2; Irving, R.E.M., *The Christian Democratic parties of Western Europe* (London, RIIA/George Allen and Unwin, 1979).

9  Amyot, G., *The Italian Communist Party* (London, Croom Helm, 1981); Sassoon, D., *The strategy of the Italian Communist Party, from the resistance to the historic compromise* (London, Frances Pinter, 1981); Tarrow, S.G., *Peasant Communism in Southern Italy* (New Haven, Conn. Yale University Press, 1967); the standard work in Italian is Spriano, P., *Storia del Partito Comunista Italiano* (5 vols, Torino, Einaudi, 1975). On relations with Moscow, see Barth Urban, J., *Moscow and the Italian Communist Party* (London, I.B. Tauris, 1986).

10  The phrase first appears in the late 1960s in the work of a constitutional lawyer close to the Moro faction in the DC, who returned to the theme over twenty years later in Elia, L., 'La forma di governo nell'Italia odierna,' pp. 26–31 in *Quaderni Costituzionali*, vol. 11 no. 1, aprile 1991.

11  See particularly Cheli, E. (ed.), 1978.

12  *Atti dell'Assemblea Costituente*, Discussioni, vol. 11 p. 3567 ff.

13  An official English translation of the text of the Constitution is in *Constitution of the Republic of Italy – Rules of the Chamber of Deputies and of the Senate of the Republic* (Rome, Research Services of the Chamber of Deputies and of the Senate of the Republic, 1979).

14  Furlong, P.F., 'The constitutional court in Italian Politics', pp. 7–23 in *West European Politics*, vol. 11 no. 3 July 1988.

15  p. 275, Calamandrei, P., 'L'ostruzionismo di maggioranza', pp. 129–136, 274–281, 433–150 in *Il Ponte*, April, May and June 1953.

16  Cheli, E., 1978; Spriano, P., *Le passioni di un decennio* (Milano, Garzanti, 1988); Togliatti, P., *On Gramsci and other writings* (London, Lawrence and Wishart, 1979).

17  Demofilo (pseudonym of A. de Gasperi), 'Idee ricostruttive della DC, luglio 1943', pp. 1–8 in *Atti e documenti della Democrazia Cristiana 1943–1967* (Rome, Edizioni Cinque Lune, 1968); a later collective view is 'Il programma della DC per la nuova costituente', pp. 23–24 in *Atti e Documenti 1968*. For the political views of one of the DC's experts, see Tosato, E., 'Sugli aspetti fondamentali dello stato', pp. 1783–1816 in *Studi in memoria di Carlo Esposito* (Padova, Cedam, 1972). Tosato and Mortati

were particularly influential in the debates in the second sub-commission of the constituent assembly, which dealt with political organisation: see *Assemblea Costituente, Commissione per la costituente*, Discussioni – seconda sottocommissione.

18 This is argued in more detail in Furlong, P.F., *The Constitution, the constitutional court and political freedom in Italy*, unpublished paper delivered to the Conference on Constitutions and political freedom, University of Warwick, September 1989. See also Adams, P. and Barile, P., *The Government of Republican Italy* (Boston, Houghton Mifflin, 1966); Adams, P. and Barile, P., 'The implementation of the Italian constitution', *American Political Science Review*, March 1953.

# Chapter 4

# The Machinery of State

## POLICY AND ADMINISTRATION

Why look at the administrative machinery at all? In particular ways which will be analysed in this chapter, the public administration determines policy through its capacity to subject substantive policy to the constraints of formal routine and of partisan determination. Italy's 'partyocracy', in other words, is expressed through a bureaucracy which though intensely politicised in some areas is able to maintain the impersonal formality of procedure in others. In general terms, the greater the degree of independence of the bureaucracy, the more likely we are to identify policy communities of relatively strong and cohesive professional interests. The more prevalent is the partisan mode of policy, the more likely we are to find the issue networks and the exchange processes associated with them. The critical qualification to this argument is that where the independence is greatest, it may rely on factors such as fragmentation of structure and legalism of procedures which mitigate against the development of policy communities.

What for the sake of argument we can call 'real policy' (as opposed to nominal or formal policy) is obviously the product of a variety of processes, including the expression of decisions by the proper authority. The difference between what political or judicial authority lays down and what is actually done by civil servants is obviously not radical in most cases taken individually. But before and after interest groups, political parties, local government, the para-state sector and ministers all have their say and reach their single or combined decisions or agreements on what should be done, when supposedly authoritative political decisions have been taken in Parliament or in the Council of Ministers, the structures and processes of Italian public administration at national and sub-national level alter the direction and scope of policy substantially.

In this context, the two most significant aspects of the power of the bureaucracy are the problem of implementation and its capacity to determine the agenda and the detail of policy formulation. Examples of the difference between formal and real policy certainly abound in the folklore of Italian politics: large sections of regional devolution legislation passed in the 1970s have been reinterpreted by ministries in Rome so as to avoid dissolution of parts of their central structures; urban planning regulations provided for in laws passed in the 1960s are inoperative because the urban plans are for the most part non-existent; European community directives on seat belts for cars and crash helmets for motor-cyclists took over a decade each to be implemented because of technical problems in the drafting, presenting and applying of the appropriate legislation; laws on the use of pesticides in agriculture are widely and freely ignored, partly because of the difficulty of monitoring and enforcing their application; and so on. The many examples tend to refer not only to positive changes in the way policy is implemented but also to the failure to carry out policy either in whole or in part. The areas affected most have been those where the machinery of the administration was instructed by law or by regulation to produce a framework for the application of future policy in the sector, as in urban planning or health, or where the administration was instructed to redistribute existing responsibilities to new or enhanced authorities, usually to its own detriment.

In comparative studies, problems such as these, which are broadly referred to as 'slippage' or 'institutional inertia', tend to be ascribed to several main sets of factors: to bureaucratic incompetence and lack of resources; or to conflicts of interest between politicians and bureaucratic agents, or to the objectives of the policy.[1] Under the first heading, logistical complications may be mishandled, co-ordination is lacking, materials, plans, skills and people may be unavailable when needed; training and supervision for new tasks may be inadequate; policies may be assigned to efficient but inappropriate agencies. Under the second, bureaucracies are seen to be responding to demands from client groups, internal sub-units, individual organisational actors; they may interpret and modify policies in the light of institutional dynamics such as changing professional preferences, dependence on unsympathetic or indifferent experts, established procedural constraints. Many small influences may interact to make the environment of implementation unstable or at least not conducive to adopted policy. Thirdly, adopted policy may be made without concern for implementation – aiming to affirm support for particular groups, to maintain values and commitments in the electorate or even to re-educate, to change public opinion. Formal policy is not always constructed entirely with a view to implementation, and may be deliberately ambiguous.

In the Italian case, all three of these types of problem may be present. Problems of genuine incompetence relate usually to bureaucracies which are given tasks beyond their scope. Some of the examples above do result from this mismatch of capacities and requirements. But the Italian institutional pattern is a rigid and traditional one, in which the tasks assigned directly to administrators are still relatively restricted. Particularly complex management tasks are usually given to separate agencies established for the purpose (autonomous agencies or public bodies). Many of the major problems with the central apparatus of the state are those associated with their difficulties in controlling these organisations, which are often far more sophisticated than they, as well as with technical incapacity, conflicts of interests and inappropriate objectives of policy. This is fostered by the recruitment and training patterns, by the forms of political control, and above all by the independence of individual ministers and by their capacity to call on legal forms to protect the jurisdictional or material interests of their ministries. In this sense, ministers are part of a highly conflictual process of policy-making whose resolution depends on the pivotal involvement of ministers or their close aides.

Italian Public Administration in its widest sense ought to be seen as a major direct influence on public policy. It is not only that the state apparatus is not under effective political control but rather that the capacity of directing public administration does not lie with the legislature, the Council of Ministers, the Prime Minister, or any other formal political body for that matter. Without stretching the point too far, it is fair to say that there is no overall control or directive capacity over the central administration in Italy, and responses to this, such as the adoption of deconcentration or decentralisation, have broadly speaking extended the location of the problem without promoting localistic solutions. There is of course political control of particular ministries and even of some policy areas, but it is fragmented, uncoordinated and unresponsive to the formal channels of legislative and executive authority; and, most important for our purposes, it is closely integrated with the traditional ways of working of the ministries. Onto this structure successive reforms have been grafted, or sometimes simply superimposed, as piecemeal administrative solutions adopted in response to rigidities and inefficiencies in the existing structures but with little attempt to integrate the new and the old. From this point of view, the system is not led by the Prime Minister or the Cabinet (which has never been seriously argued for post-war Italy), nor is it parliamentary (which has been argued by a persistent minority) nor even ruled by the parties (as argued by the overwhelming majority of commentators). Considered as a policy-making process, this is a two-headed system in which, when all other influences are taken into account, and with qualifications which will follow, the predominant actors are the individual ministers and the officials of their individual ministries, who combine to make policy, sometimes by genuine combination, sometimes by mere division of sectors. It is they who control the delivery of the bargains struck in the process of exchange, and they do so either as interested parties or as instruments for policies they are unable fully to deliver. They can determine the development of interest group relations, and are integral components of the networks and policy communities which make up the fabric of policy.

## THE ADMINISTRATION IN NATIONAL DEVELOPMENT: THE STATE APPARATUS AS THE ABSOLUTE SERVANT

One way to untangle the patterns of policy-making is to ask what rationale the functionaries themselves give to what they are doing, and what the political significance of this may be. In this case, the answer is that while the administrative process is usually regarded as intensely politicised, the ethos of the state apparatus is profoundly anti-political. This may very well be a means of preserving identity or of marking off territory from the interventions of political masters, a defensive strategy for the apparatus of central government, but it has high political costs in efficiency and political integration.

One of the most important supports for this anti-political ethos is in the predominant academic mode of understanding the machinery of state, which is highly legalistic, not open to ready public comprehension, and averse to pragmatic analysis of methods, objectives and results. Because of the predominance of legal forms, this academic perspective feeds directly into the way Public Administration sees itself, its modes of operation, and its recruitment, training and internal organisation. Characteristics of this mode of analysis are that it concentrates on formal rules and rule-making to the neglect of what actually happens, that it tends to describe essentially political choices in terms of their legal form rather than their political antecedents and consequences, and that it criticises political action in terms of formal conceptual coherence.

This results mainly from the origins of the state apparatus and its role in political development. At least one of the major distinguishing characteristics of Continental European policy processes is the complete formal coverage of law and of regulations having the force of law. Strictly speaking, there can be no action of public administration within the Italian framework which is not directly mandated by a law or by a quasi-legal norm. If this logic were to be applied fully, we would have to treat law and policy as co-terminous. This mode of administration is by no means unique to Italy, nor is it a twentieth-century invention. With a rather different theoretical background, it was a frequent response of nineteenth-century liberal elites to the problem of constraining the absolute power of the sovereign. The practice does however differ from country to country, in accordance with contingent factors. In most cases, and certainly in the Italian, the inflexibility and the universalistic pretensions of law are mitigated by considerable degrees of administrative discretion, judicial tact and political fiat.

In the early stages of the development of a national public administration, norms referring to the executive branch were treated as if assimilable to ordinary civil law in terminology and procedures, with the important exception that they referred directly to the absolute will of the sovereign, which implied that they could not be treated the same way in the civil courts.[2] One of the very first of the 'separate powers' to be established in various regimes in nineteenth-century Italy was the Council of State, whose function was to keep administrative law outside the ordinary civil and criminal procedures and thus to protect the special status of the executive. The modern Council of State in Italy is a direct descendent of these, and dates from the 1861 Ricasoli Law which (adopting the conservative view) extended the centralised and uniform Piedmontese executive structure to the new kingdom of Italy. With the important addition of regional government in 1968 this is still the basis of the state organisation. The alternative view in 1861, that of the Radicals, was that considerable autonomy should be given to regional government in recognition of the diversity of the country.

The 1861 Act introduced the office of Prefect as the representative of the state in each province. This was a measure of administrative decentralisation. The Prefect, usually an official of the Ministry of the Interior but sometimes a career politician, was supposed to co-ordinate the work of all ministries in the province, but the growth of goverment was not usually matched by institutional arrangements to enable the Prefects to maintain this role. The main tasks of the Prefect initially related to public order and internal security, including the conduct of elections, and this remained the core of prefectoral authority. The local machinery of state therefore reflected the priorities of the Liberal elites, in which political will (the Italian term is *indirizzo politico*) was a function of the central government; local political autonomy was limited, and local administration was supposedly under the close control of the Prefect. The machinery of state had mainly regulatory functions, and its structures and procedures emphasised the importance of acting with proper authority rather than responding to particular circumstances in the light of general objectives. The main function of the Council of State was to provide a prior check on the legitimacy and effectiveness of executive action, not to act as an administrative court for aggrieved citizens after the event.

The ethos of Public Administration reflected strongly the tensions associated with the process of national development. On the one hand, it was the instrument, even the servant of the monarch, separate from Parliament and answerable to the political dictates of the King's ministers. In the absence of a rigid or guaranteed constitution, the jurisdiction of the state apparatus was absolute, at least in principle. The Piedmontese state to which this originally applied was not large. The jurisdiction of its administrative machinery was geographically limited, and its control structures were relatively simple. It had no colonies, little need to develop a powerful administrative class, and no experience of the pressures of holding together a nation-state.[3]

On the other hand, the *Statuto Albertino* of 1848 established the principle of the separation of powers, together with the guarantee of the comprehensiveness of the legal system, covering all forms of executive action. This implies an absolutism of a different sort, in which the law's writ is uniform and universal, paying no regard to individual circumstances and excluding entirely the element of arbitrariness inherent in the instrumental notion of Public Administration. So from the beginning there has been tension inherent in the role of Public Administration, between the state as the embodiment of absolute political will and the state as the embodiment of law.

In practice what emerged in the process of national development was a state apparatus characterised both by absolutism and by legalism, which justified its function as an instrument of national unification only by asserting this to be the work of an abstract system of law dedicated to neutrality and to uniformity. Some elements in the state apparatus, particularly those associated with the military and with internal order functions, had a much looser interpretation of their role and were willing to use reasons of state as a justification for extra-legal actions. Though this was not the dominant tradition, it was certainly one which found favour with active and ambitious politicians: those on the Right used it to justify the severity of repressive measures against dissent, whereas those on the Left were more likely to use it to loosen the purse-strings of the state in favour of national economic objectives. Political will came to be associated, in the ethos of the public administration, with attempts by elected politicians to interfere with proper procedures. Law became a protection for the official against the efforts of ministers to use the absolute power of the state in an arbitrary manner. Hence officials came to see themselves as the embodiment of law, opposed to the partial and inconsistent operations of transitory politicians. The justification of the system lay precisely in its rigidity, its lack of consideration for particular circumstances, its unconcern for social contingencies – at least in principle.

Potentially, this was a powerful instrument of state authority. But the minority itself was divided over the priorities of unification, and there was constant suspicion that the legal absolutism was degenerating into political partiality as different factions of the Liberal elites won and lost control of executive office. Another consequence of the concern with the legal correctness of the actions of state functionaries was that the effectiveness of the policies could not be a primary concern for them. The crucial criterion by which policy was judged within the administration was the legal authority of the officials concerned, that is to say, their offices and the procedures appropriate to them.

The initial response of politicians was to try to tighten ministerial control, partly to make flexible use of the machinery and partly to prevent the development of an independent non-elected source of power. So a variety of reforms occurred during the early Liberal period which were initially aimed at enhancing the internal control mechanisms of central government. Later reforms recognised the failure of these efforts and tried to mitigate some of their consequences.

The most notable of the early reforms was the Cambray-Digny reform in 1869 which established central control over spending within ministries with the institution of the *Ragioneria Centrale dello Stato*.[4] In the late 1880s, concern over the extension of state activity in the fields of education and the economy, and over the weakness of political control by ministers, produced a series of reforms which abolished the position of secretary-general as administrative head of a ministry. These reforms, under the moderate Prime Minister Crispi, established the modern structure based on separate departments known as *direzioni generali* within each ministry. This more fragmented structure normally makes it difficult for the senior officials in a ministry to develop a single cohesive view with which to approach the minister, but it does preserve the form of ministerial responsibility and is a major obstacle to the development of an independent relatively homogeneous administrative class. Its rationale has its origins in the traditional Liberal suspicion of centres of public power, a suspicion which was predominant over the need, acknowledged in the Liberal period, for an efficient dynamic instrument of intervention in economic and social development. The legacy it passes on is of independent sections developing procedures and policies in a relationship of reciprocal suspicion with ministers.

The chronology here is significant. Italy differed in this from the other major continental European bureaucracies of the period, such as France, Germany and the Austro-Hungarian Empire. In all of these the legal framework was imposed on an apparatus which had already developed, to a greater or lesser extent, as an instrument of an executive absolutism wielding considerable power over large territories. The political instrument, in this sense, already existed in these countries, and was the early target of Liberal reforms. In Italy, the development of Public Administration and the assertion of Liberal authority occurred simultaneously, presenting the Liberals with the problem of creating for their own use an instrument of which they were inherently suspicious. To paraphrase Cassese's argument, other continental European bureaucracies had the legal straitjacket thrust on them, the Italian bureaucracy was born with it.[5]

The Crispi reforms also reflected the increasing heterogeneity of the administrative personnel, as the old Piedmontese elites gave way to a wider geographical recruitment with considerable cultural and class differences. A consequence of the widening of recruitment and the increased range of functions was the breakdown of the basic homogeneity between the political elites and the administrative elites, a homogeneity which was certainly present in the Piedmontese structures and which was initially transferred to the national government in Rome. The homogeneity of the personnel had helped make workable the informal authority relationships between the minister and his functionaries. It had permitted the survival of the non-contractual, retainer-style relationship between minister and administrator, and encouraged the development of a variety of non-uniform practices, based often on long-standing personal relationships within ministries. These had mitigated the difficulties inherent in the politician–administrator relationship. The increasing heterogeneity of the political and administrative classes closed off this solution, and compelled the politicians to acknowledge that they also needed the legal framework to control Public Administration. The political pressures militated in favour of a more categorical separation of politician from bureaucrat, and administrative demands were in the direction of greater legalisation and formalisation of practices. Mutual mistrust between bureaucracy and political elites, sharpened by the evident inadequacies of both, worked in favour of the reform of the old Piedmontese system.

The Crispi reforms are the first incomplete recognition of this. As we have seen in chapter 2, Italy began to industrialise quite rapidly from the 1890s onwards, in a manner which exposed even more sharply the limitations of the administrative system. There thus occurred from the 1890s, on a radical shift of emphasis, a greater separation of bureaucracy and politicians, and a strong impetus to seek administrative solutions outside the central organisation. These later reforms are an implicit admission of the failure of the Crispi efforts to make a flexible political instrument out of the state apparatus; they are also an acknowledgement of the supremacy of the legal framework. The administrators had won the first battles, but the war continued on different terrain.

## DEVELOPMENT AND REFORM

On the one hand, the emerging administrative groups sought greater protection from political interference in working conditions through greater stability in employment, through clearer separation between administration and elected representatives, and through greater uniformity of procedures. On the other hand, politicians and industrialists involved in the extension of state power into new areas of the economy and society wanted greater flexibility in management, particularly in recruitment and in capital spending. Two diverse trends therefore showed themselves from the turn of the century onwards, as Italy's economic growth rates began to match those of its competitors.

One set of reforms concentrated on the internal mechanisms of central government, but another way of approaching the problem was to construct new entities less closely integrated with the ministries, or even located completely outside the realm of public law altogether. The internal reforms took shape from the turn of the century to the onset of Fascism. In 1904, reversing the aims of the Crispi reforms, authority to increase the staffing establishment and to modify the administrative structure was removed from the Council of Ministers and passed to Parliament. In 1908, with similar objectives and as a pre-emptive move to avoid the spread of trade union membership, state employees were given a so-called 'statute' of employment. Without actually providing the employee with a contract of employment, this guaranteed certain conditions of tenure, promotion and pay for some restricted categories. The consolidation of much of this took place in 1923, when De Stefani, with a wide mandate from Mussolini but operating largely on Liberal reform proposals, introduced a rigid hierarchical personnel structure, uniform across almost all ministries, aiming at standard pay and strict controls on promotion. De Stefani also established the *Ragioneria Generale* with the function of controlling and co-ordinating the Finance Offices (*ragionerie centrali*) of the individual ministries; this was located eventually (in 1944) in the Treasury, where it sealed the victory of the financial control function over the territorial control function within Public Administration – in other words, the predominance of the Treasury over the traditionally prestigious Ministry of the Interior.

This haphazard and halting development, of which I have given here only the bare outlines, was not fundamentally altered by the new constitutional settlement in 1947. Some outstanding intra-ministerial arguments were settled, such as the separation of the Treasury from the Ministry of Finance in 1944, and old ministries were reconstituted from the Fascist conglomerates, so that the Ministry of the Corporations divided into its two former elements, the Ministry of Labour and the Ministry of Industry and Commerce. Similar changes occurred to the Ministry of Communications, which became the Ministry of Merchant Shipping and the Ministry of Transport.

These alterations were largely the result of internal administrative pressure, not of any strategic renewal by the new political classes. This was partly because the new elites, returning physically or meta-phorically from exile, accepted uncritically the Liberal ethos of Public Administration, and partly because they underestimated the extent to which the public sector in industry and finance (exemplified by IRI and IMI) now required radically different forms of political control. The leading authority on Italian Public Administration, Sabino Cassese, argues that the new constitution marks a return to Liberalism on this issue:

> in the relevant section, the Constitution does not go beyond the regulation of relations between the rights of citizens and the exercise of administrative powers having some impact on those rights. So what emerges is a typically nineteenth-century perspective, in which the clear separation between state and civil society is resolved by the confirmation of a set of principles of a rigidly (and reductively) 'guarantee' orientation.[6]

We might want to go further than this and argue that the Constitution continues the ambiguity of the previous regimes. Article 95 re-affirms the principle of ministerial responsibility for the conduct of the ministry, confirming implicitly that public administration is the potentially arbitrary servant of political masters and therefore in need of judicial and legislative restraint, which in fact is provided by other clauses scattered through the text. Article 97 adopts the other view, places the organisation and procedures of ministries entirely under the disposition of law, and enjoins impartiality and neutrality on them. In an unusual phrase, which seems to corroborate the previous article but may implicitly extend it, Article 98 affirms that 'public employees are at the exclusive service of the Nation.' What is remarkable about this, at first blush, is the use of the term 'the Nation' to refer to the collective interest, whereas in more overtly political contexts the term used is either 'the people' or 'the Republic'. Not too much should be read into this particular coinage, since as we have seen the text is notable for its inconsistencies and variations of expression. What is clear both from the text and from the debates in the drafting Commission is that the intention was to emphasise the separation of the machinery of state both from the private interests of its employees and from the political interests of the government. In this pre-occupation, the new Republic was maintaining the priorities and ethos of the Liberal elites, and implicitly recognising their lack of success in enforcing them.

The extent of the changes introduced into central public administration since 1945 bears little positive relationship to the volume of concern and constant debate over these issues. In 1957, a major effort of legislative drafting (from the Prime Minister's office) produced a consolidated text integrating all the various pieces of legislation since 1904 without modifying the substance or intentions radically. This was partly because of the political divisions over the role of public administration which had been reflected in the Constitution, and partly because the DC, now firmly in control, was developing its own policy style which prevented it taking radical action against its own clientele in public administration. The most important clientele are the employees themselves, the staff of the mass public sector organisations of the Postal Service, the Railways, and the Education service particularly.

From 1963 onwards, the centre-left coalitions renewed interest in the issue of reform particularly because of the introduction of planning legislation which required radically new functions in key ministries. But this experience, which we discuss in chapter 6, did not result in radical changes in administrative practice. An example of the strategic resistance put up by public administration was their response to the much-vaunted Gaspari reforms of 1972. Among other objectives, these were aimed at reducing the over-staffing at junior levels, but their most important effect was the exodus of a large proportion of senior functionaries on very favourable financial terms. It was left to a public law professor turned politician, Massimo Giannini, to bring in a radical re-organisation of the career structure.[7] As Minister for Public Administration in 1980, Giannini pushed through legislation which replaced the rigid and ineffective De Stefani categories with an entirely new 'functional' grading system based on a uniform and integrated career progression.

The purposes of the Giannini reforms were several: to open the career to outsiders at all levels by reducing the scope for ad hoc arrangements, to encourage individual responsibility at each level by ensuring reasonable salary progressions inside each grade, to prevent the increase in the number of higher posts beyond those actually needed, and to encourage a professional and functional orientation, among others. But Giannini was not able to see his reforms through to implementation, and evidence of later enquiries suggests that individual ministries successfully evaded the standardising and professionalising intentions of the law by careful control over job definitions in the transitory period, so as to ensure minimum disruption to established structures and procedures. The Giannini reforms were the first major attempt in the post-war period to resolve the conflict in Italian public administration between political will and legal authority, and may have been more important for educational purposes than in direct attainment of reform objectives. In the short and medium term, there can be little doubt that they have been ingested and integrated into the old processes much as previous efforts in other regimes.

In view of the difficulties in using central administration for the purposes of modern government and in view of the intractability of its structures, the other approach is to try to bypass the formal apparatus. In 1904, the government was preparing to take the railways under public control, and there was considerable concern both about efficiency and about the potential problems involved in the assumption of large numbers of manual workers. The obvious if controversial solution was to run the railways as a separate legal entity. This freed it from some of the more restrictive aspects of public employment such as the obligation to fill all permanent posts by formal open competition. It also kept the ministerial employees isolated from possible contagion by new industrial relations practices. The nationalisation of railways produced the first major deconcentration of authority with the establishment of an independent agency to manage the new business, responsible through a management board to what became the Ministry of Transport. This is now a well-trodden path for the provision of public services, though the specific administrative relationships vary widely. A preliminary census on behalf of the Minister for Public Administration in 1980 identified over 100 independent agencies or administrations (*Aziende Autonome*), ranging in size and scope from the railways with over 200,000 employees to institutes of geology with less than ten.[8] These are to be distinguished from the far more numerous Public Bodies (*Enti Pubblici*), of which there are at least 54,000, again of very different sizes and functions. The term *Enti Pubblici* is even looser than *Azienda Autonoma*, and they tend to be further removed from administrative control; whereas the independent agency is essentially a Liberal response to the inefficiencies of the system, the public bodies, though they originated before the First World War, were found most useful by the Fascists and later by the early Republican governments. Many of them in fact had pension and welfare functions associated with the rapid development of social security and social services from the 1920s on.

The third wave of reform we have already referred to in chapter 2. The State Participation system developed in the inter-war period as a support for private industry, supposedly holding shares in private companies under various ministries, whose holdings were eventually unified in the Ministry of State Participation in 1956. State-owned holding companies now control firms responsible for about one third of Italy's industrial output. Though many of them have a formal equity structure as if they were in the private sector, their owner is in fact the state acting through the Minister of State Participation. This may be seen as the logical conclusion of the development begun in 1904 with the railways. The final reform came with the phased introduction of the Regions in 1970, requiring further implementing legislation since then, and resulting at least on paper in the devolution of political responsibility in agriculture, health care, public works, transport and tourism. The previous three innovations – independent agencies, public bodies, and the State Participation system – all related mainly to functions new to the state. The regional reform for the first time took existing functions of central ministries and attempted to pass them down the line to more local administrations, integrated with central government by a complex planning procedure.[9]

## THE PERSONNEL OF PUBLIC ADMINISTRATION

Having considered the principles behind the development of the modern administrative system, we should now look at what we might loosely term 'the administrative class' itself. It is striking and significant how little recent research has been carried out in this area. Apart from the large-scale comparative survey by Putnam in the 1970s, and several more restricted surveys recently, there is little reliable material available on the attitudes and social characteristics of senior and middle-ranking functionaries. The limited official material on provenance, training, and career patterns is very uneven. This in itself reflects the lack of strategic control of personnel policy. As if to counterbalance this lack of hard evidence, there is a mass of anecdote and folklore in popular currency which mainly relates to the supposed absenteeism, extraordinary privileges and other scandalous features believed to be present. These at least testify to widespread public concern about the condition of Italian Public Administration. To what extent this is justified is largely a matter for conjecture. Two general characteristics can at least be ascribed with relative confidence. First, the senior functionaries until recently have in Putnam's terms been 'classical bureaucrats' rather than 'political bureaucrats'.[10] Second, in training and origin the administrative grades, which includes middle-ranking functionaries as well, are drawn predominantly though by no means exclusively from Southern regions, and a relative majority are graduates of law faculties.

The classical bureaucrat in this context is one who sees his or her role in a way which approximates to the ideal-typical model of the

Weberian bureaucrat: a Weberian bureaucracy may be described for these purposes as one organised as a fixed hierarchical legitimate authority, where the authority rests on stable abstract consistent and exhaustive rules; the functionary is subject to the impersonal discipline of the office, which also protects the functionary from arbitrary intervention (for example, from politicians) and which guarantees pay and career conditions. We have already seen that the Italian state apparatus is organised on principles very close to those identified by Weber, typical in particular of nineteenth-century liberal states. Putnam's survey indicates that the Italian senior bureaucrats were distinctly ambivalent about democratic processes and saw their role as separate from and opposed to that of politicians, in that the bureaucrats tended to regard themselves as representing the non-partisan, objective and superior application of general laws. In this sense, they resist the application of political control and base their work patterns on the legal jurisdiction defined by the office held. One of the most striking and perhaps surprising features of the results of the survey is the homogeneity in the attitudes and ethos of the administrative elite. This homogeneity is not so marked in social provenance and education. But in political attitudes and in career development, the pattern is that of an isolated and exclusive group profoundly at odds with the ideals and values of post-war Italian society and united in its pursuit of exempt status.

But this anti-political perspective should not mislead us into regarding the bureaucratic elite as segregated from the disorderly unstable world of party politics.[11] On the contrary, their rejection of the pluralist world of modern Italy, their disdain for interdependence or interaction with it, could be seen as a consequence of the conflict between their internal organisation and procedures and the over-weening unavoidable demands of the political system.

Appointment to the senior levels of public administration, the director-generals or equivalent ranks, is by the Council of Ministers. Precise figures are not available, but most estimates number them at about 600, a relatively high proportion compared with other countries in Western Europe. In all ministries without exception, the number of functionaries having director-general status exceeds the number of such posts actually available, a clear indication of the pressure both from politicians and from the civil service to use senior positions as a personal privilege or reward rather than solely as a function related to the aims and objectives of the departmental brief. The highest-ranking director-generals until very recently have been almost without exception career civil servants, not drawn from outside and not usually sought by private-sector employers. Despite their provenance and the security of their tenure, and despite the emphasis on legality and automaticity in the formal career structure, they are widely regarded as essentially political appointments. Those director-generals who actually have posts appropriate to their pay and status occupy a crucial mediating role between the Minister and the rest of the ministry. They are the gatekeepers between the disruptive demands of political direction and the legal order which is supposed to determine the pattern, objectives and pace of bureaucratic tasks. There is insufficient detailed information to enable us to describe the routine of relations with Ministers, but material from other surveys suggests that Ministers are not expected to pay great attention to the practice of their departments. Power of initiative rests predominantly with the departmental heads, the *direttori generali*. Ministers are encouraged in this 'arm's length' approach by the automaticity and formalism of the procedures, but also by the lack of effective parliamentary accountability for individual cases, the lengthy and cumbersome procedures of the Council of State, and not least the lack of electoral stimulus. What the Minister can do is to impose on the director-generals his or her own limited partisan concerns which will usually relate to territorial or sectoral patronage issues. There is therefore a distinction between partisan policy and administrative policy. Partisan policy concerns those areas affected directly by the concerns of the Minister, while administrative policy is the province of issues left to the formal competence of administrators. The separation between the two is not fixed, but varies between ministers and between ministries. It is partisan policy that is characterised by continuing conflict, while administrative policy reflects the institutionalised compromises ratified by legal status and therefore relatively settled distributions of political resources.

The type of legislation produced by the legislative system helps continue this separation. In the tradition of uniformity and impartiality which pervades the formal legislative procedures, legislation is often drafted in absolute and rigid terms which may make it difficult to apply later. There is no central control, for example in the Prime Minister's office or in the Treasury, of the text of legislative proposals. There is a drafting office in the Ministry of Justice, whose functions relate to the requirement that all laws have to be countersigned by the Minister of Justice who certifies as to their formal correctness. This is not therefore an editing, standardising or co-ordinating function.

Whatever may be the financial or other political implications of a Bill, the quality of the drafting of legislation is often poor, so that Parliament finds itself obliged either to engage in considerable editing of the text of government bills or, if it has failed to do so, to pass later amendments making good defects not identified when the bill was first passed. Hence a significant proportion of Parliament's work is occasioned by administrative inflexibility or poor drafting. This results in small-scale bills which contain clarifications or authoritative interpretations, or which allow specific exceptions to excessively narrow laws, or which allow such exceptions to be made by ministerial regulation – which may very well mean by director-generals. It is laws such as these which actually make up the bulk of the *leggine*, the little laws of limited sectoral interest which often merely extend privileges from one group in the public sector to another. This system, in which an originally narrow law is amended extensively by the addition of exceptions and clarifications, has been referred to as 'government by juxtaposition'.[12]

Of course, Ministers could not restrict themselves entirely to such interests even if they wished to; but outside the major policy-oriented Ministries such as Interior, Treasury, Defence and Foreign Affairs, the political content of ministerial work seems to be dominated by relatively narrow concerns, and only rarely are ministers with departmental responsibility expected to show more competence than is demanded to keep the machine moving at its usual pace. Control of the director-generals is therefore more important than a practical knowledge of the ministry. Ministers are able to maintain this control through their involvement at key points in the conditions of work of the ministry as well as through the more enduring political links which are part of the promotion profile for elected representatives. Standardisation and stability of terms of employment have been a priority for all the administrative reforms of the post-war, particularly the Gaspari and Giannini reforms of 1972 and 1980. The continuation of previous policy processes (and of previous recruitment methods) indicates that these reforms have been undermined, not least by the vulnerability of the employment system to intra-ministerial exemptions and privileges. Ministerial approval is required on a regular basis for the many expenses, overtime payments and special payments which top up the otherwise relatively low pay of their senior officials. The same process of ministerial patronage allows ministers to determine part-time paid appointments of civil servants to the boards of administration of para-state organisations.

The other aspect of this which is a recurrent if spasmodic subject of debate is the regional and educational bias in recruitment. Appointment to posts in public administration has to be by open competition. This was considered so important in the Constituent Assembly that it was written into the Constitution, in Article 98, which however includes the crucial qualification 'except in cases established by law'. This can be regarded as a very early post-war example (there are several others in the Constitution) of the government by juxtaposition to which we referred earlier. Such competitions, imposed for the purpose of preventing patronage and political interference, tend to be extremely time-consuming for all concerned, and are often criticised for the abstract academic nature of the examinations, particularly for access to the higher grades of the administration (the *quadri direttivi*). It is therefore not uncommon for more informal recruitment methods to be used, so as to avoid the delays and inadequacy of the official procedure. A 1978 survey (before the Giannini reforms, therefore) found that 58.5 per cent of all employees in central administration had been recruited by open competition and 41.5 per cent by special regulation or law.[13] One of the services a minister may render to his or her department is to regularise the position of the individuals or groups who have thus been taken on temporarily or designated *fuori ruolo*, *incaricati*, *sovranumerari* or one of the other euphemisms.[14]

The ease with which this may be done is one of the reasons why reforms of personnel are rendered innocuous. However they are recruited, once employed in the state system individuals tend to remain in it for the rest of their career, and in a very restricted sector. Movement horizontally, between roles, is possible but rare in practice, and not necessarily beneficial to a career. Movement vertically from one type of career to another (for example, from administrative or 'conceptual' to directive) used to be difficult because of the different formal qualifications required. The Giannini reforms introduced an integrated structure based theoretically on an entirely new scale of functional levels, which ought to have allowed easier progress through the hierarchy on the basis on professional competence. In practice, the persistence of old formal distributions of authority, the maintenance of promotion by seniority within each level and the lack of central control of staffing levels have meant that the new post-Giannini administration appears little more functional or flexible than its predecessor. There is also a widespread lack of proper in-service training and other forms of personnel development, a need recognised but not met by the establishment of the Central College for Training in the Gaspari reforms of 1972. It is scarcely surprising that there is little evidence of pantouflage, the easy movement between civil service and industry which is a feature of the French administrative elites. Italian civil servants do not have high status and are not readily employable outside their own ministries.

Two persistent themes in Italian political debate are the supposed excessive numbers in the state apparatus and the 'meridionalisation' of the state – the increasing domination by southerners. There is undoubtedly an element of exaggeration in much of the comment in this regard, and there is also a tendency to confuse rates of growth in public employment with absolute levels. On the skimpy evidence available, it would be difficult for a reasonable person to come to categorical conclusions on general over-staffing. On the other hand, the figures on the growth of public employment in particular periods are impressive. Under Fascism, for example, the expansion of the Public Bodies and the Independent Agencies resulted, from 1935 to 1940, in an increase of over 100 per cent in the clerical and administrative grades; according to a survey carried out for CNEL in the 1970s, following the introduction of the planning reforms, employment in the public sector increased by about 20 per cent between 1970 and 1976, while employment in the private sector increased in the same period by about 4 per cent.[15] This does not demonstrate that there is general over-staffing, and in fact the evidence does not suggest at all that the state apparatus is over equipped with qualified computer experts, for example. It may suggest, however, that at particular periods the expansion of public employment has been determined to some extent by difficult conditions in the labour market rather than by identifiable state requirements. In other words, there have been occasions (for example, at the end of the 1930s and in the mid-1970s) when the state has been seen by politicians and by those seeking work as a job pool. Despite the relatively low pay, jobs in the ministries are sought after because of the security of tenure and the generally undemanding nature of the work – in particular the lack of control of the hours worked. A survey carried out by ISAP in 1965, rather before the extraordinary growth in the numbers of graduates available, found that the predominant motive for choosing a career in the public administration was 'lack of alternative', followed closely by 'job security'. Service to the community, status and good pay were referred to by very few of the respondents.[16] Such is the lack of adequate selection criteria and so great is the disparity between the number of applications and the number of posts that the recruitment procedure is best regarded as a managed lottery, in which prior knowledge and contacts are essential but unpredictable in their effects.

As suggested above, two specific characteristics are well-attested. Recruitment into the *quadri direttivi*, the highest formal level of entry, is dominated by southerners and by law graduates. A 1979 survey of all employees of four ministries found that 44 per cent of the sample were of southern origin; the ISAP survey of a decade previously of *quadri direttivi* in all ministries found that 77 per cent of its sample were born in the South.[17] The difference between the two findings may be due to a decrease in the phenomenon, but it is more likely to be the result of the different samples. Southerners, in other words, were over-represented in the senior grades, an imbalance that has been attested by every one of the admittedly infrequent surveys since 1918. Modern data on the university degree of the entrants is not available, but a 1961 survey of all administrative entrants found 40 per cent of its sample had degrees in law.[18] Law remains the single most popular university course in Italian universities, and there is no indication that its predominance at the upper levels of public administration is waning. The 1979 survey found that 40 per cent of all competitions to Public Administration required a degree in law as a condition of entry. These amounted to only 6 per cent of the posts competed for.

The patchy character of the data available must induce caution. There is obviously public concern about the so-called 'southernisation of the state'. The significance of the figures is not that lawyers or southerners are in some strange way deemed incapable of staffing a modern bureaucracy. Certainly the predominance of legal training in a system already characterised by formalism and lacking practical management skills is hardly ideal; but the breadth of the law degree in Italian universities allows a considerable variation in the content. The lack of quality of the teaching, the unreliability of the examination procedures and the inadequacy of the recruitment process have all been subject to considerable criticism. Technical improvements could certainly be made, but behind the technicalities are important political problems. The state is a major employer in the national economy, and the direction of its personnel policy is subject to immediate political pressures not likely to affect other large employers. Public administration has to operate as a sponge for the labour market. Its intake to the most influential administrative grades is generally strongest in the area and in the sector most affected by graduate unemployment – respectively, the south and the legal profession.

The increase in the numbers of public employees (including military personnel and teachers) from 649,972 in 1946 to 1,415,239 in 1975 resulted in part from the great increase in the range of activities undertaken by the state, particularly in the welfare sector, and from the expansion of the education system. But the specific way in which it took place enabled the governing parties, particularly the DC, to use public sector employment as part of the solution, albeit a short-term and costly one, to the new post-war southern question. The aims and capacities of the state apparatus were subordinated directly to the demands of economic management as an employment resource rather than mainly as an administrative instrument. It was particularly useful in the context of the problems of under-employment and land-hunger in the South immediately after the war, but also as a response to the problems of industrial unemployment when the recession of the 1970s affected the vulnerable Southern industrial sites first. But the political context of the period demanded also that the political parties attend to the need to build up party organisation and support, a demand which was especially pressing for the Church-dominated DC. Detailed personal control over recruitment into the public sector was one way in which government ministers and those associated with them could extend the base of the party and render it independent of large well-established interest groups such as the Church and *Confindustria*. Networks of bureaucratic patronage, once established, are difficult for parties to grow out of, and it may be that the DC is now thoroughly dependent on these instruments. Hence public administration should be seen not only as a tool by which government policy is carried out, more or less efficiently as the case may be, but also as a political resource in itself, a means of integrating marginalised sectors and securing their consent. Apart from the strains this imposes on the effectiveness of administration, this co-option of discrete groups – mainly young graduates, mainly from the South, mainly with legal training – is necessarily limited and partial, and excludes some as well as integrating others. It also maintains the contested tradition of party-political involvement in the state apparatus.

## STRUCTURES AND PROCESSES

Historically, as we have seen, the Italian administrative system was based on direct territorial control from the centre through a single hierarchical structure of multi-purpose territorial divisions. Though vestiges of this remain, successive reforms have changed the relationships within government and between government and society. The system now combines residual central control particularly over finance, with regional devolution of democratic accountability, and with the unchecked multiplication of a horde of functional field agencies, semi-autonomous national and local bodies, and ad hoc territorial divisions.

The initial centralising impetus has been fundamentally changed. What we have hitherto referred to as if it were a single entity transpires on closer inspection to be a collection of many individual components. The great formal authority exercised by central government and the scope of its intervention, bestowed on it in the early Liberal period, are mitigated in a variety of ways, but above all by the sheer diversity of political and administrative relationships. Though the formal structures emphasise uniformity, standardisation and clear lines of authority, the practice which developed even before the regional reforms is very different.

If we leave on one side offices directly answering to the elected representatives of local government at communal, provincial and regional level, the machinery of state can be identified as the organisations and personnel directly or indirectly responsible to the public authority of the national government. Italy has a vast range of such organisations of many different types, having diverse relationships with central government and employing personnel who share nothing in working conditions and careers except that they are all ultimately employees in the public sector, broadly understood. The core would normally be thought to be made up of the central bureaucratic apparatus of the ministries, located in Rome. This is no longer very helpful in many industrialised countries, and in Italy probably less so than most. Table 4.1 is a simple tabular representation of the peripheral organisational structure of Italian government. It includes only employees in offices directly dependent on ministries, and therefore excludes from the head-count almost all the *Enti Pubblici* and the State Participation system.[19]

A simple view of the administrative layering of Italian government might describe it as composed of national, regional, provincial and communal levels. These certainly exist, and their divisions cover the entire national territory. But there are many other territorial divisions also, such as local health units, school districts, tax districts, planning consortia, transport areas, and 'mountain communities'. This list is not exhaustive. These divisions occur at different levels – inter-regional, sub-regional, inter-provincial, sub-provincial, inter-communal, and

*Table 4.1* Ministerial branch organisation 1984

| Ministry | All Staff | Branch Staff | Geog. level | Status of Branch Office | Types of Branch Function |
|---|---|---|---|---|---|
| Foreign Affairs | 7717 | n.av. | SP | 2,3 | 2,3,5 |
| Agric. & For. | 8818 | n.av. | SP,EP | 1,4 | 3,5 |
| Heritage | 23014 | 74% | SP,P,EP,R | 2,3,4 | 1,3,4 |
| Budget | 256 | none | – | – | – |
| Foreign Trade | 516 | n.av. | EP | 1 | 2 |
| Defence | 272937 | 80% | EP,IR | 2 | 1,3 |
| Finance | 108274 | 67% | P | 3 | 1,3,4 |
| Justice | 62036 | 60% | EP,R | 1,2 | 1,2 |
| Industry | 1452 | 35% | SP,P,R,IR | 1,2,3 | 1,2,3,4,5 |
| Interior | 112520 | 84% | P,R,IR | 1,2,3,4 | 1,3,4 |
| Public Works | 4873 | 68% | SP,EP | 3,4 | 3,5 |
| Labour | 16747 | 87% | SP,P,EP,R | 2,3,4 | 2,3,4 |
| Mercht. Marine | 1712 | 64% | SP,EP | 3 | 4 |
| State Part. | 148 | none | – | – | – |
| Posts & T.com. | 6 | none | – | – | – |
| Education | 1154104 | 88% | SP,P,R,IR | 1,3 | 1,2,5 |
| Health | 4713 | 18% | SP, | 3,4 | 1,5 |
| Treasury | 13873 | 49% | SP,P,R | 3 | 3,4 |
| Transport | 5431 | 65% | P,EP,R,IR | 3 | 1,4 |
| Tourism & Arts | 307 | none | – | – | – |
| P.M.'s Office | 3861 | none | – | – | – |

*Independent Agencies*

| | |
|---|---|
| State Monopolies | 16587 (Finance) |
| ANAS (Roads) | 13549 (Public Works) |
| Flight control | 2483 (Transport) |
| Posts & Telecomm. | 216454 (P & T) |
| Telephone services | 12133 (P & T) |
| Railways | 222714 (Transport) |
| [Forestry | 1006 (formerly A & F)] |
| (n.av. = not available) | |

DEFINITIONS

*Geographical level*
SP – Sub-provincial
P – Provincial
EP – Extra-provincial (not necessarily respecting provincial boundaries)
R–Regional
IR–Inter-regional

(*Table 4.1 continued*)

*Status*
1 Independent agency
2 Operational independence, central policy supervision
3 Branch offices, directly dependent
4 Shared with regional authority or transferred wholly to region

*Type of function*
1 Own function, not shared with centre (usually regulatory)
2 Consultative or promotional functions for centre
3 Own functions, under general co-ordination of centre (e.g. monitoring environmental pollution)
4 Execution of functions for centre (e.g. tax collection)
5 Sharing of functions with centre under central control (e.g. building works)

*Note*: Categorisation of the status and type of local organisation of the ministries is bound to be problematic, because of the range and because of the general uncertainty about the functions of some of the offices. The categorisation offered here is therefore to be regarded as illustrative and descriptive, rather than exhaustive and analytical.

*Sources*: *Compendio Statistico Italiano 1984* and Cassese 1983

sub-communal (for neighbourhood organisations in large cities). For the most part, these are purely administrative divisions of local or national government, without direct local accountability. As can be seen in Table 4.1, in 1984, 16 of the 22 ministries had peripheral offices or field agencies. These operate under regimes which are almost entirely ad hoc, not uniform and not repeated for other peripheral offices of other ministries, or even for other peripheral offices of the same ministry. Eight ministries have some peripheral offices, having geographical jurisdiction based on the provincial tier of local administration. As with other peripheral offices, these are often associated functionally with a particular *Direzione Generale* in the central ministry in Rome, and the career structures, pay and training will be determined through this central office. It is normal (despite the Giannini reforms) for functionaries to spend their entire careers not only in the same ministry but even in the same *Direzione*, so that the fragmentation of the ministerial system, with little co-ordination at Cabinet level, is compounded by further fragmentation of policy within the ministries.

The peripheral structure matches the central in this pattern. Where ministries have more than one peripheral function, each function in so far as it belongs to a separate *Direzione* within the ministry may have a separate office or set of offices, often not occupying the same premises as one another or indeed communicating with one another except through the centre. A typical example of this would be the Ministry of Finance, where the different taxes (income tax, VAT, customs, company taxes, inheritance duties) are operated by different *Direzioni* within the central offices in Rome and by different offices at provincial or district level. These are also entirely separate from the Services organisation for the ministry, which is organised regionally, and from the Inspectorate of Finance, which has its own geographical divisions. This pattern usually applies for all ministries which have formal branch structures – multiple branches, multiple levels, little horizontal connection. The structure of ministries is therefore extremely complex, and not systematically so.

It must not be thought that the apparently 'Branch-less' ministries escape. Two of those characterised as having no formal branch structure, namely Posts and State Participation, have in fact very large numbers of employees under their indirect supervision: the Ministry of Posts has only six functionaries formally in its central office, but a further 228,587 employed in the independent agencies which actually deliver the post or operate the telephone system. This Ministry also has ultimate responsibility for the conduct of the public radio and TV service, operated on permanent concession by RAI, which is actually a subsidiary of the state-owned public sector company IRI, itself responsible formally to the Ministry of State Participation. Both the Ministry of State Participation and the Ministry of Posts with their minute numbers of staff are extreme examples of how an otherwise inflexible system responds to the pressures associated with the growth of government. The Ministry of Posts is a shell whose structure is explained not by the need for formal accountability but by historic management concerns together with the contemporary political opportunities provided by the employment, communications and concessionary business of the policy sector. The Ministry of State Participation is branch-less for different reasons. Founded in 1956, it is intended to be a modern ministry, the central co-ordinator of a range of responsibilities executed by technocratic managers in public enterprises. That it has not yet succeeded in this need not mean that the model is faulty, but it does suggest that traditional methods of administration have not adapted easily to the newer climate.

The other ministries particularly characterised by the colonial structure of the *Aziende* and the *Enti* are the Ministry of Transport and the Ministry of Labour and Social Insurance. In the first case, the Ministry of Transport owns the stock and land of the railways directly, and is responsible for the service indirectly through the Railways Agency. This structure should be compared with the administration of other aspects of Transport in the same ministry: responsibility for air transport is shared with the Ministry of Defence, who own several airports in civil use and who maintain considerable residual interest in air traffic control; a major client group in the sector is of course Alitalia, owned yet again by IRI and thus formally responsible to State Participation, not to Transport; policy and regulation of inland waterway navigation has now been devolved at least nominally to the regional authorities, and sea transport is the responsibility of the Ministry of Merchant Shipping, though the Ministry of Finance's interest in customs duties gives it leverage, usually exercised through its police force the *Guardia di Finanza*; and responsibility for road transport is divided between the Ministry of Transport and the Ministry of Public Works both directly and with the road-building agency ANAS, part of the Public Works sector. The problem of intra-ministerial division is thus added to the complexity of inter-ministerial divisions and overlap of responsibility. The Ministry of Transport has a variety of *Enti* which deal with individual aspects of its work, such as registration of motor vehicles, driving licences, registration of road freight transporters, and so on. These functions, together with the concessions and contracts involved in the management of civil airports, give the Ministry of Transport enormous scope for patronage. It is scarcely surprising that in view of the divided responsibilities of the sector it is to this aspect of its work that more attention seems to have been given, rather than to the development of integrated sectoral transport policies, of which there is little evidence. It is not clear, however, that even the relatively routine aspects of its work are handled effectively. In 1981, the Permanent Commission of the Chamber of Deputies dealing with Transport found on its agenda a single clause bill sponsored by the Ministry of Transport which extended for a further three years the register of road freight transporters whose original year of compilation had been 1967. A complete reform of the criteria for registration had been under discussion for over ten years, and the extension requested was in fact the third such. Agreement on the new register had not been possible, and the Committee grudgingly assented to the bill, though for most practical purposes of regulation the register was useless.[20] The reports of the debates of the Permanent Commissions demonstrate clearly that this procedure is far from infrequent, and appears to be needed by all ministries on occasions. The Ministry of Transport is not uniquely ineffective or uniquely dilatory.

The Ministry of Labour has a different pathology. In this case the fragmentation of functions typical of the *Azienda/Ente* structure relates not to concessions, contracts and jobs but on the one hand to the diversification of the pensions and welfare system, and on the other hand to the use of employment exchanges for purposes of controlling access to the jobs market – hence the very large proportion of employees of this ministry who work in peripheral offices. These functions of employment exchange and social insurance supervision thus involve the Ministry's officials in direct contact with individual voters and make the Ministry an unspectacular but remunerative ally for aspiring local politicians. The point should not be exaggerated, for this is only one of many different channels by which patronage relations can be nourished, but the presence of former provincial employment directors and social insurance inspectors on the back benches of Parliament suggests how the role of the Ministry may be interpreted.[21] In the midst of this voluminous and electorally import-ant work, it is scarcely surprising that the Ministry of Labour has difficulty fulfilling the planning roles attributed to it (with the Ministry of Industry) by the 1977 law on industrial reconstruction, and that it has not yet been able to produce an acceptable draft Bill to implement Article 39 of the Constitution on trade union registration. This omission, however, is a matter ultimately of political responsibility, and could not be laid entirely at the door of the functionaries.

Of the 22 established ministries in 1986, only one, the Ministry for the Budget and Economic Planning, had no branch offices or dependent agencies of any kind. The only subsidiary organisation identifiable for this ministry from official sources was ISPE, the Institute for the Study of Economic Planning. The Budget Ministry is a relatively new ministry, established in 1967 with the function of co-ordinating the activities of all other ministries to meet national budgetary objectives and to supervise the implementation of the Economic Plan. The Ministry was set up in the flush of planning enthusiasm during the first centre-Left coalition including the socialists in the 1960s.[22] Its power should have lain not in the size of its own resources or in its capacity to take binding decisions, but in its central role as effective co-ordinator of the inter-ministerial planning committees set up at the same time – in particular, the *Comitato Interministeriale per la Programmazione Economica*, usually known as CIPE, and the *Comitato Interministeriale per Credito e Risparmio*. It has never been able to carry out this role successfully, partly because of major political differences between the parties over the scope, powers and objectives of planning, but also because the fledgling ministry, despite the individual talents at its disposal, was never able to exercise significant influence over the other ministries which had established interests and direct authority over spending.

The fragmentation of the branch structures derives in part from the central ministerial organisation. The law establishing the institutional format for the ministry should also specify the numbers and categories of personnel by *direzione generale*. These allocations can only be added to by further laws, or (since the Giannini reforms) by the directive of the Prime Minister's Office. In some but not all cases the further modifications may be made by ministerial decree rather than requiring the full force of legislation. The approach to such legislation relies to some extent on the political objectives of the minister of the day, but mainly on the senior functionaries themselves. The internal arrangement of functions varies widely between ministries. Consider, for example, the main divisions established by law in the Ministry of Foreign Affairs and the Ministry of Industry, Commerce and Artisanship. These two ministries are given here on the grounds that they represent typical examples of two different problems, though from this point of view there is no one typical ministry. Each presents its own specific conformation. Foreign Affairs is characterised by the iron predominance of the Directorate Generals organised by policy sector. These override the geographical concerns of the individual embassies and subordinate geo-political strategy to sectoral divisions. The sectoral control was introduced in the 1930s to replace the geographical organisation, itself a reform dating from immediately after the first world war.[23] Industry and Commerce has highly complex central and peripheral structures, the result of incremental addition of functions (in particular in price control and investment subsidies) in the 1960s and 1970s. The original core of its activities was its responsibility for small and artisan industry, but this directorate was dissolved in 1977 and the functions were transferred to the regions. The new functions of Industry and Commerce require it to cover a wide spread of sectors, to report to several different statutory inter-ministerial committees, and to consult extensively with local and national interest groups. In contrast to Foreign Affairs, which retains its traditional elitist policy style, Industry and Commerce has different approaches for different sectors, reflecting the periodic encrustations of successive regimes – regulatory, corporatist, technocratic, sub-ventionary. The existence of specific consultative or technical committees established by law for the private insurance and petro-chemical sectors reflects the political leverage of the interests in these areas.[24]

The Ministry of Foreign Affairs also retains the post of secretary-general from the period before the Crispi reforms, a privilege shared only with the Ministry of Defence and with the two Chambers of Parliament. But in both cases the authority to agree spending and to approve regulations rests with the directors-general. This position is the summit of administrative responsibility within the administrative career, and carries with it significant statutory powers (and therefore political influence). In Foreign Affairs, helped by the separation of foreign policy from other aspects of government activity (and despite the reform efforts of 1967), the traditional structure has survived and integrated the new demands in its own way, while Industry and Commerce had no such clear ethos to impose on its new divisions. What these two examples indicate is that the formal structure of Italian Public Administration, despite the commonly accepted view, is neither entirely unresponsive nor grossly and simply centralised. The effectiveness and appropriateness of its responses and of its procedures are more debatable.

## CONCLUSION

The purpose of this excursion into the undergrowth of the individual ministries is not to pretend to describe even one of them completely. It is rather to identify some of the salient features common to the structures taken together. One of these features, salient not least because traditional views of the subject suggest otherwise, is the very diversity of the geographical organisation and of the channels of authority. There is no a priori reason why the diverse structures referred to here are necessarily inefficient or ill-adapted for their function. On the contrary, in many cases the diversity is demanded by the different jobs to be done, as identified by the individual ministry. The provincial structure which it breaches was based not on historical entities or on practical assessment of differing needs in the post-unification period; the provincial boundaries were a nineteenth-century product of the Royal Statistical Office, whose categories and priorities they reflected. In fact, there has been repeated debate about the continued existence of provinces, particularly since the regional reforms, but it is apparently a constant of Italian politics that the establishment of new administrative institutions is much easier than the dissolution of old ones. Dissolution of the provinces would not do away with the formal centralisation of public administration, but it would remove the remaining residual element of the Liberal structure which originally was intended to give uniformity and standardisation to the central control. As we have seen, that function is no longer served by the provinces, and they are now one among several ways in which central public administration implements its policies and controls local government.

The difficulty lies in the fact that the political, administrative and financial control structures operate mainly through the central ministries in such a way that the diversity is never subject to co-ordination and rarely to strategic control, either by the central apparatus or by local elected representative institutions, and yet are insulated almost entirely from market pressures towards different kinds of efficiency. The diversity of the structures would not matter from this perspective were it not for the fact that each level and each function seems to have separate and often split accountability which in practice defies mastery. The problem then is that flexibility appears to achievable only through fragmentation, at the cost of lack of co-ordination at peripheral or central level, and through lack of political or administrative control over implementation.

The control exercised by the finance offices is always prior to spending, and checks the legal correctness of the expenditure in terms of authorisation procedures not efficiency. The same applies to the control of the Court of Accounts (*Corte dei Conti*) and in its different sphere to the Council of State. Ministerial control of the central or peripheral offices is limited by political and formal constraints. These procedures have been established as much for the protection of officials from politicians as for public service, and they can only be circumvented with the direct complicity of senior functionaries. Ministers thus may develop a practical compromise with their officials. In return for non-interference in the privileged working conditions and general organisation of the ministry, in return for not disrupting established practices and the hierarchical power structures of the permanent administrators, Ministers may achieve their individual political goals in particular sectors, always provided that these do not upset normal working arrangements. The easiest way for a Minister to make this compromise work is not to have strategic goals which differ from the consensus within the individual *Direzioni*, but rather to interest himself or herself in the much more manageable business of patronage and to leave the rest to normal administration. Only the occasional sectoral crisis, or a particularly active minister, will disturb this pattern.

Individual ministries are occasionally cohesive integrated groups of professionals pursuing strategic continuous objectives. The effective decision-making is fragmented within the ministries at the level of the directorates (*direzioni*). The communities, networks or scattered groups with whom they relate are structured in accordance with relatively specific and unstable political needs. Typical examples are industry, education and agriculture. The main exceptions to the lack of cohesion, as we have seen, occur in those areas where the state has separated service providers such as railways, health provision or state participation companies from central control. Only in these is the conflict relatively attenuated and the policy formation continuous.

Formal administration for most ministries is not policy development. It is made up of the contracts, concessions, pension cases, licences, transfer payments, subsidies, registrations appertaining to the policy sectors. One of the results of the mechanisms described is that the demands of efficiency may compel the conscientious manager to short-circuit the procedures, where the inefficient or corrupt can take refuge in the formalities.[25] The result of the structure overall is a lack of political responsibility since the Minister will be excluded by the working compromise from intervention in the policy of the sectors, though he or she will certainly be able to intervene in individual cases. There is also a lack of financial responsibility, since the budgetary system provides little incentive either to restrain spending or to spend efficiently. In its extreme form the system would lead to interference without co-ordination, dispersion of roles without independence of decision-making, duplication and overlap of responsibility without effective consultation. That it does not always do so may, without too much of a flight of fancy, be described as yet another victory of the real Italy over the legal Italy, but this is not without its costs.

## NOTES

1 Pressman, J.L. and Wildavsky, A.B., *Implementation* (Berkeley, Calif., University of California Press, 1973); Niskanen, W.A., *Bureaucracy and representative government* (Chicago, Aldine Press, 1971); Lindblom, C., 'The science of muddling through', pp. 79–88 in *Public Administration Review*, vol. 19, 1958.
2 Cappelletti, M. *et al.*, 1967; Ferraresi, F., *Burocrazia e politica in Italia* (Bologna, Il Mulino, 1980) pp. 148–162; a political scientist's perspective is

Graziano, L., 'Vecchia e nuova scienza politica in Italia', pp. 109–137 in Graziano, L., Easton, D. and Gunnell, J. (eds), *Fra scienza e professione – saggi sullo sviluppo della scienza politica* (Milano, Franco Angeli, 1991); Graziano, L., 'The development and institutionalisation of political science in Italy', pp. 41–57 in *International Political Science Review*, vol, 8 no. 1, 1987.

3  Ferraresi, F., 1980, pp. 162–165; Cassese, S., *Il sistèma amministrativo italiano* (Bologna, Il Mulino, 1983) pp. 55–56.

4  Cassese, S., 1983, p. 43 ff.; Mignella Calvosa, F., 'Stato e burocrazia in Italia: un'analisi storico-sociale (1923–1975)', pp. 158–197 in *Revue Internationale de Sociologie*, vol. 14, 1978.

5  On the Liberals' administrative policies, see Calandra, P., *Storia dell'Amministrazione Pubblica in Italia* (Bologna, Il Mulino, 1978) p. 33 ff.

6  Cassese, S., 1983, p. 59.

7  Berti, G., 'La riforma dello stato', pp. 447–492 in Graziano, L. and Tarrow, S.G., *La crisi italiana* (Torino, Einaudi, 1979); Berti, G., 'La politique de choix des fonctionnaires en Italie', pp. 137–147 in Debrasch, C., *La fonction publique en Europe* (Paris, Editions du CNRS, 1981); Cassese, S., *Burocrazia ed economia pubblica – cronache degli anni '70* (Bologna, Il Mulino, 1978); Balducci, M., 'Fonction publique en transition: le cas italien', pp. 322–330 in *Revue Internationale des Sciences Administratives*, no. 3–4 1982; Petroni, G., 'La Pubblica Amministrazione: analisi delle disfunzioni e indirizzi di riforma', pp. 749–824 in Miglio, G.F. (ed.), 1983.

8  Giannini, M.S., *Rapporto sui principali problemi dell'amministrazione dello stato*, Atti Parlamentari, Senato della Repubblica 11 July 1980; see also Consiglio dello Stato, *La Riforma della Pubblica Amministrazione – stato di attuazione del Rapporto Giannini*, vol. 1, 21 febbraio 1984 (Roma, Servizio Studi del Consiglio dello Stato, 1984).

9  Barbera, A. and Bassanini, F. (eds), *I nuovi poteri delle regioni e degli enti locali* (Bologna, Il Mulino, 1978); Dente, B., 'Centre-local relations in Italy: the impact of the legal and political structures', pp. 125–148 in Meny, Y. and Wright, V. (eds), *Centre-Periphery relations in Western Europe* (London, Allen and Unwin, 1985); Leonardi, R., Nanetti, R.Y. and Putnam, R.D., 'Italy – territorial politics in the post-war years: the case of regional reform', pp. 88–107 in *West European Politics*, special edition on 'Tensions in the territorial politics of Western Europe', vol. 10, no. 4 1987.

10  Putnam, R., 'The political attitudes of senior civil servants in Britain, Germany and Italy', pp. 86–126 in Dogan, M., *The Mandarins of Western Europe* (New York, Sage, 1975); also Aberbach, J.D., Putnam, R.D. and Rockman, B.A., *Bureaucrats and politicians in Western Democracies* (London, Harvard U.P., 1981); Putnam, R.D., *The comparative study of political elites* (Englewood Cliffs, New Jersey, Prentice-Hall, 1976).

11  Cassese, S., 'The higher civil service in Italy', pp. 35–71 in Suleiman, E. (ed.), *Bureaucrats and policymaking – a comparative overview* (London, Holmes and Maier, 1984).

12  Amato, G., *Economia, politica e istituzioni in Italia* (Bologna, Il Mulino, 1976) pp. 169–170. See chapter 5, p. 125 ff., for a more extended discussion of the problem of *leggine*.

13  Original research by Scarselli, M., quoted by Balducci, M., 1982, p. 323.

14  Literally 'not established', 'engaged', 'supranumerary'.

15  Mignella Calvosa, F., 1978.

16  Ammassari, P., Garzonio dell'Orto, F. and Ferraresi, F., *Il burocrate di fronte alla burocrazia* (ISAP Archivio 1968, Milano, Giuffrè, 1969) p. 296.

17  Ammassari, P. *et al.*, 1969, p. 7.

18  Quoted in Cassese, S., 1983, p. 118.

19  The analysis in this section and in the associated tables is based on data compiled from *Compendio Statistico Italiano 1985* (Roma, ISTAT, 1985); Cassese, S., 1983, pp. 137–170; Bianchi, G., *L'Italia dei ministeri: lo sfascio guidato* (Roma, Editori Riuniti, 1981).

20  *Atti Parlamentari*, VIIIa Legislatura, Commissione Permanente X, discussioni, p. 1224 ff.

21  For bibliographical data on parliamentarians, the basic source for each legislature is *La Navicella – I Deputati e Senatori del Parlamento Repubblicano* (Roma, La Navicella, various years). The data is elaborated from my own database drawn from this source.

22  Ruffolo, G., *Rapporto sulla programmazione* (Bari, Laterza, 1973);by the same author 'Project for Socialist planning', pp. 69–84 in Holland, S., *Beyond capitalist planning* (Oxford, Blackwell, 1978).

23  Kogan, N., *The Politics of Italian Foreign Policy* (London, Pall Mall Press, 1963)

24  Momigliano, F. (ed.), *Le Leggi della Politica Industriale in Italia* (Bologna, Il Mulino, 1986); Morisi, M., *Parlamento e politiche pubbliche* (Roma, Edizioni Lavoro, 1988); also Del Monte, A., 'The impact of Italian industrial policy 1960–1980' pp. 128–164 in Scase,R., *The State in Western Europe* (London, Croom Helm, 1980).

25  The argument that inefficiency and corruption may lie more in the observance of the formalities than in obviating them was put forcefully by Myrdal, G., *Asian drama – an enquiry into the poverty of nations* (London, Penguin, 1968); see also Clarke, M., *Corruption – causes, consequences and control* (London, Frances Pinter, 1983); for a discussion of the particular 'vicious circle' of the Italian bureaucratic process, see Cassese, S., 1983, ch.9; also Galli, G., *L'Italia sotteranea: storia, politica e scandali* (Bari, Laterza, 1983).

# Chapter 5

# Government and Parliament

In terms of the analysis proposed in Chapter 1, the Liberal state and Fascist regime in their different ways can be seen as exercises in state-building which retained the structures of the regulatory state and had only very limited success in developing more sophisticated ways of resolving the state–civil society relationship. The more complex forms which I have typified as issue networks and policy communities only began to develop with the post-war Republican system. But they did so in ways which inherited some of the weaknesses of the past, particularly the anachronistic state apparatus and the divisive representative relationships associated with clientelism. To these, the post-war system brought universal suffrage, a complex party structure, and rapid socio-economic growth, but the impact of these potentially positive innovations was limited by the exclusion of the second largest party from government and by the development of further informal but rigid controls on participation in policy-making. Hence formal politics in and outside Parliament remain expressions of confrontation. This has impeded balanced political growth, and has distorted the ways the state responds to political and civil society. The political system has circumvented this 'roadblock' only by dint of some potentially hazardous manoeuvres.

The opening up of civil society, the new freedoms of association, of the press, of opinion, the constitutional safeguards against abuse of political power, all these provided an unprecedented opportunity for political development, and offered the hope that this could occur in such a way as to resolve the traditional profound conflicts in the relationship between civil society and the state. Summarising the analysis of the previous chapters, we can regard these conflicts as concentrated round a set of dichotomies, as shown in Table 5.1.

*Table 5.1* State–civil society conflicts

| Policy process | State | Civil society |
| --- | --- | --- |
| Location of activity | Central ministries, peripheral offices | National and local trade associations, interest groups, churches |
| Historical origins | Traditional, Liberal | Modern, post-war |
| Framework of operations | Public, impersonal formal norms | Private, personalised informal conventions |
| Pace of development, adaptability | Low, rigid | High, flexible |
| Scope of access for individuals | Limited | Open |

Between these two spheres lies a hybrid world, comprising not only the political organisations in the narrow sense but also those elements of the state which operate outside the traditional framework – particularly the autonomous agencies, the public bodies and the public sector in industry; we should also include in this intermediate sphere the new instruments of local government, particularly the regional governments. In the process of managing the boundaries between the two arenas, the political parties especially have a pivotal role. Political parties form the main link between the apparatus of the state and the organisation of civil society. They determine which routes issues are to follow in the intricate paths which make up the very varied modes of policy-making. It is the governing parties who exercise discretion over access to public resources, whether these are material, moral, legal or hierarchical. It is they who control the gates between the formal and the informal, who mediate between the rigidity of the bureaucracy and the dynamism of an active and expanding economy, who maintain and develop the conventions by which the political system operates.[1]

Overall, the internal weaknesses of the governing parties require them to moderate their public inflexibility in private. Groups formally excluded have to be allowed the minimum access necessary for the routine management of policy, within the limits set by the established balance of forces. The contrast and interaction between the formal and the informal, between the public and the private, between legal norms and practical short-cuts, between the traditional and the modern, give shape and meaning to the entire policy process. These contrasts are most visible in the central political institutions. Policy-making entails a complex process of exchange between conflicting groups mediated by the political parties, who use public resources as currency to contain and to reduce societal conflict. Contrasts permeate the way politics works, and serve an important function, that of stabilising and enforcing the rules for the distribution of public spoils among conflictual sectional interests. They can serve this purpose because they give *de facto* legitimacy to the disjunctures and irrationalities inherent in them, against which there is no appeal. They are needed above all to maintain the conventional balance among parties and among interest groups, by enforcing the disparity of treatment to be expected for particular interests, and by providing a sanction against excessive opportunism on the part of those most favoured.

Against the background of the process of exchange of resources, how does the specific structure of government, Parliament and the parties affect policy? This chapter considers the most important institutional instruments with which the parties work directly, namely government and Parliament, while chapter 6 analyses the policy processes of the parties themselves.

## GOVERNMENT

### The ministerial cadre

We have seen in chapter 4 that ministers have important functions within a clearly delimited range of activity. If the policy process is likened to the functions of a market, the ministers are the main selling agents, controlling the flow of the primary product which is the access to public resources. The parties in this analogy could be described as the market-makers, bringing buyers and sellers together and controlling the rates of exchange. Where the analogy with the pure market breaks down is that the political leaders, whether they are ministers or not, may also deal directly with clients, are not separated from them, and therefore can seek to weight the markets in their own favour. Also the market does not operate with a common currency; it is a system of barter, a process of exchange in which the primary product is based on the use of public resources for particularistic objectives. The capacity to determine this use is at the core of the political process.

Granted that most ministers are not independent, their role in transmitting demands and in acting on the deals struck is still an important one. Recruitment to ministerial rank or to other posts open to politicians is clearly controlled from above. The control is exercised by party leaders, the most important brokers in our metaphorical market, who are not necessarily the party office-holders but rather the politicians who control the largest or best-placed factions. The structure and operations of the factions are discussed in more detail in chapter 6. Their guiding role in government formation was first recognised overtly in 1954, when the leader of the right-wing DC faction Giuseppe Pella formally objected to the structure of a new coalition government on the grounds that the Republicans were not included. Pella ordered his faction not to accept posts in the government, but two of his supporters did join 'in a personal capacity'.[2] This episode and the fact that the two rebels both went on to sustain occupation of high office in future governments gave an early indication of the pretensions and limits of factional organisation. Factional leaders are expected to be the prime disposers of ministerial office, which they use to reward supporters; denying their supporters access to office weakens the government only if factional discipline holds. The temptation of office is a strong one, and factions withdraw their support at their own peril.

The Cabinet, known formally as 'the Council of Ministers', does not usually have a co-ordinating role. This results partly from the traditional institutional autonomy of ministers and partly (if para-doxically) from the weakness of the Prime Minister's office, since the Head of Government is not generally strong enough to bind the Cabinet together as a cohesive unit, and still less to impress a clear unifying political vision on it. The Constitution (Art. 95) is ambiguous on the functions of the Prime Minister:

> The President of the Council of Ministers conducts and is responsible for the general policy of the government. He assures the unity and consistency of the political and administrative pro-gramme by promoting and coordinating the activity of the Ministers.

For most of the post-war period, this has not been sufficient to sustain Prime Ministers if they wished to impose their own unalloyed political direction on a coalition cabinet. Almost without exception, govern-ments will omit some important party leaders to whom individual cabinet members owe allegiance, and the Prime Minister of the day can usually only rely implicitly on the support of his own faction. The final clause of Article 95 calls for further legislation to lay day the organisation of the Prime Minister's Office. In the absence of this, Prime Ministers have lacked the detailed statutory powers to control individual ministers or the increasingly independent regional authorities. The political conditions for the formalisation of the Prime Minister's office also were lacking, since all DC Prime Ministers had to work within the limits set by factional demands within the DC. These rendered politically irrelevant the inadequate statutory position of the Prime Minister. It was only when the DC lost control of the appointment to the office of Prime Minister that the ambiguity of the office became significant – both for its holder and for the coalition partners. In 1988, after a lengthy gestation period, Parliament finally passed an integrated law (Law no. 400/1988) which reorganised the Prime Minister's Office, extended its personnel to cover the activity of individual ministries, gave the Prime Minister's Office particular powers in relation to regional government, and established Prime Ministerial authority to use delegated powers to co-ordinate and simplify fragmentary legislation.[3] In part, Law 400 followed the practices already developed during the Craxi premierships (1983–1987), during which the Socialist Prime Minister extended the numbers of staff at his own disposal, took on experts to monitor individual sectors, and attempted to get ministers to co-ordinate their legislative and budgetary requirements bilaterally with his office. A Socialist interpretation of Law 400 argued that it constituted a positive enhancement of the directive capacity of the Prime Minister, something they had sought for a considerable time; the mainstream view, however, was that it formalised and regularised the existing conventions on the Prime Minister's co-ordinating role, rather than creating the new dimension to the office which the Socialists sought.

These recent changes may result in long-term redistribution of power from individual ministers towards the Prime Minister, though they are unlikely to enhance the role of the Council of Ministers as such. But for most purposes, it is reasonable to assume that the individual ministers will continue to be of critical importance in the understanding of the policy process. Because of their autonomy, control of their appointment is a critical aspect of policy determination. The process of ministerial recruitment is concentrated almost exclusively on Parliament. It is not unknown for ministers to originate from outside Parliament, and usually these are referred to as independents or as technocrats, though this does not imply freedom from party constraints or exceptional expertise, merely that they are not initially parliamentarians. Independents or technocrats are generally recruited from a background of experience in industry, commerce and banking, so they generally come from the para-state sector or from private industry. Examples of *pantouflage* from the senior ranks of public administration to ministerial office are extremely rare.[4]

Party support is an essential condition even for those from outside Parliament and, in many such cases, ministerial office is the prelude to a parliamentary seat if the minister is at all successful. Usually 'technocrats' are resorted to if the crisis has been particularly difficult to resolve or if for particular reasons the ministry is not attractive enough at the time to the available factions. Though 'a government of technocrats' is often mooted as a means of imposing a truce between conflicting parties in government, the principle has never yet been fully applied. The nearest approach to such a government, that is a government staffed partly by ministers who were not members of Parliament, occurred before the 1987 elections after a particularly difficult government crisis which resulted in an early general election. The interim government was led by the veteran DC leader Amintore Fanfani, President of the Senate. It contained a total of nine non-parliamentarians out of 27 ministers, all of them regarded as close to the Christian Democrat party, and all occupying posts with a high technical content and relatively low patronage potential (such as Foreign Trade, Finance, and Reform of Public Administration). Of the nine, only one had previously been a functionary in a ministry, and six of the remainder were university professors of law.

For most serious purposes, the route to ministerial office runs through Parliament at some stage, and a long stay in Parliament is the best route of all.[5] Why Parliament should be so important is not entirely clear, since it does not provide any obvious training in ministerial skills, and expertise in the management of parliamentary business is not directly relevant to the intra-party competition which determines career movements. On the contrary, vigorous participation in parliamentary business is likely to rule out the network-building which junior members need if they wish to accumulate preference votes in their constituency and to place themselves well in a strong faction. Election to Parliament is part of this process: it gives aspiring politicians informal access to influential national figures, and provides the opportunity to measure their local strength in direct competition with others in the same party and in other parties. It also enables future ministers to try out the limits to independent action, and to assimilate the culture and values of the ministerial elite. Ministerial office is a further stage in the career, since it gives the politician a degree of independent control over public resources and therefore an opportunity to develop further a personal power-base.

Statistical evidence over a forty-year period suggests the existence of a 'super-elite' of ministers, about 20 Christian Democrats and four Social Democrats, who had held office on more than ten occasions, including four DC deputies whose offices numbered between 20 and 32 up to 1983.[6] One of the factors which maintains these leaders in office, though certainly not the only one, is the consistency and size of their preference vote at election time.[7] This is significant not only for the security it grants to the particular leader, but also because a preference vote following can to a certain extent be used to build up support within the parliamentary group and within the local and regional party. Maintenance of the preference vote requires access to patronage resources, and therefore to ministerial influence. There is a direct interaction between control of ministerial office and depth of support within the party. The most successful party leaders are those who can claim office consistently for themselves and for their supporters.

As we would expect from these figures, Italian government ministers are characterised by a high degree of continuity in office, thought not necessarily in the same post. A survey of changes in ministerial personnel between governments for the period 1946 to 1976 found an average continuity rate of 58.6 per cent among all government ministers including under-secretaries. This means that nearly six out of ten ministers or under-secretaries in each government were re-appointed to the following one, though usually to different posts. It is not surprising therefore that, as well as the super-elite, there is a large group of politicians who hold office a few times. These may be politicians in any of the governing parties. For example, just under 60 per cent of all Social Democrat deputies from 1946 to 1983 held ministerial office at some stage in their parliamentary career. The equivalent figure for Christian Democrat deputies (a much larger absolute number) was 40 per cent.

The pattern therefore combines elite stability with relatively easy access for certain politicians to the lower ranks. The crucial characteristics of the ministerial cadre as a whole are that the minister is a member of one of the governing parties (obviously, but with particular weighting for DC and PSDI members), retains the seat over several elections (typically at least three), and represents a 'heartland' DC constituency – the Veneto region has more ministers than would be expected, while Tuscany and Emilia-Romagna, regions dominated by the Communists, are under-represented in the Cabinet in proportion to their number of DC deputies.

## Cabinet formation

A recruitment pattern characterised by structured but informal parliamentary co-option is common in its general features to most West European legislatures. In Italy it is mediated directly and entirely through the political parties, so that it is not possible to talk of Parliament as an independent variable in this context, and only to a very limited extent can the Prime Minister exercise discretion. Cabinets are constructed by negotiation between the Prime Minister designate, the secretary-generals of the governing parties, and their factional leaders. These negotiations require the participants to agree a weight for the posts available and to distribute them in accordance with the prevailing distribution of power between the factions. By the early 1970s, the process was stable and frequent enough for these complex negotiations to be fairly predictable in their general pattern. It is commonly believed (though never reliably confirmed) that an unofficial handbook exists to guide the participants. Known as the *Manuale Cencelli*, it is named after its supposed originator, a director of the personal office of the DC leader Mariano Rumor, who was Prime Minister five times in the 1960s and 1970s.[8] Whether or not such a handbook was ever used, it is clear that these ministerial positions figure prominently in the exchanges of resources which actually determine who gets what policies; also that this part of the exchange occurs in accordance with relatively stable currency values.

Because of the importance of this process, and bearing in mind the inevitably speculative nature of the enterprise, we can attempt to describe what the relative values of the ministries appear to be and on what basis the values are established. All ministries have a substantial policy element and a patronage element in varying proportions. Some also have either exceptional status, which is obviously an advantage, or exceptional administrative content, which is not. Finally, posts 'without portfolio' exist within the Prime Minister's office which mainly provide places for junior entrants to the cadre and which help to balance the equation. More rarely, ministries are established to meet this need or because of the political salience of a problem. Unless there is a strong patronage element, these two sub-categories are the least valuable of all, since their formal powers are limited and their political position is dependent on senior figures. We can thus identify four separate groupings of ministries, as shown in Table 5.2.

Table 5.2 Categorisation of ministries

| Group A Status | Group B Politics | Group C Patronage | Group D Dependence |
|---|---|---|---|
| Foreign Affairs Interior Treasury | Budget Defence Finance* Industry Justice* Labour | Agriculture Education Health Merchant Marine Post and Telecom. Public Works Southn. Dev. (wp) State Participation. Transport | Culture Environment Foreign Trade* Tourism wp: Civil Defence EC Policy Parliament. Rel. Pub. Admin.* Regional Affairs Science Research |

Note:  wp  without portfolio
   *   ministries with exceptional administrative content

This categorisation is based on the posts usually allocated in the governments of the 1980s. There has been a gradual increase in the number of Cabinet posts throughout the post-war period, from an average of 18 in the first legislature (1949–53) to an average of 29 from 1983 to 1990. New ministries may only be created by law, but ministerial posts may be merged and new posts 'without portfolio' created without recourse to complex procedures, so the structure of individual governments may vary considerably at the margins. For example, in the Goria government which followed the 1987 elections, the new Prime Minister Giovanni Goria took personal responsibility for Southern Development; to acknowledge the weight of the Socialists, the post of Deputy Prime Minister was resuscitated and given to the Socialist Treasury minister Giuliano Amato; and a new 'without portfolio' post was established for Urban Problems.

The ranking proposed in Table 5.2 should not be taken to imply that Group B posts have no significant patronage content, or that the Group C posts lack political profile. The ranking refers to how the posts are valued in the negotiations, with particular reference to the demands of factional leaders and to the salient issues at the time. On occasions, the Group C posts can achieve considerable political importance, especially Health and Education. On the whole, however, the fact that these are 'mainly patronage, with some policy' rather than 'mainly policy, with some patronage' means that they are given to second-ranking figures in DC factions, not to factional leaders. Group A and Group B posts are posts with significant decision-making responsibilities for policy. They are usually sought by factional leaders for themselves or for their immediate lieutenants, exceptions being the Ministries of Justice and Finance, which may on occasions be difficult to fill because of the technical requirements of the posts. The other exception in Group B is the post of Budget minister. This post retains considerable status and has wide formal powers, but the patronage element is very low indeed, and the real political clout of the ministry is restricted. Hence the Budget ministry tends to attract senior figures, but they do not stay in the post for long and the rate of change of Budget ministers is high. In terms of relationships with interest groups, those in Group C are characterised by the predominance of clientelist networks, while those in Group B have at times shown considerable evidence of cohesive policy communities.

The general conclusions to be drawn from this analysis are two-fold. First, patronage issues do not dominate Cabinet formation to the exclusion of other considerations, though they do make it difficult for policy issues to be given priority in all ministries. This is corroborated by the phenomenon of politicians who are able to build up large local bases of support without participating in the super-elite.[9] Contrary perhaps to popular belief, the support of a large client-base manifested through preference-votes is not enough of itself to guarantee a continuous role in the Cabinet. It is a necessary but not sufficient condition. Second, in a comparatively large Cabinet, the recruitment process stimulates the development of a clear pecking-order among ministries and of an inner grouping composed of senior ministers engaged in policy issues over the long term (Groups A and B). We now go on to consider these issues of the pecking-order and internal differentiation within the Council of Ministers.

## Parties and Ministries

Most of the above analysis refers to the processes involved in the allocation of individual ministries when governments are being constructed. A further issue in the context of Cabinet formation is the overall distribution between parties. Nominations to specific ministerial and under-secretarial posts are made formally by the Prime Minister, but in practice he usually has to negotiate within the constraints of lists presented to him by the party secretaries, and for some posts may have no choice at all. The question therefore arises, to what extent can we identify party links with particular ministries? Aside from the individual decisions concerned, is there any long- term pattern in the distribution of ministries to parties, and how does this affect the policies associated with them?

The number of posts allocated to each party depends on which parties are making up the coalition. As we saw in the previous section, the number of ministers has increased gradually over the post-war period, and by the end of the 1980s had reached a new record with thirty-one in the De Mita and Andreotti governments. The number has historically tended to be larger the more parties are actually participating fully with ministers, as opposed to merely supporting in Parliament. For example, the Craxi and Goria governments of the mid-1980s, five-party coalitions, all had twenty-nine ministers, while the only minority government since 1979, that of Fanfani, had twenty-five.

Prior to 1981, the conventions governing the general distribution appeared relatively straightforward. Three simple rules apply, in descending order of priority:

1  The DC always had the Prime Minister's office.
2  The DC always had at least 50 per cent + 1 of the cabinet posts.
3  The ratios between the parties respected very approximately their relative strengths in parliamentary seats, but never so as to threaten the DC's majority in Cabinet posts.

The DC also maintained a majority of all under-secretaryships. The most important additional rules which apply for these minor posts are that in coalition governments no party should hold both the ministerial office and all the under-secretaryships, and, second, that the DC should have at least one representative in each ministry.

Since the relative strengths of the parties in Parliament changed very little, the conventional ratio *DC:PSI:PSDI:PRI:PLI* was quite stable at 8:4:2:2:1, which was understood as a minimum beyond which the DC's share could not be reduced in relation to any of the other parties individually. In practice, sharing the available posts among the coalition parties without infringing the rules was usually not a problem. Only in a five-party coalition would it be difficult to maintain the conventional distribution, and the political differences between the Liberals and Socialists ruled out the full five-party coalition. After 1981, three factors intervened to disturb the convention:

1  The DC lost the monopoly control of the Prime Minister's office.

Table 5.3 Distribution of ministries by government, 1980–90

| Prime Minister | Took Office | Ministers | | | | | |
|---|---|---|---|---|---|---|---|
| | | DC | PSI | PSDI | PRI | PLI | Total |
| Cossiga (DC) | 4/4/80 | 16 | 8 | – | 3 | – | 27 |
| Forlani (DC) | 18/10/80 | 14 | 7 | 3 | 3 | – | 27 |
| Spadolini (PRI) | 28/6/81 | 15 | 7 | 3 | 1 | 1 | 27 |
| Spadolini (PRI) | 24/8/82 | 15 | 7 | 3 | 1 | 1 | 27 |
| Fanfani (DC) | 1/12/82 | 14 | 8 | 4 | – | 2 | 28 |
| Craxi (PSI) | 4/8/83 | 16 | 5 | 3 | 3 | 2 | 29 |
| Craxi (PSI) | 1/8/86 | 16 | 5 | 3 | 3 | 2 | 29 |
| Fanfani (DC) | 17/4/87 | 16, + 9 indepdts | – | – | – | – | 25 |
| Goria (DC) | 28/7/87 | 14 | 8 | 3 | 3 | 1 | 29 |
| De Mita (DC) | 13/4/88 | 15 | 9 | 3 | 3 | 1 | 31 |
| Andreotti (DC) | 23/7/89 | 14 | 9 | 3 | 3 | 2 | 31 |
| Amato (PSI) | 18/6/92 | 10, + 4 indepdts | 7 | 2 | – | 2 | 25 |

2 The five-party coalition including all available parties became politically possible.
3 The electoral strengths of the parties began to vary more widely.

As a result, the conventions regarding overall distribution have lost their applicability, and the balance of power within the Cabinets has shown greater changes. Tables 5.3 and 5.4 indicate the distributions of posts in Cabinets since 1980 and the under-secretaryships, beginning with the last two under the old conventions.

The most obvious immediate adjustment in response to the new political conditions is the need to include the Prime Ministership in the calculations. The office seems to be treated as equivalent now to two Cabinet posts and three under-secretary posts. This applies to all parties, so that in 1987 when the DC recaptured the Prime Ministership they lost their overall majority in Cabinet. This does not

*Table 5.4* Distribution of under-secretaryships by government, 1980–90

| Prime Minister | Took Office | Under-Secretaries | | | | | |
| --- | --- | --- | --- | --- | --- | --- | --- |
| | | DC | PSI | PSDI | PRI | PLI | Total |
| Cossiga (DC) | 4/4/80 | | | | | | |
| Forlani (DC) | 18/10/80 | 31 | 16 | 6 | 4 | – | 57 |
| Spadolini (PRI) | 28/6/81 | 31 | 15 | 5 | 3 | 3 | 57 |
| Spadolini (PRI) | 24/8/82 | 31 | 15 | 5 | 3 | 3 | 57 |
| Fanfani (DC) | 1/12/82 | 28 | 15 | 5 | – | 3 | 51 |
| Craxi (PSI) | 4/8/83 | 31 | 12 | 5 | 6 | 4 | 58 |
| Craxi (PSI) | 1/8/86 | 31 | 12 | 5 | 6 | 4 | 58 |
| Fanfani (DC) | 17/4/87 | 33 | – | – | – | – | 33 |
| Goria (DC) | 28/7/87 | 30 | 20 | 3 | 4 | 3 | 60 |
| De Mita (DC) | 13/4/88 | 38 | 20 | 3 | 4 | 3 | 68 |
| Andreotti (DC) | 23/7/89 | 37 | 21 | 5 | – | 5 | 68 |
| Amato (PSI) | 18/6/92 | 19 | 11 | 3 | – | 2 | 35 |

signify a greater Cabinet instability or a loss of direction, since the Cabinet as such has never provided a strategic political direction. The loss of more Cabinet posts signifies a loss of control over more individual ministries, not necessarily a change in overall Cabinet policy.

These methods of Cabinet formation have led to a clear long-term pattern in the relationship of ministries to parties (see Table 5.5). We should leave on one side the post of Deputy Prime Minister, as this does not usually carry specific administrative responsibilities and is mainly a means of recognising the weight of a particular party or particular leader in the coalition. The most striking result of the long process of accumulation of offices under the unwritten conventions is the dominance of the Christian Democrats over almost the entire ministerial apparatus.

Table 5.5 Allocation of ministries, 1945–92

| | DC | PSI | PSDI | PRI | PLI | IND | Other | Total |
|---|---|---|---|---|---|---|---|---|
| Dep. PM. | 9 | 7 | 3 | 3 | 2 | – | – | 24 |
| Foreign Affairs | 41 | 3 | 2 | 4 | 1 | – | – | 51 |
| Interior | 48 | 1 | – | – | – | – | 1 | 50 |
| Treasury | 40 | 2 | 1 | 1 | 5 | 1 | –1 | 50 |
| Budget | 28 | 8 | 3 | 6 | 1 | – | – | 45 |
| Defence | 29 | 6 | 4 | 6 | 3 | 1 | 1 | 50 |
| Finance | 29 | 4 | 6 | 3 | – | 5 | 3 | 50 |
| Justice | 29 | 6 | – | 3 | 2 | 6 | 4 | 50 |
| Industry | 35 | 3 | 3 | 3 | 4 | 2 | – | 50 |
| Labour | 33 | 11 | 5 | – | – | 1 | – | 50 |
| Agriculture | 48 | – | – | – | – | – | 2 | 50 |
| Education | 45 | – | 1 | 1 | 2 | 1 | 1 | 51 |
| Health | 23 | 7 | – | – | 6 | – | – | 36 |
| Merchnt Marine | 38 | 2 | 5 | 2 | – | 3 | – | 50 |
| Posts & Telecom | 43 | 1 | 2 | 4 | – | 1 | – | 50 |
| Public Works | 25 | 9 | 9 | 3 | 1 | 1 | 1 | 50 |
| Southn.Dev. (wp) | 32 | 7 | 3 | – | – | – | – | 42 |
| State Part.ption | 31 | 5 | 1 | – | – | 1 | – | 38 |
| Transport | 30 | 10 | 4 | – | 1 | 1 | 4 | 50 |
| Culture | 13 | – | 3 | 3 | – | 1 | – | 20 |
| Environment. | 1 | 4 | – | – | 2 | 1 | | 8 |
| Foreign Trade | 23 | 13 | 4 | 2 | – | 6 | 1 | 49 |
| Tourism | 23 | 9 | 1 | – | 1 | 1 | – | 35 |
| Civil Defence. (wp) | 8 | 1 | 1 | – | – | – | – | 10 |
| EC Policy (wp) | 5 | 2 | – | – | 2 | – | 3 | 12 |
| Parl. Relns (wp) | 26 | – | – | 2 | 3 | 1 | – | 32 |
| Pub. Admn. (wp) | 29 | – | 4 | 2 | – | 1 | – | 36 |
| Reg. Aff. (wp) | 10 | 3 | 2 | 1 | – | 3 | – | 19 |
| Sci. Res. (wp) | 14 | 5 | 3 | 1 | – | 3 | – | 26 |
| Spc. Prbs. (wp) | 14 | – | 1 | – | 1 | – | – | 16 |
| UN Policy (wp) | 7 | – | – | – | – | – | – | 7 |
| Urb. Prbs. (wp) | – | 4 | – | – | – | – | – | 4 |

*See* note to Table 5.6

This shows itself in two ways. First, there are four ministries which have been controlled by the DC almost without interruption since the war. They are Interior, Education, Agriculture, and Posts. Table 5.5 begins in June 1945, with the first post-war CLN government, but if the table were pruned to begin the count in May 1947, after the break-up of the Tripartite coalition, Interior and Agriculture would have had 45 DC ministers out of 45 governments, Education 42 out of 45, and Posts 41 out of 45. Two other ministries have almost as long a record of DC control: they are Foreign Affairs and the Treasury, in

*Table 5.6* Occupation of ministries, 1945–92, as percentage of total period

| | DC | PSI | PSDI | PRI | PLI | IND | Other |
|---|---|---|---|---|---|---|---|
| Foreign Affairs | 82.7 | 2.9 | 5.2 | 8.4 | 2.2 | – | – |
| Interior | 97.5 | 1.4 | – | – | – | – | 1.1 |
| Treasury | 81.9 | 4.5 | 3.0 | 2.0 | 8.5 | – | – |
| Budget * | 57.9 | 18.9 | 9.6 | 11.3 | 2.4 | – | – |
| Defence | 54.8 | 8.3 | 8.8 | 19.3 | 5.8 | 2.3 | 0.7 |
| Finance | 60.8 | 8.3 | 12.3 | 11.5 | – | 3.3 | 3.8 |
| Justice | 75.1 | 8.1 | – | 7.2 | 3.9 | 1.1 | 4.6 |
| Industry | 70.8 | 3.7 | 4.9 | 4.7 | 15.5 | 0.7 | – |
| Labour | 66.1 | 16.0 | 17.2 | – | – | 0.7 | – |
| Agriculture | 97.5 | – | – | – | – | – | 2.5 |
| Education | 90.1 | – | 3.7 | 0.9 | 2.8 | 1.1 | 1.3 |
| Health* | 67.3 | 23.5 | – | – | 9.1 | – | – |
| Merchnt Marine | 82.8 | 3.6 | 6.4 | 4.7 | – | 2.5 | – |
| Posts & Telecom. | 90.7 | 0.7 | 3.1 | 4.5 | – | 1.0 | – |
| Public Works | 47.2 | 22.1 | 20.4 | 5.2 | 1.4 | 3.0 | 0.7 |
| Southn. Dev. (wp) | 81.9 | 12.1 | 5.9 | – | – | – | – |
| State Part.ption * | 69.8 | 10.1 | 20.1 | – | – | – | – |
| Transport | 64.4 | 22.6 | 6.1 | – | 2.4 | 0.7 | 3.8 |
| Culture * | 72.9 | – | 11.6 | 15.4 | – | – | – |
| Foreign Trade * | 38.5 | 30.9 | 9.1 | 7.8 | – | 12.2 | 1.4 |
| Tourism * | 62.8 | 31.8 | 1.3 | – | 3.3 | 0.9 | – |
| Civil Defence (wp) | 91.7 | 8.3 | – | – | – | – | – |
| EC Policy (wp) | 33.4 | 39.1 | – | – | 7.2 | 20.3 | – |
| Parl. Rel.s (wp) | 69.8 | 6.9 | 3.7 | 13.4 | 5.2 | 1.0 | – |
| Pub. Admin. (wp) | 83.5 | – | 15.5 | – | – | 1.0 | – |
| Reg. Affairs (wp) | 42.3 | 15.9 | 26.3 | 4.5 | – | 11.1 | – |
| Science Res. (wp) | 60.0 | 15.2 | 10.7 | 5.5 | – | 8.6 | – |
| Spec. Probs. (wp) | 89.5 | – | 2.6 | 7.9 | – | – | – |

Percentages refer to the total period during which the ministry has formally been in existence since June 1945. Ministries established in the intervening period are indicated(*). Omitted from Table 5.6 are the Ministry for the Environment and the Ministers without portfolio for the UN and for Urban Problems, for which the figures are too small to be properly comparable. The Ministry for Culture, established in 1974, was represented by a Minister without portfolio from 1973 until 1976. Responsibility for environmental protection was covered by the Ministry for Culture until 1983, and then by a Minister without portfolio until the establishment of a separate ministry in 1987.

which the Christian Democrat occupation begins in earnest after 1948 and is then broken only for brief periods by isolated individual ministers from other parties. Second, there is no indication that, to compensate for this, other parties might have been able to establish similar 'squatter's rights' in other ministries. The DC strategy, wittingly or unwittingly, has been 'divide and rule'. By concentrating on only a few important ministries, the DC has been able to claim each of the other ministries sufficiently frequently to prevent concentrations of power in other ministries by other parties. As a result, the nearest any party comes to matching the DC record of presences is in the Ministry of Foreign Trade, a Group D ministry, where the PSI has reached 13 to the DC's 22. Table 5.6 gives the percentages for the lengths of time in which ministries have actually been occupied. This broadly shows the same pattern of Christian Democrat domination, and reveals that the maximum occupation achieved by any other party is 23.5 per cent by the Socialists in the Ministry of Health.

Purely in terms of Cabinet formation and periods of office, without reference therefore to how ministers actually spend their time, the Christian Democrats exercise strategic control over Cabinet posts, maintain almost exclusive rights to particular ministries, and prevent other parties claiming or occupying other ministries with any significant degree of frequency or continuity. What is significant about the ministries on which the DC has concentrated since May 1947? Put simply, they are either status or patronage. The Christian Democrats are relatively uninterested in the powerful but second-ranking policy ministries. None of the six ministries in the Group B category is among those preferred in the long term by the Christian Democrats. The DC have concentrated their attention on the three Group A ministries (Foreign Affairs, Interior and Treasury) and on three out of the Group C patronage-based ministries (Agriculture, Education and Posts). The marginal case in this categorisation is provided by the Ministry of Merchant Marine, another Group C ministry, where the DC has 38 out of 49 presences. Whether by default or by design, the DC strategy shares decision-making on major issues of state with coalition partners, by allowing them relatively frequent access to the policy ministries. But the DC also recognises that the other governing parties may need access to the patronage-based ministries, and in a general sense barters this in exchange for political support in government. The ministries most used by the DC for barter are Public Works, Health and Transport. The marginal case here is the Ministry of Labour and Social Insurance, which combines a high profile (the industrial relations issues) with control of pensions and employment benefit cases. The Ministry of Labour is therefore one of the most sensitive to changes in the balance of power between the parties, a ministry where the Socialists and Social Democrats (with 10 and 5 presences respectively) between them have come relatively close to challenging the DC on both policy and patronage terms.

The barter for these offices takes place under terms set by the DC in the early years of the Republic, terms which have only begun to be questioned since 1981. The DC is still able to claim nearly half the ministries in any government, and more if it does not hold the Prime Ministership. It has usually been able to maintain the other terms of the barter, including unchallenged control of Education, Agriculture and Posts, together with the capacity to break up potential 'occupation' of ministries by other parties through the weight of numbers. The loss of the office of Prime Minister has not so far destabilised the process of exchange and control, partly because the DC has been able to exchange the office of Head of Government for an extra weighting of ministerial office. The problem occurs for the DC when it recovers the office of Prime Minister, and therefore has to relinquish important positions under the amended rules of distribution. First signs that this might be happening came in the DC-led governments of 1987 to 1990, with the loss of the Ministry of Posts and Telecommunications to the Republicans, associated with the loss of first the Treasury Ministry and then of the Foreign Affairs Ministry to Socialists.

This is partly corroborated by the reorganisation of the Prime Minister's Office in the Law 400 reform referred to earlier, which formalised the position of the Cabinet Council (*Consiglio di Gabinetto*).[10] The Cabinet Council had developed under the first Craxi government as a restricted group of ministers meeting irregularly for the purpose not of supplanting the full Council of Ministers but of assisting the co-ordinating role of the Prime Minister. Under the two Craxi governments and the Goria and De Mita governments, the membership of the Cabinet Council assumed a clear pattern. As we might expect, its membership is fluid between governments, and based on a mixture of policy and party considerations. Permanent members seem to be the three Group A ministers, together with the Ministers of Defence, of the Budget and of Industry from Group B. Other ministers may be included to adjust party representation as described above, with the DC having the majority of seats when it does not hold the Prime Ministership. The need for proportionality appears to override the importance of the ministries – for example, in the Goria government, the highest-ranking PSDI minister in the Cabinet was the Minister for Public Works, who was therefore included in the Cabinet Council; in the Craxi governments, the Minister of Finance, a Republican, was excluded from the Cabinet Council since the PRI were already represented by the Minister of Defence, but when the Ministry of Finance passed to a Christian Democrat in the Goria and

De Mita governments the Minister of Finance joined the club. The role of the inner Cabinet during these four governments in the 1980s seemed to be mainly to handle government policy during particularly difficult times for coalition relations. Though information about its meetings was not always clear, it appeared to meet frequently at times of political crisis but infrequently otherwise. It certainly is a more powerful actor than the full Cabinet, but it does not rule out the need for the traditional meetings between party secretaries and Prime Minister, and its use depends very much on the style and requirements of the particular coalition. With the return therefore to the much more conventional Prime Ministership of Andreotti from July 1989, the inner Cabinet lost ground to the traditional bilateralism of Christian Democrat party management.

In conclusion to this section on the role of Ministers, we should refer briefly to the collective functions of the Council of Ministers, that is, the full Cabinet. In the terms of the Constitution, the Council of Ministers and the President of the Council together make up the government. Ministers are responsible collectively for the decisions of the Council of Ministers, and should normally support government policy. In practice, the Council of Ministers has found it difficult to intervene effectively in policy-making.

The first and most obvious reason for this is that party differences over strategic issues, such as support for the government, tend to find their immediate institutional expression in the proceedings of the Cabinet, resulting in open and widely publicised disagreement between Cabinet ministers from different parties over the general conduct of the government of which they are all part. Secondly, policy differences between the minor parties are not unusual – for example, Socialists and Republicans disagreed strongly with one another for much of the 1970s over economic priorities, and the separation of macro-economic responsibilities into three separate ministries allowed these differences to be aired fully in Cabinet.

Thirdly, the Cabinet has generally lacked sufficient information about the budgetary affairs of government to be able to consider the full implications of legislation. General financial management is the prerogative of the Ministry of the Treasury through the *Ragioneria Generale*, and the individual ministries as we have seen often lack the facilities properly to cost their own policies, still less to pass judgement on wider policies. This is particularly important when the economic policy ministers seek to have emergency legislation approved through the decree-law system. Under this system, a decree approved by

Cabinet as an urgent measure passes into law immediately and has to be approved by Parliament within sixty days. As we discuss in the next section, government has had increasing resort to this method, but ministers outside the core of economic policy-makers have neither the time nor the information to enable them to query the measures in Cabinet, despite the fact that they are politically if not formally exercising a legislative power, albeit one subject to parliamentary review.

Fourthly, the volume of legislation and the form of its presentation are not conducive to thorough policy assessment by the Ministers acting collectively. Until the 1988 reform there was no central office to ensure that legislation was drafted properly, nor was there any overall coordination of the calendar for presentation of bills to Parliament. On occasions Ministers have complained in public of draft bills appearing before them in Cabinet with obvious errors and omissions, including omission of the source of the funds to pay for the proposals. Another complaint has been that on grounds of the urgency of the material, bills sometimes have to approved *in copertina*, literally 'in the folder', with little more for ministers to go on than the title and a summary of the main provisions.[11]

There is a well-developed system of inter-ministerial Cabinet committees, particularly CIPE, CIPI and CIPCC dealing with economic planning, industrial policy and credit control. There are also inter-ministerial committees for the South, and for other special problems. These committees usually have major statutory responsibilities deriving from original legislation. For example, under Law 675 of 1978, CIPI has the job of approving plans for long-term industrial restructuring under which public and private sector firms may qualify for substantial loans and grants. Though in some cases the responsibilities are clearly beyond the administrative capacity of the committees, nevertheless these can exercise independent decision-making power. Even where their decisions have to go to full Cabinet, the practice is that their deliberations are rarely overturned. The membership of these inter-ministerial committees is restricted to specific ministers, who may however allow senior civil servants to substitute for them. It is not difficult to see in the inter-ministerial committee structure a further example of the tendency in the Italian policy process to treat the major institutions as arenas for set-piece formal functions and to relinquish effective policy-making to less public, more restricted groups, where compromise is easier to achieve and where, if necessary, discussions with favoured interest groups can carry on without raising public concerns about representativity.

## PARLIAMENT

### Parliamentary recruitment and organisation

Like most modern legislative assemblies in industrialised countries, the Italian Parliament is overwhelmingly male, middle-class, middle-aged and University-educated (see Table 5.8). In this it reflects accurately not the balance of such characteristics in society at large but rather the requirements for access to positions of authority in most sectors of activity. A detailed study in the 1970s found that 28 per cent of all parliamentarians had previously been full or part-time party officials, and a significant proportion had had careers in the trade unions or in the para-state sector. Many had previously held elected office in local government. The general career patterns of the elected representatives suggests strongly that those who make a career in Parliament are professional politicians undergoing a process of central and regional co-option, relatively homogeneous in background and imbued with the values and outlook of their specific political sub-cultures.[12] This is particularly important in the Italian context because of the weight of the unwritten rules and conventions by which the policy process is dominated. Though election to Parliament obviously depends on a popular vote, the parties appear able to control recruitment to a limited extent so as to maintain a population which will observe the boundaries of accepted behaviour. This is assisted by the electoral system, whose large constituencies enable regional and national party organisations to determine the ranking of candidates on the party lists.

The formal regulations and conventions under which Parliament operates dictate a clear separation of roles between Parliament and the executive. The timetables and agendas of the two Houses are decided in each case by the Conference of the leaders of the parliamentary groups for the Senate or for the Chamber of Deputies, which are separately organised. The Conferences of the leaders in each House, who are known as the *capigruppi*, are chaired by the President of the Senate and the President of the Chamber of Deputies respectively.[13] The two Chambers (Senate and Chamber of Deputies) have equal constitutional status and equal powers over legislation. The Senate has 315 members (half that of the Chamber), a slightly different electoral system, and its electors are all adults over 25 years of age, not 18 as in

*Table 5.7* Legislative output, Chamber of Deputies, 1948–87

| Legislatures | 1 | 2 | 3 | 4 | 5 | 6 | 7 | 8 | 9 |
|---|---|---|---|---|---|---|---|---|---|
| Govt bills proposed | 1168 | 782 | 758 | 805 | 494 | 627 | 797 | 975 | 754 |
| Other bills proposed | 1028 | 1920 | 2964 | 3333 | 3063 | 3205 | 2129 | 3344 | 3618 |
| Govt bills passed in Assembly | 500 | 433 | 421 | 398 | 189 | 324 | 337 | 384 | 326 |
| Other bills passed in Assembly | 87 | 63 | 63 | 47 | 16 | 42 | 84 | 42 | 48 |
| Govt bills passed in Committee | 1496 | 1006 | 919 | 861 | 663 | 617 | 307 | 477 | 424 |
| Other bills passed in Committee | 344 | 592 | 639 | 743 | 480 | 493 | 145 | 369 | 337 |
| Decree Laws presented | 29 | 60 | 30 | 94 | 69 | 124 | 167 | 477 | 424 |

*Source: Le legislature repubblicane nelle statistiche parlamentari*, and *Resoconti Sommari delle Legislature VII, VIII, e IX* (Roma, Servizio documentazione e statistiche parlamentari, Camera dei Deputati, various years)

*Note*: this refers only to the Chamber of Deputies. It therefore ignores the considerable (though smaller) volume of legislation first presented in the Senate. Hence also the category 'total bills passed' in any legislature includes some bills first presented in the Senate.

*Legislatures*: 1 – 1948–53    6 – 1972–76
2 – 1953–58    7 – 1976–79
3 – 1958–63    8 – 1979–83
4 – 1963–68    9 – 1983–87
5 – 1968–72

the Chamber of Deputies. But for most practical political purposes, other than those referred to below, there is little difference between them. All legislation has to go through the same procedures in both houses, and conflict between them, which is rare, is resolved by joint bilateral committees.

Whenever the *capigruppi* cannot agree among themselves, the President has the formal authority to apply solutions which will keep the institution functioning. In the Chamber of Deputies, where these matters are usually more difficult than in the Senate, the timetable and agenda should be set in advance by unanimous decision of the conference of the *capigruppi* for a period of three months. The purpose of the unanimity provision, introduced in 1971, was to ensure stability and predictability of the Chamber's agenda by ensuring that all groups were involved in agreeing to it. This effort at integrating minority groups into the decision-making process was associated also with the planning reforms of the same period, into which the parliamentary procedures were supposed to fit. For reasons not directly associated with Parliament, the planning mechanisms were never operated properly by the bureaucracy and soon fell into disuse. The parliamentary procedures remained, however, and proved vulnerable to disruption by the smaller parliamentary groups, particularly those such as the Radicals who regarded themselves as outside the parliamentary game.

The government has the right to send a representative to meetings of the Conference, but cannot impose its own priorities and cannot even rely entirely on the support of the *capigruppi* of the coalition parties. When agreement is not possible by unanimity, the President of the Chamber may put the programme to the plenary assembly, in this case to over a period of no longer than two months. If the programme is defeated, it is then the responsibility of the President to determine the programme and detailed calendar on a daily basis, until agreement can be reached, but even in this case the timetable has to be put to the assembly. The need to secure a wide basis of agreement among the *capigruppi*, the vulnerability to 'ambushes' from the smaller parties, and the difficulties of ensuring a cohesive coalition majority, all have stimulated an increasing dependence on the disciplined resources of the Communists, whose co-operation has become essential to keep Parliament running.

The offices of the presidencies carry considerable authority. This arises from their constitutional status and from their practical role. Both Presidents have the right to be consulted by the President of the

Republic during the process of government formation, and the Head of State also has to consult the Presidents if he is considering dissolution of Parliament. If for any reason the Head of State is unable to carry out his functions, he may be substituted by the President of the Senate, and if the Head of the State resigns office or dies in office, it is the responsibility of the President of the Chamber of Deputies to call the election for his successor. The two offices constitute in effect the second and third ranking positions in status in the Republic. The Presidents of the Senate and of the Chamber of Deputies are responsible for the administration and organisation of their institutions, with the help of several elected vice-Presidents and a battery of permanent parliamentary officials, whose status, salary and levels of qualification differentiate them sharply from the ordinary ranks of public administration. The Presidents, who also have the more mundane if sometimes vexatious task of chairing sessions of the plenary assembly, are elected in both cases by the Senate or the Chamber of Deputies from among their own members. The holders of the positions are generally regarded as being obliged to display impartiality and to act as representatives of their institutions, not of their parties.

But despite this, and notwithstanding the concern of successive Presidents to maintain the impartiality of the position, the importance of the offices as of other parliamentary positions is such that in their method of appointment at least they are integrated into the general system of spoils allocation. The most important single advance made by the PCI in its march through the institutions since 1947 was the election in 1976 of the veteran Communist left-winger Pietro Ingrao to the office of President of the Chamber of Deputies. This was part of the general redistribution of posts which occurs after every election, and at the same time several Communist deputies and senators were elected to chair the permanent legislative committees. Occupation of these offices is an important resource by which parties can influence policy, and it provides a barometer of their status in the complex world of negotiation and barter in which all (excluding the neo-Fascists) are involved. At the end of the seventh legislature in 1979 the historic compromise between DC and PCI collapsed, and since then the PCI have not been allocated any chairmanships of the committees. However, they have retained control of the Presidency of the Chamber of Deputies and are still able to command one of the two vice-chairmanships in each of the fourteen permanent legislative committees.

## Decision-making in Parliament

The co-operation which is needed to keep Parliament functioning in its normal operations is also required in particular to keep government bills moving through the legislative system. The legislative function of Parliament has been the object of considerable criticism – the institution seems unable to respect its own timetable established by regulation, still less that of a government anxious on occasions to get major changes passed without undue delay. Also, the legislature is repeatedly criticised for the quality of its output – bad drafting and incomplete consideration mean that laws too often have to be returned to Parliament for an *interpretazione autentica* (definitive interpretation), or for harmonisation with other laws covering similar ground. The model which legislation is intended to pursue, a model described in the juridical textbooks, would have Parliament working on governmental drafts to produce relatively few laws of a general nature, providing the structural framework for more detailed legislation which would be the work of regional assemblies or of ministerial regulation. But as Table 5.7 indicates, Parliament produces a great number of laws, from a variety of sources, in several different ways. Much of the debate about the need to reform Parliament concentrates on its output of so-called 'little laws' (*leggine*), brief pieces of legislation with a restricted scope, usually concerned with issues of public employment or social security, which despite their narrowness might have a significant patronage implication for specific groups of parliamentarians.[14] Those opposed to the use of Parliament for these restricted sectional objectives coined the sarcastic reference to them as *leggi con fotografie* – laws whose impact was so limited that the photographs of all the citizens concerned could have been attached to the draft bill as supporting information. But often the individual case may be justified by the fragmentary nature of a previous reform, by the discovery of a group unintentionally omitted through careless drafting, or by the casual outdating of long-established legislation. In all such cases, a more appropriate answer might be for ministries to undertake a thorough consolidation of fragmentary texts and to submit single complete bills to Parliament in place of the dozens of partial amendments. This, however, seems to be beyond the normal capacity of public administration. In any case, the procedure provides grist for political mills, and there is little evidence of the firm political intention which would be required to prevent it.

Since the dominant mode of policy-making places great emphasis on implicit public support for covert private agreement, Parliamentarians of all parties are generally reluctant to vote down such

*Table 5.8* Deputies – social and educational background (all deputies, 1972–83, 6th 7th and 8th legislatures).
Figures are percentages of total deputies in the three legislatures (aggregate = 1105) and of deputies who were also ministers (aggregate = 268)

|  |  | All Deputies | Ministers only |
|---|---|---|---|
| Female |  | 6.6 | 1.9 |
| Education: | primary | 4.3 | 0.4 |
|  | secondary | 18.5 | 9.3 |
|  | higher | 63.7 | 84.0 |
|  | unknown | 13.5 | 6.3 |
| Age 1st leg.: | <35 | 18.2 | 26.1 |
|  | 35–44 | 44.0 | 55.9 |
|  | >44 | 37.8 | 18.0 |
| Univ. degree: | n.a./n.k. | 35.9 | 16.0 |
|  | Law | 30.6 | 46.3 |
|  | Humanities | 9.0 | 8.6 |
|  | Economics | 5.2 | 8.6 |
|  | Medicine | 4.0 | 4.1 |
|  | Others | 15.3 | 16.4 |

measures, though abstention is more common. The difficulties in which they find themselves can be exemplified briefly with one specific case, with the comments of a senior Communist deputy, Antonio Caruso, vice-chair of the Constitutional Affairs permanent committee from 1976 to 1979. In May 1977 the committee had to consider a bill designed to provide adequate pension rights for former local government civil servants from the Italian colonies. Caruso said:

> The Communist group is generally not in favour of 'little laws', especially if they are of personal nature. But in this case we are dealing with people who belong to a group which has been forgotten for years. It is necessary finally to give them a stable and permanent juridical status.[15]

The bill was delegated to a sub-committee, and was eventually passed by the committee without a contrary vote. It directly affected a total of 12 people. It is typical of the *leggine* that they are difficult to argue against, since very often (as in this case) they concern the extension of rights already granted in favour of one group to another similar group. The responsibility for this lies not in the multitude of individual decisions passing the *leggine* but in the weakness of the public administration and the permeability of legislative procedures.

The *leggine* must therefore be seen as part of a wider problem of decision-making in Parliament. Bills put forward by the government have no guaranteed place on the timetable, as we have already seen, and the government cannot usually control the detail of the text once the bill is before the permanent committees. Many proposals originate from backbench parliamentarians, who can find a variety of different channels for exercising influence, and who have the right to submit proposals freely – though securing a place on the timetable for them depends on the Chairs of committees and on the *capigruppi*. Some of these backbench proposals are individual *leggine*, but many non-government proposals are reactive and unoriginal, in the sense that they are put forward by individual parliamentarians or by party groups seeking to attach themselves to a more substantial proposal. This is encouraged by the practice of *abbinamento*, by which proposals on the same subject may be 'composited' (in effect, merged) in committee. By this means, opportunist backbenchers and their sponsors may seek to claim part-authorship of major bills.

The structure of Parliament, particularly of the lower House, is highly polycentric, and most notably through the committee structure. In both Houses the permanent committees, organised by policy sector, can consider all bills in detail and have the authority to pass certain kinds of bill directly into law without further reference to the plenary assembly. There are also joint committees of the Senate and the Chamber together, which cover a variety of sectoral activities and which are usually involved in monitoring the operations of specific agencies or reform programmes (see Table 5.9 for a full list of the committees). When the permanent committees are passing law, this is referred to as *in sede legislativa* or *in sede deliberante*. When they consider draft bills in detail before referring them back to the full Assembly, this is *in sede referente*.

With the changes in planning legislation after 1966, and particularly with the changes in parliamentary regulations in 1971, the permanent committees began to develop other functions – presenting unsolicited reports to the full Assembly, providing opinions on legislation going through other committees, interrogating ministers and senior civil servants, investigating problems and developments in specific sectors. Most of these functions were already available in the regulations but only began to develop independently in the mid-1960s, as the volume of Parliament's work increased and the difficulties of

*Table 5.9* Permanent committees in Parliament

*Chamber of Deputies*

Committee No. and Subjects

| | |
|---|---|
| I. | Constitutional affairs, organisation of the State, regions, public sector employment |
| II. | Prime Minister's business, internal and religious affairs, public agencies |
| III. | Foreign affairs and emigration |
| IV. | Justice |
| V. | Budget, planning and State participation |
| VI. | Finance and Treasury |
| VII. | Defence |
| VIII. | Education and Fine Arts |
| IX. | Public Works |
| X. | Transport, civil aviation, merchant shipping, posts and telecommunications |
| XI. | Agriculture and forestry |
| XII. | Industry, trade, artisan affairs, foreign trade |
| XIII. | Labour, welfare, social insurance, co-operation |
| XIV. | Hygiene and public health |

Also: Special committee for the reform of the pension system

*Senate*

Committee No. and Subjects

| | |
|---|---|
| I. | Constitutional affairs, Prime Minister's business, internal affairs, organisation of the state and of public employment |
| II. | Justice |
| III. | Foreign affairs |
| IV. | Defence |
| V. | Economic planning, budget, State participation |
| VI. | Finance and Treasury |
| VII. | Public education, fine arts, scientific research, culture and sport |
| VIII. | Public works, communications |
| IX. | Agriculture |
| X. | Industry, commerce, tourism |
| XI. | Labour, emigration, social insurance |
| XII. | Hygiene and health |

Also: Commission for European Community affairs

*Joint Committees (Senate and Chamber combined)*

1. Committees established by constitution or by constitutional law:

Parliamentary committee for regional questions
Parliamentary committee for criminal proceedings

*(Table 5.9 continued)*

2. Committees for political control, monitoring and supervision:

Parliamentary committee for general control and supervision of radio and television services
Permanent sub-committee for monitoring of access to radio and television services
Parliamentary committee for monitoring tax registers
Parliamentary committee for monitoring intervention in the South
Parliamentary committee for industrial restructuring and conversion and for state participation planning
Parliamentary committee for the intelligence and security services and for state secrets
Parliamentary committee on the phenomenon of the Mafia

3. 'Mixed' monitoring committees (including some non-elected members)

Committee for monitoring issue of currency and banknotes
Committee for monitoring savings banks and pension funds
Committee for monitoring the administration of public debt

4. Consultative committees

Parliamentary committee for advice to the Government on delegated legislation related to tax reform
Parliamentary committee for advice to the Government on the use of funds for the reconstruction of Belice
Parliamentary committee for advice to the Government on decrees related to indirect taxation resulting from EC obligations
Consultative committee for the award of civil and military honours (mixed)

This list excludes the occasional committees of enquiry which are established for specific short-term purposes – for example, the parliamentary committee of enquiry into the P2 affair (1982–83) and the parliamentary committee of enquiry into the reconstruction after the 1980 earthquake.

managing public sector operations became more evident. These additional functions are not widely publicised, but they enhance significantly what has been referred to as the polycentric character of parliamentary decision-making. As we discuss later, polycentrism is a common characteristic of other parts of the system too, but in this case it means that deputies and senators, a relatively restricted group by most standards, are able to exercise influence through several different channels. In the Italian Parliament, defeat and victory are rarely complete. The time is long gone when the Italian Parliament could be regarded simply as a rather inefficient law-making machine. Though law-making remains its most salient activity, the ways in which it

*Table 5.10* Activities of permanent committees, 1976–85 (% of total)

|  | referente | legislativa | consultiva | 'other' |
|---|---|---|---|---|
| **7th Legislature.** | | | | |
| Meetings | 37.4 | 28.4 | 19.0 | 15.2 |
| Time spent | 34.6 | 24.8 | 19.3 | 21.3 |
| | | | | |
| **8th Legislature.** | | | | |
| Meetings | 30.5 | 24.4 | 18.9 | 22.1 |
| Time spent | 34.0 | 23.4 | 18.4 | 24.2 |
| | | | | |
| **9th (to Nov.1985)** | | | | |
| Meetings | 31.1 | 24.8 | 17.3 | 26.8 |
| Time spent | 32.6 | 22.9 | 18.2 | 26.3 |

*Sources: Le legislature repubblicane nelle statistiche parlamentari, 1985; Notiziarie di statistiche 8a legislatura no.23; Notiziarie di statistiche 9a legislatura no.14, Camera dei Deputati, Roma, 1983 and 1985*

exercises power are now very numerous – through enquiries, resolutions, reports, as well as the traditional questions to ministers. Its willingness to seek other forms of influence clearly reflects the difficulties associated with its law-making function – cumbersome procedures, delays, inadequate drafting, insufficient information. The law-making function must remain the central one in a law-based system such as the Italian, but the other forms of policy development available to Parliament make it more open and more accessible.[16]

This increasing range of activities applies particularly to the permanent committees. Originally dominated by activities directly related to legislative proposals in their own sectors, these are now multi-functional, able to intervene in different ways and across a variety of sectors. The relative majority of their time is spent on consideration of bills *in sede referente*, but to a diminishing extent. For example, in the first legislature, 57 per cent of all permanent committee meetings were *in sede referente*, and the remainder were *in sede legislativa*, the only other category reported. By the 1980s, as Table 5.10 indicates, *sede consultiva* and 'other functions' accounted for about 40 per cent of the time spent in permanent committees. *Consultiva* (consultative functions) refers to consideration of bills allocated to other committees which touch on the competence of the committee, while 'other functions' mainly refers to enquiry, to political resolutions and to budgetary procedures.

The openness of the internal workings of the two chambers results from two basic principles: representativity and proportionality.[17]

There is some difference in the application of these between the Senate and the Chamber. Abstracting from the differences, these principles have two important implications: first, that deputies and senators have to be able to participate in debates on any issue which concerns them, even if they cannot vote, and, second, that if a full member of a committee cannot attend, his or her place may be taken by a substitute from the same party, with full voting and speaking rights. The regulations of the Chamber of Deputies do not allow deputies to belong to more than one permanent committee, but this is not applied rigorously by the Chairs of the committees, particularly where (as is the norm) a minister is permanently substituted by a deputy from the same party who is also a full member of another committee. The governing parties suffer from considerable problems of absenteeism, and all the smaller parties have difficulties maintaining their numbers on committees. The preference vote system ensures that many individual deputies will have particular interests in issues which properly belong to committees not their own. Absenteeism and conventional practice ensure that it is not difficult for such deputies to find the opportunity to speak and to vote as substitutes outside of their own committee. Furthermore, if the backbencher is the proposer of a bill coming before another committee, he or she has the right to attend the appropriate meeting without a vote, and can act as reporter on the bill both to the committee and to the full assembly. The core membership of the committee may consist of regular attenders (including the officers) who have built up expertise and long-standing contacts in the subject area. But irrespective of this, the openness of the membership, and the breadth of the subjects covered, make it possible for more local and more narrow sectional interests to get a hearing and to exert an influence through the intervention of deputies whose involvement in the committee is more temporary.

The permanent committees publish minutes containing full versions of their debates and lists of those present, but these are not readily available to the general public, and the documents provide no indication of how members vote. Television cameras, allowed with relative freedom into the full Assembly, do not cover the workings of the committees, and only on rare occasions is there radio coverage. So the activities of the committees, particularly those under the headings of 'other functions', take place almost entirely outside the public gaze. Where there are particular political or technical difficulties, the full committee may delegate a small sub-committee (*comitato ristretto*) to resolve the problems and to report back. It is difficult to identify what activities these sub-committees engage in, as their meetings take place entirely outside the sphere of public accountability. From reports and references in published minutes it appears that their considerations are not limited to internal negotiation and that they may take evidence from interest groups, from functionaries within ministries, and from other government agencies, in a flexible and informal manner not available to the full committees. The sub-committee may also provide the institutional location for frank negotiation between the parties, of the sort which never appears in the minutes of the full committees. Certainly they appear to be a useful means of identifying whether a compromise is possible and of breaking a deadlock within a committee, as generally their reports are unanimous and are accepted in full by the committee. They also enhance the seclusion of committee work.

The permanent committees can be seen to have taken over many of the legislative and non-legislative functions of the full Assembly. Their influence depends above all on their capacity to dictate the place and the content of all legislation. That this is practical, not merely formal, is corroborated by the frequent letters of complaint particularly from the President of the Chamber directed at committees whose failure to come to decisions on proposals holds up the work of the full Assembly. There is a four-month deadline for report back from a Committee *in sede referente*, but this is unenforceable under current regulations and is frequently ignored. Difficulties with the timetable, with the complexity of business and with the political salience of Assembly debate mean that *sede legislativa* is the preferred route, but this is only available where the proposal 'does not have special relevance of a general nature' (Art. 92, CD regulations). When it is used, the larger parties on the committees are in an even stronger position. Referral back of a proposal allocated *in sede legislativa* occurs if requested by one-fifth of the members of the committee or one-tenth of all deputies. In practice only the Christian Democrats and the Communists can muster sufficient forces to require a referral. The referral back of a proposal to the full assembly without a decision on its merits would be tantamount to consigning the proposal to parliamentary oblivion, which helps explain why so much of the legislation approved in committee (both *referente* and *legislativa*) is passed without opposition. This degree of consensus is only rarely possible in full assembly.

Finally, just as there is a hierarchy of ministries, so there is a hierarchy of permanent committees. Committees I and V in both Houses (which deal with constitutional matters and budgetary policy respectively) have to be consulted on any proposals which involve their competence – in practice, checking for constitutional legitimacy and for budgetary implications. In *sede legislativa*, if the originating committee disagrees with Committee I or V and neither side is willing to compromise, the proposal is automatically referred back to the full Assembly. These two committees therefore occupy pivotal roles at the centre of the decision-making process, and even *in sede referente* their opinions are difficult for other committees (or the full Assembly) to ignore. Their power is used sparingly, for two main reasons, both of which are common in differing degrees to all the committees: first, they do not usually have sufficient information about the practical implications of proposals (especially the budgetary provisions) to be able to comment with full authority, and, second, the members are reluctant to disturb agreements and compromises reached in other committees. The other major point of differentiation between the committees mirrors the status/policy/patronage distinction between the ministries, though the committees are too broad for this distinction to be rigorously applied. In general, the committee to which senior parliamentarians and ministers temporarily out of office gravitate, having the appropriate mix of status and policy, is Committee III, dealing with foreign affairs, which has the lowest workload of any of the committees. Correspondingly, the busiest, with the highest number of bills *in sede referente* and the most sittings, is usually Committee VI, dealing with Finance and Treasury matters. Clearly in the category 'predominantly patronage with some policy' (equivalent to group C in the ministries) are the committees dealing with agriculture, education, public works and health.

So the individual permanent committees which consider bills in detail suffer from the same problems in microcosm as do the conferences of the group leaders, and for the same reasons their work is characterised by a high level of co-operation between government representatives, senior DC parliamentary figures and the leaders of the largest opposition party. Also, for technical reasons, as we have seen, opposition agreement may be necessary to keep bills progressing through the committee system. Finally, the absenteeism from the government benches in committee and in the full assembly, contrasting as it does with the disciplined organisation of the Communists, puts the government in need of frequent Communist support to get a majority for its proposals. Hence the system which in public excluded the PCI from office came to rely on their support for routine functions out of the public eye.

The highly developed role of the permanent committees can be seen as one of the means by which the party-political obstacles in the system can be circumvented, within a restricted political market structured in accordance with the long-term coalition requirements of the governing parties. They therefore provide a point of access for networks and interest groups outside the normal range of acceptable exchange. Some of the committees are clearly characterised by a high degree of interchange with professional groups – those dealing with tax policy, and industrial policy particularly. Others such as agriculture and education appear to have a much wider range of acquaintances, and tend to have a larger floating membership of substitute deputies. These should not be seen as operating in conflict with the administrative organisation of interest groups – on the contrary they seem to reflect the same pressures that were referred to in Chapter 4. They provide an alternative point of access for all groups, and may be of use to those unable to secure a footing in the ministries, though insufficient is known of interest group activities in the committees to be able to argue this with confidence. In any case, the permanent committees operate within the same general conventions and constraints of decision-making. Though they may be able to widen the party-political exchange somewhat, they can contribute little to resolving the problems of delays, bad drafting, and constant barter of text and budget which characterise the normative procedures of Italian decision-making.

The decree-law procedure is a much more drastic instrument, by which governments have attempted to impose their wills directly on the parties. Traditionally all governments have complained about the lack of sense of responsibility of Parliament, particularly when faced with urgent legislation. As we have seen, governments are hardly blameless in this regard. But there is no doubt that frustration at the failings of the procedures has led government to an increasing use of the decree-law in an effort both to ensure the speedy passage of their proposals and to get them through in a form close to the original text.

Decree-laws are provisional measures approved by the Council of Ministers, which go into effect immediately.[18] According to the Constitution (Article 77), the procedure can be used only in cases of 'emergency and necessity'. It requires the proposal to be presented to Parliament on the day of publication, and consideration of the proposal must begin in Parliament within five days. If it is not converted into law within sixty days, the decree loses validity and is automatically nullified. The procedure has conventionally been used by government to introduce urgent measures in macro-economic policy. It has also been used to apply particular instruments of financial control which need to be introduced without warning, such as restrictions on exports of capital, though these can also be introduced by delegated legislation.

As Table 5.8 indicates, from 1979 onwards governments began to use decree-laws with much greater frequency, and for many different kinds of measures. Examples of decree-laws approved by the Council of Ministers in the 1980s included increases in the costs of medical prescriptions, provisions relating to promotions in the Armed Forces, extensions of deadlines for recruitment procedures in various ministries and public agencies, streamlining of procedures for the validation of signatures in referendum petitions, and provisions on private radio stations (three successive decree-laws in this last case). It is not easy to escape the conclusion that this has developed into an alternative procedure, a conventional part of the armoury, rather than an exceptional route. Governments have also begun to approve decree-laws after their own resignation, when convention dictates that they should engage only in routine continuing business. This particular practice has excited the vigorous criticism of the opposition, and the disapproval of the Head of State, neither of whom, however, can prevent it in most cases. In 1988 (sentence no. 302) the Constitutional Court warned the Council of Ministers that it had grave doubts about the constitutional legitimacy of reiterations of decree-laws. It also said it was concerned about specific provisions in them which retrospectively enforced any norms which may have lapsed in the meantime. In response to the general increase in the use of the procedure, Parliament has begun to treat decree-laws as ordinary legislation, declining to give them favoured passage through the timetable or to treat the texts as unamendable. But Parliament has to find a place for the decree-law immediately after publication, even if thereafter it moves at its own pace; also, the effect of 'anticipated legislation' such as this is immediately to create a client-group of those favoured by the provisions, who can be relied on to remind Parliament how difficult it is to remove rights once granted. And if Parliament should fail to pass the decree-law within the required 60 days, the government has shown itself willing to re-issue it repeatedly, if necessary in an amended form, Constitutional Court sentences notwithstanding. For the government, the benefits of the decree-law are diminished but not removed by Parliament's increasing resistance to this conventional arm-twisting.

The fact that the Communists are not acceptable coalition partners yet occupy influential positions in the legislature does not mean that the relationship between executive and legislature is necessarily characterised by confrontation. On the contrary, the two major developments of the rise of the permanent committees and the governmental use of decree-laws suggest that their relationship is intricate and fluid, marked by conflict and by reciprocal dependence in proportions which vary over time, between the different parties involved, and in accordance with the different institutional locations. To refer to the metaphor of the market-place, within Parliament the governing parties are engaged in a complex barter of resources with the second-largest party. The Communists give co-operation in making the institution work, and in passing government bills in committee, and in return for these major items get the opportunity to influence policy outside the full assembly and recognition of their legitimacy as a constitutional party. What the Communists also give, implicitly of course, is toleration of the informal rules and conventions by which the governing parties maintain their internal relationships, in particular tacit acceptance of the sharing out of public appointments (*lottiz-zazione*) and of the equivalent activity in Parliament, the little laws. But all the constitutional parties within Parliament are also engaged in exchanges with the government of the day. If the permanent committees are the open market for government business, where government, as selling agent, is acting in rough parity with the parties, the decree-law mechanism can be seen as one of the means by which the government attempts to maintain the boundaries of the market, to remove some goods from the barter so as to impose them directly at a price determined by the seller. The responses of Parliament, parties, Head of State and pressure-groups show how difficult it is prevent the processes of the market-place from spreading beyond their conventional boundaries.

But governments know that in propaganda terms it is relatively easy for them to attribute the responsibility for policy failures to Parliament as a whole. The critical literature on the legislative assembly is vast if rather general, that on the government much more limited. Whatever the nature of the private transactions in the forum of the committees, Parliament's formal decision-making procedures are generally open, visible and subject to considerable media attention; Government's are not, partly because government chooses to make them so. Further-more, the premiss supporting the entire structure of the market is that governing parties will not normally be penalised by the electorate for poor performance, mainly because of the lack of alternative. The debate about political change in Italy has therefore increasingly become a debate about institutional reform, in which Parliament is cast in the role of villain, and the priority of enhancing governmental power (as it is seen) is paramount. Underlying this, however, the power of the governing parties has until recently remained largely unquestioned. In the next chapter we consider the parties, their societal bases, their interaction.

## NOTES

1 The best introduction to the party–civil society relationship remains Farneti, P., *Il sistema politico italiano* (Bologna, il Mulino, 1973); English translation and adaptation, Farneti, P., 1985. But see also Mannheimer, R., *Il Mercato elettorale, identikit dell'elettore italiano* (Bologna, il Mulino, 1987), and the discussion in chapter 6.

2 *I programmi dei governi repubblicani* (Roma, Centro Romano Editoriale, 1978) pp.91–178.

3 Fusaro, C., 'La legge sulla presidenza del Consiglio, primi adempimenti a otto mesi dall'entrata in vigore', pp.349–373 in *Quaderni Costituzionali* a.IX n.2 agosto 1989.

4 The most notable exception to this was the former Chief Accountant Gaetano Stammati, who became a DC Treasury minister in the late 1970s. Mario Sarcinelli, former deputy governor of the Bank of Italy, was Minister of Foreign Trade in the Craxi governments in the mid-1980s, where his main brief was to prepare Italy's finance markets for liberalisation. The political career of both these men was short-lived, albeit for different reasons.

5 See particularly Cotta, M., *Classe politica a parlamento in Italia* (Bologna, Il Mulino, 1979); also Rose, R., *Ministers and ministries – a functional analysis* (Oxford, Clarendon Press, 1987).

6 This is taken from my own unpublished research into the biographies of Deputies. For a summary, see Furlong, P.F., 'Parliament in Italian Politics' pp.52–66 in *West European Politics*, vol. 13 no. 3, July 1990.

7 See ch. 1 for a detailed explanation of the preference vote.

8 Venditti, R., *Il Manuale Cencelli* (Roma, Editori Riuniti, 1981). For an example of the power of the party secretaries over a weak Prime Minister, see *La Repubblica* 31 July 1987 pp.2–4. This describes how the PM-designate Giovanni Goria had to wait with his prospective ministers while the party secretaries or their deputies haggled over under-secretaryships.

9 For discussion of the importance of local power bases see Chubb, J., *Patronage, power and poverty in southern Italy* (Cambridge, Cambridge U.P., 1982); Allum, 1973.

10 Fusaro, 1989.

11 On the processes within the Council of Ministers, Cassese, 1983, pp.193–197; also Cassese, S., 'Special problems of budgetary decision-making in Italy,' pp.254–267 in Coombes, D. (ed.), *The power of the purse* (London,

George Allen and Unwin, 1976); Ferraresi, F., *Burocrazia e politica in Italia* (Bologna, Il Mulino, 1980).

12  Di Palma, G., *Surviving without governing – the Italian parties in Parliament* (Berkeley, Calif., University of California Press, 1977); see also Meynaud, J., *Rapport sur la classe dirigeante italienne* (Lausanne, Etudes de Science Politique, 1964).

13  On the organisation of Parliament, see Manzella, A., *Il Parlamento* (Bologna, Il Mulino, 1977); also the series edited by A. Predieri, *Il processo legislativo nel Parlamento italiano* (Milano, Giuffre, 1974), the research for which, however, largely predates the regulation changes of 1971.

14  On the phenomenon of the *leggine*, the *locus classicus* is Predieri 1974. For a discussion in English, see Di Palma 1977.

15  *Atti Parlamentari* Legislatura VII, Resoconto Stenografico, Comm. Permanente I, p. 24.

16  On the multiplicity of access, see Manzella 1977.

17  The discussion which follows is drawn from my own unpublished research in the Chamber of Deputies, and is based on the *Atti Parlamentari*, Discussioni, Commissioni Permanenti, VI, VII, and VIII legislature.

18  Della Sala, V., 'Government by decree: the Craxi government and the use of decree legislation in the Italian Parliament', pp.8–24 in Nanetti 1988. See also Furlong 1990.

# Chapter 6

# Parties, interests and policy

## THE PARTY SYSTEM

### The Sartori–Galli debate

Most modern discussions of the Italian parties begin by acknowledging the influence of Giovanni Sartori, whose description of the party system as 'polarised pluralism' was first published in 1966 (see Table 6.1 for a summary of general election results).[1] Though voting patterns have altered considerably since then, his description is often used as a starting point for discussion of the way Italian parties interact. The basic features of this model are straightforward: a polarised pluralist system such as Italy has a plurality of parties represented in Parliament (at least five), anti-system extremist parties ('poles') at both ends of the political spectrum, intense disagreement between the remaining parties, and no party able to win an overall majority.

The effect of the anti-system or extremist parties, according to Sartori, is to deprive the political system of an alternative government to that of the centre parties. The existence of the anti-system parties ensures the permanence in office of the largest centre party or of the centre grouping, since no coalition can be formed without it. The coalition partners cannot be held responsible for their actions by the electorate, and they tend to have no commitment to support the government beyond the purely tactical. The minor parties thus have no serious incentive to pursue moderate centrist policies or to resolve their serious differences. Even worse, they also, like the anti-system parties, are under pressure to maintain their electoral identity in the face of the permanent dominance of the major centre party, and so they tend to adopt unrealistic policies – a tactic Sartori refers to as 'outbidding'. A party system characterised by polarised pluralism is literally centrifugal: the parties flee from the centre. This makes the

Table 6.1 Constituent Assembly and parliamentary election results, 1946–87 (% of valid votes)

| | 1946 | 1948 | 1953 | 1958 | 1963 | 1968 | 1972 | 1976 | 1979 | 1983 | 1987 | 1992 |
|---|---|---|---|---|---|---|---|---|---|---|---|---|
| DC | 35.2 | 48.4 | 40.1 | 42.3 | 38.3 | 39.1 | 38.8 | 38.7 | 38.3 | 32.9 | 34.3 | 29.7 |
| PCI | 18.9 | 31.0 | 22.6 | 22.7 | 25.3 | 26.9 | 27.2 | 34.4 | 30.4 | 29.9 | 26.6 | 16.1(3) |
| PSI | 20.7 | (1) | 12.7 | 14.2 | 13.8 | 14.5 | 9.6 | 9.6 | 9.8 | 11.4 | 14.3 | 13.6 |
| MSI | – | 2.0 | 5.8 | 4.7 | 5.1 | 4.5 | 8.7 | 6.1 | 5.3 | 6.8 | 5.9 | 5.4 |
| PSDI | – | 7.0 | 4.5 | 4.6 | 6.1 | (2) | 5.1 | 3.4 | 3.8 | 4.1 | 3.0 | 2.7 |
| PRI | 4.4 | 2.5 | 1.6 | 1.4 | 1.4 | 2.0 | 2.9 | 3.1 | 3.0 | 5.1 | 3.7 | 4.4 |
| PLI | 6.8 | 3.8 | 3.0 | 3.5 | 7.0 | 5.8 | 3.9 | 1.3 | 1.9 | 2.9 | 2.1 | 2.8 |
| Rifondazione | | | | | | | | | | | | 5.6 |
| Leagues | | | | | | | | | | 0.5 | 0.5 | 8.7 |
| DP | | | | | | | | 1.5 | 1.4 | 1.5 | 1.7 | – |
| PRad | | | | | | | | 1.1 | 3.4 | 2.2 | 2.6 | 1.2 |
| LVerde | | | | | | | | | | | 2.5 | 2.8 |
| SVP | | 0.5 | 0.5 | 0.5 | 0.5 | 0.5 | 0.5 | 0.5 | 0.6 | 0.5 | 0.5 | 0.5 |
| PSdA | 0.3 | – | – | – | – | – | – | – | – | 0.2 | 0.4 | 0.2 |
| PNM | 2.8 | 2.7 | 6.9 | 4.8 | 1.7 | 1.3 | – | – | – | – | – | – |

Party acronyms and abbreviations

| | | | |
|---|---|---|---|
| DC | Christian Democracy | DP | Proletarian Democracy |
| PC | Italian Communist Party (see note 3) | PRad | Radical Party |
| PSI | Italian Socialist Party | LVerde | Green List |
| MSI | Italian Social Movement | SVP | South Tyrol People's Party |
| PSDI | Italian Social Democratic Party | PSdA | Sardinian Action Party |
| PRI | Italian Republican Party | PNM | National Monarchist Party |
| PLI | Italian Liberal Party | | |

(1) PSI in coalition with PCI in Fronte Popolare
(2) PSDI united with PSI in 1967 to form the PSU, disbanded shortly after 1968 elections
(3) Renamed PDS (Democratic Party of the Left) in 1991
(4) Others winning seats included Uomo Qualunque 30 seats in 1946; 6 other minor parties a total of twenty seats in 1946; Union Valdotaine 1 seat in Val d'Aosta at every election except 1976; Unità della sinistra 1 seat in Val d'Aosta in 1976; Associazione per Trieste 1 seat in 1979.

formation of government coalitions difficult and their survival precarious. Even the centre party or grouping has no incentive to give priority to government stability, because the dynamics of the party system, together with the relative stability of the electorate, ensure its permanence in office. Sartori does not have much to say directly about the policy effects of this model, except that the anti-system parties can be identified as such not only because of their propaganda and rhetoric but also because of the way they use their numerical strength in Parliament to block much-needed reforms. Their strategy is thus clearly aimed at delegitimising and destabilising the system. Sartori does not provide direct evidence for either of these two assertions. He also does not have much to say about the stability of the electorate, though he clearly attributes a considerable importance to the electoral system in maintaining the contours of the model.

The alternative view to that of Sartori is rather less theoretical. One of its clearest proponents is Giorgio Galli, whose argument is sometimes referred to as the 'imperfect bipartism' model, though it does not constitute a model with the same kind of aspirations as Sartori's.[2] Like that of Sartori, the Galli analysis begins with the assumption that the major problem is governmental instability, and that this is in some way associated with the permanence in office of one party or of one group of parties. However, Galli's research into party organisation and voting in Italy in the 1960s led him to observe that political participation is dominated not by many parties of roughly equal strength, as polarised pluralism might suggest, but by two parties, namely the Christian Democrats and the Communists. These parties won more than 60 per cent of the total vote at every election from 1948 to 1987, and the electoral system ensured that this dominance was translated faithfully into parliamentary seats.

The DC and the PCI sustained their position through their control over what Galli refers to as 'sub-cultures'. Sub-cultures are complex networks of social organisation in specific regions. The networks are dense and widespread, and can have the effect of 'encapsulating' significant proportions of the population, so that most important aspects of their lives are influenced by the ethos and objectives of the political movements predominant in the region. These sub-cultures have usually been identified as the Veneto, the area round Venice in the North-east, for the Christian Democrats, and the two central regions of Tuscany and Emilia-Romagna for the PCI. The sub-cultures are the source of the enduring strength of the PCI and the DC, and are responsible for the extraordinary stability of the electorate until the 1980s.[3]

A consequence of this model is that both main parties are to some extent inter-class, differentiated from one another by region and ideology more than by sectoral interest. Both have to appeal to similar socio-economic groups. The DC has significant working-class Catholic support organised in CISL, and the PCI has middle-class professional support in the central regions, and support from the small entre-preneurs who rely on the flexible model of industrial specialisation characteristic of the 'third Italy'.[4] Hence, while the rhetoric may appear different, policies in some sectors converge. This is enhanced by the fact that both the Veneto and the Red Belt have relatively modern agricultural sectors and profitable small industry. The polarised pluralist model predicted outbidding and centrifugality; imperfect bipartism predicted convergence and centripetality. In both models, interest groups are acknowledged not to have a monopoly of representation of a particular sector. They have to compete with the interest groups of other parties for public support and for access to government.

In the bipartism model, unlike that of Sartori, the problem of government instability is not the result of the electoral system, but neither does it follow directly from the characteristics of Galli's main interest, the sub-cultures. According to Galli, government instability is directly associated with the permanence in office of one party, the Christian Democrats (together with their smaller partners), and with the fact that there is no acceptable alternative to them. In the Italian case (but not necessarily elsewhere), continuity in office is associated with unregulated factionalism in all the governing parties, and with the use of public office to maintain these factions. The Christian Democrats and their allies (Socialist, Social Democrats, Republicans and Liberals) are in effect not accountable to the electorate for their record in office. They are not penalised for inefficiency, and may with impunity use government office for narrow party-political ends. The underlying obstacle to alternation in government, to the replacement of the DC by a loyal opposition, is not the lack of a large enough opposition party. The PCI have normally had sufficient seats to form the basis of a multi-party governing coalition, all other things being equal. If the system is viewed as 'imperfect bipartism', the problem at the core of the way the parties work is the historical exclusion of the major opposition party from government.

Whatever conclusions we may wish to draw about the ailments afflicting the Italian party system, it is difficult to deny the reliance of the two mass parties on complex and deep-rooted social structures, or to deny the importance of their decline. In their different ways, the Catholic and Communist social bases were composed and to an extent still are composed of organisations and informal networks which have so strong a political affiliation that their entire activity is permeated with it. The political affiliation is more than just a symbolic adherence or a formal link. It carries with it an ethos, a logic, a particular way of looking at the world, not necessarily dogmatic or intolerant, but nevertheless connecting the social identity of large sectors of the population with the particular political party. At their peak, in the 1950s and 1960s, the sub-cultures were estimated by Galli to account for 70 per cent of the vote of the DC and the PCI within their respective regions. The forms of social organisation directly linked to the two parties have a major impact on their relationships with the electorate and on the way in which interest-groups are organised. Their strength also helps explain the different strategies of the two parties, both of which have now been thrown into disarray by the decline of the social organisations on which they rested.

Implicitly both these models adopt the notion that the institutions of state are dependent on the parties; if there is a crisis, it is not a crisis of the state as such but is attributable to the interaction between the party system and other aspects of politics. In the Sartori view, there is considerable vertical mobility in the political system, but the recruit-ment function is dominated by the special relationship between the DC and the Church, with the result that 'the modernising potential elites tend to adopt a radical protest attitude or are left aside in a wasteful position of estrangement'.[5] We might amend this to say that the Church's favoured position has now been usurped by a few powerful lay interest-groups, closely associated with the governing parties. In the sub-cultural perspective, the elites have to confront one another over fundamental choices because of the deep ethical differences separating their social organisation. In either case, political representation through interest-groups was regarded as determined strictly on party lines. Functional representation was subordinated to representation based on territory and party affiliation. Policy on most issues operated on the automatic pilot of ministerial routine, against the permanent danger that major change might raise the spectre of divisive fundamental conflict over values. The development of this pattern of interest-group relations followed the deliberate choices of both mass parties to use organised groups and associations of all kinds to maintain their social support.

Party platforms and party performance have been of secondary importance as a determinant of electoral behaviour and therefore of electoral success or failure. This assumption of a lack of correlation between perceptions of government performance and voting behaviour is corroborated by survey evidence over a long period.[6] This has consistently shown Italians to have the lowest levels of satisfaction with the functioning of the state, and with the honesty and competence of politicians, of any country in the European Community, over decades characterised by considerable electoral stability. Galli and Prandi concluded in the English language version of their study, 'Catholic and socialist traditions have exerted more influence in determining the attitudes of people than have income levels, party platforms or the party's ability to protect or further social and economic interests.'[7]

Sartori has little to say about policy, and its lack of significance for his model is itself an indication of its lowly status within his terms. In Sartori's world of polarised pluralism, just as in imperfect bipartism, policy is derived endogenously, dependent on factors internal to the party system, not on contending perceptions of public interest or on strategic responses to political and economic modernisation. In general terms, it was a common point to the two orthodoxies that there was no direct relationship between specific policy and electoral success. This assumption of course did not mean that policy was of no concern to ministers and parties, nor did it mean that there was no connection between what governments did and how people voted. Rather it meant that for the first thirty years of the Republic policy formation and implementation were subject to intense but very specific electoral pressures, of a kind that most systems do not have to sustain over such long periods. These electoral pressures related either to 'grand politics' – the nature of the system, Italy's international role, the moral choices implied in the formation of alliances – or to very low politics indeed – what Tarrow has described as 'the distribution of public spoils to a host of private claimants'.[8] Embedded social organisation and clientelism bound the system together.

## Party politics in the 1970s and 1980s

But the political crises of the 1970s questioned the relevance of the two models – both of sub-cultural analysis based on a cultural similarity between the Christian Democrats and the Communists, and of the spatial mechanics of polarised pluralism – because of the effects of secularisation on the Catholic vote, and because of the strategic development of the PCI. In 1977 Parisi and Pasquino proposed a different way of explaining the vote, which also implicitly directed attention away from party systems towards the newly volatile electorate itself.[9] The Parisi–Pasquino model concentrated on the relationship between the voter and the vote, in other words on the type of representation involved in voting rather than on the more mechanistic party-centred approaches of Sartori and Galli. Parisi and Pasquino identify three distinct types of vote: first, the vote of opinion, based on a reasoned choice of programmes and policies; second, the vote of identity, based on affiliation to a party or movement seen as a general cultural association in the broadest sense; and third, the vote of exchange, based on mass clientele networks held together with public resources. This model suggests that a major shift in forms of representation is taking place, with reduction in the proportion of voting behaviour which can be explained by traditional political culture and an increase in the importance of issue-based voting. This would be an important conclusion to draw, because it would imply a stronger link at least in a general sense between governmental performance and the way people vote. But the Parisi–Pasquino model, though intuitively plausible, has been difficult to verify one way or the other. For researchers of Italian voting behaviour the clientele vote remains a potent obstacle to explanations framed in more conventional terms.

One conclusion from which few would now dissent is that far from being dominated by one or two heavyweight influences the Italian electorate is actually responding to a plurality of pressures. Generically, they can be classified as cultural, socio-economic, ideological, and clientelistic, but within and between these headings relationships are complex and overlapping. Local political cultures and their social networks have not been entirely swept away by secularisation or by the development of national means of mass communication: very wide regional diversity and homogeneity within regions are still visible. Even in the difficult electoral climate of the 1980s, the Christian Democrats could count on over 40 per cent support in all the provinces of the Veneto, and the same held true for the Communists in the provinces of Emilia-Romagna in the centre. The weight of socio-economic factors is strong despite the pace and scope of economic growth: research by Sani and Barnes has suggested that the three major cleavages identified by Rokkan – religion, the urban/rural split, and the labour market – all remained important in Italy in the 1970s and 1980s, though at a diminished level of intensity.[10] At the level of individual attitudes, research has repeatedly demonstrated the continuing significance of ideological factors, in the sense that Italians continue to be able to place themselves on a Left–Right continuum and in particular are still able to locate themselves with reference to the major division between the Christian Democrats and the Communists. Research quoted by Daalder in 1983 found that those who identified quite strongly or very strongly with a particular party were clearly differentiated from supporters of other parties by self-location along a Left–Right continuum.[11]

This does not mean that the Italian electorate is unconcerned about the quality of government performance. As we saw in the previous chapter, survey data from several sources over a long period suggests that Italians have the lowest level of satisfaction with their governments of any country in the European Community (see Table 6.2). But this does not translate itself into clear electoral responses to specific problems. Survey data fail to elicit any persistent correlation between attitudes on issues and voting intentions, though this may be because of the difficulty of asking direct questions about the latter, with large proportions of 'don't know/refuse to answer' still appearing in most surveys. When marked changes do occur in the electorate, as in the mid-1970s or in the late 1980s, these appear to follow the emergence of concerns about the way politics operates rather than sectoral policy crises or opportunities.

Ecological data based on more general consumer surveys and on censuses have been more successfully used. It is therefore possible to describe the socio-demographic characteristics of the electorate with rather more plausibility (see Table 6.3). In general terms, and hardly surprisingly, it is the two largest parties which are the most representative in a socio-demographic sense. The data suggest that the DC has a strongly female electorate, and one that is strongest outside the major conurbations. It is also a less well-educated electorate, a characteristic shared with the Communist voters. The Communist vote otherwise is close to a mirror-image of the DC electorate, being predominantly male, younger than the mean, and more likely to reside in large cities. These results are as one might expect from traditional electoral analysis, particularly since religious observance is significantly higher among women than among men, in the countryside than in the cities, and among the old than among the

*Table 6.2* Attitudes to politics in Europe – Eurobarometer surveys: 'How satisfied are you with the way democracy works in your country?' (% of those answering)

|  | France | FRG | Italy | UK |
|---|---|---|---|---|
| **a. September 1973** | | | | |
| Very satisfied | 14 | 5 | 2 | 7 |
| Fairly satisfied | 37 | 39 | 25 | 37 |
| Not very satisfied | 30 | 44 | 42 | 34 |
| Not at all satisfied | 16 | 11 | 30 | 20 |
| Don't know | 13 | 1 | 1 | 2 |
| **b. Autumn 1978** | | | | |
| Very satisfied | 4 | 9 | 1 | 6 |
| Fairly satisfied | 36 | 68 | 18 | 45 |
| Not very satisfied | 34 | 15 | 46 | 28 |
| Not at all satisfied | 17 | 2 | 32 | 12 |
| Don't know | 9 | 6 | 3 | 9 |
| **c. October 1983** | | | | |
| Very satisfied | 7 | 7 | 1 | 12 |
| Fairly satisfied | 39 | 59 | 19 | 49 |
| Not very satisfied | 30 | 21 | 46 | 20 |
| Not at all satisfied | 13 | 3 | 31 | 11 |
| Don't know | 11 | 10 | 3 | 7 |
| **d. April 1988** | | | | |
| Very satisfied | 5 | 13 | 2 | 10 |
| Fairly satisfied | 42 | 64 | 25 | 47 |
| Not very satisfied | 36 | 18 | 46 | 27 |
| Not at all satisfied | 10 | 2 | 25 | 11 |
| Don't know | 7 | 3 | 2 | 5 |

young. The survey data from the mid-1980s therefore corroborated the argument that electoral change in Italy has so far been gradual rather than cataclysmic, and that the electorate is still characterised by many elements of continuity.

## Parties and social interests

Another way of looking at this is to ask what is the relationship between the parties and organised social interests. The main link between groups and governmental decision-making is personal, through the

Table 6.3 Socio-demographic profile of electorate by major party

|  | DC | PCI | PSI | PRI | MSI | Italy |
|---|---|---|---|---|---|---|
| Female | 57 | 45 | 45 | 47 | 33 | 52 |
| Rural | 41 | 27 | 31 | 32 | 37 | 35 |
| Provincial Urban | 47 | 49 | 45 | 39 | 46 | 44 |
| Major Urban | 12 | 24 | 24 | 29 | 17 | 21 |
| 18–34 age group | 27 | 38 | 34 | 39 | 37 | 33 |
| 35–54 age group | 31 | 37 | 36 | 37 | 34 | 35 |
| 55 years or more | 42 | 25 | 30 | 24 | 29 | 32 |
| Primary educ. or less | 55 | 48 | 41 | 17 | 37 | 46 |

Source: DOXA surveys, 1985–88. Figures are percentages of total support for each party and for the total electorate. 'Rural' means residing in a village or town with fewer than 10,000 inhabitants. 'Major urban' refers to residence in city with 250,000 or more inhabitants.

factions. The relationship depends on access to positions of power at the national level, but this is mainly because of the regulatory power of ministers and their control over the big decisions of investment and spending. It is also important for a party to have a solid base of local elected representatives, because the opportunities for direct patronage are much more frequent at the regional and communal level. One participant, a DC local councillor, wrote in 1976 in a study of the preference vote:

> It is not necessary to believe that central power is more profitable for detailed clientelist operations. The contrary is probably more correct, that now local power is becoming more significant . . . The availability of the appropriate centres of decision-making (communes, municipal enterprises, provinces, regions, hospitals, welfare organisation) provides the opportunity to respond to an infinite number of personal problems. The requests can involve a job, a promotion, a building licence, a commercial or craft licence, a grant, a subsidy, surfacing a road, filling in a pot-hole . . .[12]

The success of local politicians in building up networks of support gives them a considerable degree of independence from the local party organisation. They are not divorced from national politics; their initial entry into elected office will almost certainly have come from membership of a faction, which will also provide them with the immediate network of contacts among other elected representatives. The power of the national leaders of the factions is not in detailed control of local patronage but in controlling the passage between levels of government, in regulating the interaction between elected representatives within the faction. The clientelist system therefore depends on relatively sophisticated linkages between local and national government, calibrated in accordance with the preference votes in party, local and national elections.

But as the previous section described, neither the parties nor the electorate are motivated entirely by clientelist impulses, and it follows that national and local policy is not either. Clientelism conditions the choice of objectives and affects the way policy is implemented, but it does not directly determine policy objectives as such. It constrains the range of choices available and sets exchange values for the substantial policy choices to be made. Above all, it sets the priorities among the interests of the existing social blocs whose interaction is at the basis of the system of exchange. As long as the established social organisations and clientelism held good, governmental policy had to be measured primarily not against the achievement of sectoral policy objectives but rather against its capacity to maintain the social consensus.

But this social consensus, based on the rural and provincial emerging middle classes embedding themselves in local government, was not static or homogeneous. On the contrary, it was increasingly fragmented by the unco-ordinated economic development of the 'Italian miracle' – the period of rapid growth from 1952 to 1963. Alessandro Pizzorno, one of the leading sociologists of the period, argued that during this process of development the main governing parties (including the socialists) did not grow into coherent and relatively unified political parties, as happened elsewhere in Western Europe.[13] Rather they turned into a series of pluralist, broad-based and loosely co-ordinated political machines. Another way of putting this might be to say that the individual parties were able to articulate diverse social interests but not to aggregate them. They were unable to act as unified organisations, had great difficulty representing, acting on behalf of, their own elected representatives at the national and at the local level. As Pizzorno says, 'Instead they mainly aimed at satisfying demands presented by individual party members, groups, *correnti*, factions – fragmented elements of a representative body.'[14]

Policy processes therefore had to be tailored to the need to service the social coalition put together by individual politicians and their factional organisations, in which the variegated 'Catholic tradition' (trade unions, peasant co-operatives, financial and academic interests, the expanding public sector management) provided core elements. In this dispersed system, major reforms and strategic programmes emerge only with difficulty and do not have a powerful electoral impulse behind them.

In the early 1970s the ending of the sustained period of growth brought into focus the imbalances in the way Italy had developed. Particular problems were the sprawling urban-industrial conglomerations of the North (particularly Milan and Turin) contrasting with the unemployment and under-employment of the southern countryside, the difficulties of sustaining export-led growth together with rising standards of living, and the neglect of social infrastructure including health and education provision. The first warnings of this came from about 1963 on, and resulted in the attempts to establish a national indicative plan for development which was the major objective of the centre-Left coalition. This also marked the first major adjustment in the post-war party settlement, since it included the Socialist Party as a full member of the governing coalition for the first time since 1947.[15]

The decline of the traditional hegemony of the DC based on a compact Catholic vote was signalled clearly by the defeat in the divorce referendum in 1974. This occurred against the background of financial scandals and evidence of DC complicity in extreme rightwing subversive conspiracies. In socio-economic terms, the other main pillar of the support for the governing coalition was a heterogeneous lay grouping of the traditional Right, made up of liberal private-sector industrialists, the self-employed and the petty bourgeoisie of the provincial cities, who had been particularly susceptible to the antiCommunist appeal of DC strategy.[16] The high inflation of the 1970s eroded the living standards of these groups particularly, with their traditionally high ratio of savings to income. The influence of the traditional Right had been pivotal in bringing the Fascists to power in the 1920s, and the strategy of all the governing parties had been to treat the anti-communism of such groups as a historical datum, an unalterable phenomenon which could be manipulated but not changed. But in response to secularisation, to international detente, and to the economic mismanagement of the DC, they showed increasing signs of accommodating themselves to the prospect of leftwing involvement in government. This showed itself not so much in the increased support for the Communists, but in the willingness of their spokesmen in *Confindustria* and in the other associational groups to acknowledge the legitimacy of the PCI and its potential competence in government.

Further electoral decline followed in the regional elections of 1975, giving the PCI a say in the governments of Italy's seven largest regions, and in the parliamentary elections of 1976, when the swing to the Communists ensured that no majority government could be formed without their co-operation. The 'historic compromise' which followed integrated the Communists further into the system, and despite its brief duration made it more difficult to sustain centrifugal models of Italian policy. But it did not resolve the existing acute problems of representation, and the economic difficulties of the 1980s appear to have exacerbated the fragmentation and sectionalism of interest-group participation.

In 1981 a referendum on abortion revealed the extent of the decline of the Catholic vote (from 41 per cent in the 1974 divorce referendum to 33 per cent in the abortion referendum). The impact of secularisation was twofold. First, it reduced the number of those voting on Catholic principles, as these referenda indicated. Second, it undermined the political unity of Catholics by releasing Catholics from their traditional post-war obligation to support the party of which the Church hierarchy approved. Prominent lay Catholics are now visible in left-wing parties, particularly the Communists. Traditional right-wing Catholics are organised through the pressure group *Comunione e Liberazione*, a scourge of progressive bishops and a critical support for the DC.[17] After the erosion of the liberal right during the 1970s, their predominance in setting the agenda for Italian government has been reasserted during the 80s, with both the DC and the Socialists adopting the rhetoric of fiscal conservatism and privatisation. The critical difference is that the pivotal role of the traditional self-employed provincial middle class is no longer interpreted by the governing parties to include the veto on Communist participation. Therefore, in summary, the social coalition on which the governing parties are based has not altered fundamentally, and still requires the patronage system to maintain its cohesion, but the ideological conditions within which it operates have changed significantly.

## PARTIES AND POLICY CHOICES

### Policy mixes in the DC

The predominant influence in policy determination is the Christian Democrat Party. The Italian state is fashioned by them for their purposes. To a greater or lesser extent, the other governing parties are integrated into the policy-making procedures through their acceptance of these purposes and methods for the DC and for themselves. The integration of the Republicans and Socialists, the two most ideologically defined parties, has not challenged the distribution of public resources to small farmers, to the provincial self-employed, to the wealthy traditional bourgeoisie of the larger cities. The policies of the DC are limited mainly in two ways: first, by the need to maintain its control over the rules and values of exchange, and second, by the requirements of the social groups on which it has depended or which it wishes to favour. The other parties brought more client groups, added to the shopping list, and eventually cut down on the resources available for distribution when growth slowed. They do not challenge the rules of exclusion, of share of jobs, of private negotiations for public office. In this sense, and with qualifications which have already emerged, the policy methods and the policy mix are a DC method and a DC mix.

The DC tended to a passive view of their own representative role. From the beginning the Christian Democrats identified themselves as an inter-class party, aggregating widely diverse interests and aiming to resolve the tensions resulting from the process of modernisation process: the political party as mass psycho-therapist. De Gasperi's successor, Amintore Fanfani, summarised this ambition at the DC congress in 1954:

> The trade union and the party must link permanently the sovereign people with the legislative power and with the executive power; they must gather together the demands of the people, assess them critically and oversee their acceptance and satisfaction . . . there must not be a commune or ward in which the electors are not informed many times throughout the year in public assemblies . . . of the events in national life, in Parliamentary life, in political life of which we the DC are the protagonists or principal motivators. We must realise a closer collaboration between the DC and Christian social forces; between the DC and free trade unions, small farmers, factory managers and militant associations and forces.[18]

For the DC the issue was not so much which particular class or group to seek to represent. In so far as this was relevant, their social base was historically given, by their own Catholic tradition and by their inheritance of the conservative vote, particularly in the South. The one tied them to rural and agricultural interests, the other to the urban self-employed, particularly outside the larger cities. But the narrowness and potential instability of these electorates made them unreliable in the long term. Also, it threatened to leave them excessively dependent on the organisation of the Church. The Christian Democrats therefore sought to develop a mode of operation which would enable them to be open to all groups without losing their own social base. This also ensured that potential rivals (particularly the lay centre parties) would have difficulty maintaining their identity in the face of a dominant party which was apparently malleable to an indefinite degree on specific issues so long as these did not affect its cultural identity or its mode of electoral mobilisation.

The modern DC, no longer dependent on the Church, four decades of government experience behind it, is a mature stable coalition of factions which are loosely organised around central offices. The main functions of the central offices are to provide a minimum of common services and an arena for the endless negotiation and compromise between the factions. The factions themselves have separate recognised organisations within the party, some with their own periodicals, newspapers and research centres. The only full-length study of the DC in English, by Leonardi and Wertman, identifies their functions in this way:

> Factions represent the mechanism through which the dialectic of power operates and makes possible the shifts from one strategy to another, shifts between ruling elites, generational change within the party, and the servicing of diverse group interests.[19]

There have been factions within the DC almost from its inception. Though the names and leaders have changed (though some do remain from the founding period), the balance of forces in general ideological terms has remained more or less constant. The factions seem impervious both to party rule changes (from majority voting to proportionality and back again) and to denunciations from every incoming secretary since 1964 – partly because the secretaries themselves are factional leaders. For a brief period from 1964, after the introduction of proportional representation throughout the party, the factions had a direct policy role to play, in that they were required to present policy programmes as part of the pre-congress preparations at local provincial and national level. This effort at encouraging substantive debate in the party did not endure beyond the next congress, that of 1967.

The Leonardi and Wertman study discusses the DC's record in power mainly in terms of shifts in alliances occasioned by electoral and intra-party changes. The mass membership of the DC, as has been shown in numerous surveys, is very inactive, has little say in the choice of candidates and can contribute little to the formation of policy.[20] But policy is not developed by the party apparatus, nor is it discussed at any length in party congresses. The party congresses are the occasion for the establishment of the pecking order within the party elite on the basis of successful mobilisation of activists. They determine the membership of the central ruling bodies (the National Council and indirectly the National Executive) and since 1982 elect the party secretary. In a speech lasting over three and a half hours at the 17th congress in 1986, the party secretary De Mita spoke mainly about values and tradition, and sent coded messages to the warring factions about their potential ranking in his grand vision. But on policy he could find room only for 'indications' about 'areas for attention' which amounted to little more than a list of issues and acknowledgement of the need for action. But in this the DC is not unique – none of the major parties uses congresses to debate policy, not even to legitimise policies already adopted. Speeches from the secretary lasting hours and proposing little are the rule rather than the exception.

The power of the factions is exercised continually between the congresses by the faction leaders. Formally, management of the party rests with the National Council, but since this meets only once every three or four months, effective political authority lies with the National Executive, a body of about forty members whose composition is kept finely attuned to the factional balance of power. The formal structures of the DC, in other words, enhance both the factional organisation and its concentration in the hands of a relatively restricted group of leaders. In the 1960s and 1970s it was customary to argue that the factions were essentially electoral and clientelistic apparatuses, driven by motivations unrelated to policy.[21] The persistence with which successive generations of factions cleave to particular strategies within the party suggests otherwise. The policy-making role of the factions is very minor in relation to their other functions, as recruiters, as electoral campaigners and as power brokers, but it is possible to identify ideological differences. Though they do not appear at party congresses, the differences result in characteristic responses to the major issues, which as we have seen interact closely with coalition strategy.

The basic structure was laid down in the 1960s, as the party consolidated its grip and reach throughout the state machinery. The simplest differentiation between the factions is between Left and Right, but this standard categorisation is not very illuminating. It does not explain why supposed left-wing factions like the *Fanfaniani* and *Forze Nuove* have adopted apparently atypical policies, like vigorous opposition to the PCI and to trade union unity. Conversely, factions usually regarded as right-wing, such as the faction supporting Giulio Andreotti, have on occasions been amenable to PCI involvement in government and to radical reforms such as the establishment of the National Health Service in 1978.

The dividing-line between the factions is not simply a class-based one, such as in an inter-class party like the DC might be summarised by the Left–Right dichotomy. It is also to do with the role of religious authority in modern politics. The conventional left-right division describes differences over the role of the state in the economy, particularly over levels of taxation and levels of public spending. Until the mid-1970s there were few within the DC willing to support radical free-market policies, and even thereafter they have been a minority, generally technocrats such as the academic economist Nino Andreatta, and the former governor of the Bank of Italy, Guido Carli. Both these have been Treasury ministers, Carli for several years from 1988 to 1992, so they were certainly not without influence, but their ministerial activities were constrained by their lack of independent power outside the factions.

The question then is of the extent and type of state intervention rather than the principle of such a policy. Cutting across this division is the division about the significance of Catholicism in politics.[22] This is not a simple divide, since all Christian Democrats until the mid-1970s paid at least token respect to the Catholic origins of the party. But the traditional factions disagreed from the outset about how the Church and Catholic teaching should relate to governmental policy. This disagreement gave an initial structure to the factions, which has remained. Significant minorities on Left and Right have always favoured a distant relationship with the Church, preferring to use Catholicism as a cultural support rather than a specific guide. These are usually known as the liberal Catholics. Those who on the contrary approve the application of clerical influence in politics are referred to as 'integralist'. These, however, are divided internally between those who hold essentially conservative views about authority, for whom clerical influence is applied through the teaching of the Popes and the bishops, and those who seek independence from the hierarchy in the integral application of what they take to be Catholic social policy. The former are referred to as traditional integralists and the latter as social integralists. This is a division of substance as well as of method, since

*Table 6.4* DC factions 1973

|  | minimum intervention | maximum intervention |
| --- | --- | --- |
| integralist | *Dorotei* (34%) (traditional) | Fanfani and Forlani group (20%); *Forze Nuove* (10%) (societal) |
| liberal Catholic | Andreotti group (16%) | Moro group (9%); *Base* (11%) |

the traditional integralists have tended to follow a line of fiscal conservatism, while the social integralists have favoured an active state role, particularly in welfare policy. Many social integralists have found themselves on the left of the party, particularly on issues such as labour relations, since one of their strengths has been in the Catholic trade union confederation CISL. This division between traditional and social integralists mirrors the split word only in the nineteenth-century origins of Christian Democracy between the paternalist and the activist wings.[23]

At the 1973 congress, the last before the major changes induced by the defeat in the 1974 divorce referendum, the delegates divided by factions as shown in Table 6.4 (the names are the traditional ones, not necessarily those under which they campaigned at the time).

After 1973, the party went through a long and intense period of fluctuations within the factions, exacerbated by the murder of Aldo Moro in 1978, by the break-up of the right-wing *Doroteo* faction into several small factions and by the long decline of the social integralist group led by Fanfani. During the same period, however, a new group of modern integralists emerged – originally in the Catholic lay group *Comunione e Liberazione*, later in its political offshoot *Movimento Politico* (MP). By the 18th congress in 1989, the balance of power had stabilised (see Table 6.5).

The 1989 congress resulted in the election of Forlani as party secretary in place of the Left leader Ciriaco De Mita. Forlani had the support of the *Andreottiani* who were allied for the occasion with the MP faction. Such fluidity is not rare. Ideological differentiation is not the predominant motive in factional organisation, and alliances are frequent across the categories. The main divide in recent years has been between the Left, led by De Mita, and the traditionalist *Doroteo* group, each of which can ally with equal facility with groups in either

*Table 6.5* DC factions 1989

|  | *minimum intervention* | *maximum intervention* |
|---|---|---|
| integralist | *Dorotei* + Forlani group (37%) | Forze Nuove (7%); *MP* (5% est.); Fanfani group (3%) |
| liberal Catholic | Andreotti group (13%) | Left group – ex-Moro, ex-Zaccagnini, *Base* (35%); |

of the two smaller categories. Andreotti in particular has demonstrated extreme tactical flexibility in supporting both major groups at different times. But the two main groups are themselves coalitions of factions, subject to splinters and defections by smaller factional leaders seeking immediate gains elsewhere.

The internal development of the party contributed to the adoption of new objectives. As the DC became a mass party of widely differing interests, its leadership became more obviously collegial. The DC has never organised an effective whipping system for its parliamentary groups, apparently relying on the factions to secure majorities. The collegial internal party discipline, never fully commensurate with its governmental responsibilities, was gradually lost to the haphazard discipline of the factions, loosely grouped around the main division between the centre-right integralist *dorotei* and the liberal-Catholic Left. The Left were organised mainly in the faction of the southern notable Aldo Moro in what was originally a splinter from the *dorotei*, hence known as the *morotei*. After his death in 1978, the ideological leadership of this area passed to his ally Benigno Zaccagnini, and then to De Mita. But no leader since the 1950s has been able to achieve the factional domination exercised for a brief period by Fanfani, against which the consensual pluralism of the *dorotei* was an explicit reaction.

Granted the overall strategy of the DC described above, they have tended to give priority to maintaining a lively economic growth rate – the purpose being to keep tax revenues buoyant in order to ensure adequate funding for the mildly redistributive welfare policies. Economic growth also ensures that strains in the labour market are kept to a minimum, but the assumption in much DC policy until very recently seems to be that Italy has a more or less permanent surplus of labour. Full employment is undesirable, because of its impact on prices and balance of payments, but it is also unlikely, because of Italy's historic problem of over-population (relative to the likely supply of home employment). Hence it falls to the DC to manage the social strains occasioned by Italy's unbalanced and uneven growth through a policy of distribution of spoils – particularly jobs, but also pensions of various kinds, housing policy, and more generally through the promise of political stability between the two extremes of Communism and Fascism. These implicit centrist objectives explain why some areas of the state are occupied by the DC with no serious attempt at reform, while others are not only occupied but also subject to activism. In the first category are Education and Reform of Public Administration: education is important for the protection it can provide for the Church's interests in teaching, and for its pivotal role in cultural policy. Most important of all, the Education ministry is one of the largest single employers in the country, and an employer furthermore of social groups who formed part of the DC's original constituency. The control of the Public Administration portfolio for many years gave DC ministers an informal veto over changes to conditions of employment, again over social groups of particular significance to them. In the second category are agriculture, state participation and to a lesser extent labour and social security. In these ministries the strategy of spoils distribution required extensive new structures to be established and supported. These included the *Federconsorzi* in agriculture to distribute state support to *Coldiretti*, the expanded state-owned conglomerates IRI, ENI, EFIM, EGAM and others, together with complex networks of state-subsidised occupational pension schemes through the Ministry of Labour. The overall DC strategy rests on the premiss of adaptation to the international environment, but the adaptation is led by the traditional private sector or by market-oriented public sector industrialists. Both sets of actors should ideally operate with considerable autonomy, making judgements in accordance with their perceptions of the market. They could be subsidised by the state to the extent that the long benevolent arm of public authority required them to adopt explicitly political objectives (as with support of employment by unprofitable investment in the South) – that at least was the relationship as envisaged by the economist Pasquale Saraceno, adviser to Aldo Moro and author of the 1964 plan.[24]

This 'best-buy' strategy of the DC came under increasing strain after the 'hot autumn' of 1969, the resurgence of trade union power, and then the delayed reaction by the major industrialists beginning in 1980 with the FIAT redundancies.[25] Over strategy, the DC retained its pivotal role, but over specific policy, it was an apparently docile participant in the plans of others, lending its majority in accordance with the tactical needs of the day. Even the reaction of the 1980s saw it following on behind the neo-liberal reforms of the Republicans and the socialists, despite the efforts of De Mita to re-fashion the DC into a more active force on the centre-right. But overall there is a striking continuity in the DC method and objectives, which perforce has stamped itself on the state, though not on society as a whole. The DC emphasises adaptation to the domestic and international environment, and requires no long-term structural intervention by governmental authorities. In this sense the tradition of pragmatism, of modest objectives and limited horizons which has characterised Italy's foreign policy, is continued and is reflected in a similarly unambitious approach to domestic issues.

Popular and paternalist, compassionate and firm, centrist and radical, the DC still seems to see itself operating within the context of a generic Catholic model of the organic society, committed to a functional individualism in which the freedom of each is found in the full development of one's social faculties. The DC is no longer integralist in its approach to Catholic doctrine, nor is it merely the instrument of the Catholic Church. But its model of society derives from Catholic corporatism, from which however it has purged any notion of a strong directing centre, so that what remains is dominated by the mediating consensual role of the inter-class political party.

Despite the flashes of Republican rhetoric, the DC's tradition is the tradition of the commonplace, of continuity and flexibility, a tradition which for forty years has helped it cobble together government alliances, for the most part without firm policy commitments. This tradition combines Catholic populism with the supposed demands of realism, which for the DC means the recognition of Italy's proper place as a stable part of the Western alliance, vulnerable, strategically significant, reliant on others to fashion the international climate within which Italy can develop. DC leaders since De Gasperi have expected and required compliance with these objectives from all their allies. From this compliance many of the characteristic features of the Italian political system follow.

## Policy mixes in the other parties

A brief mention must be made of the impact of the other governing parties. Within the general context of the domination exercised by the

DC factional majority, it is possible to trace a clear division between the social managerialism of the socialists and the liberal managerialism of the Republican Party. This has had its effects both on government stability and on the reform programmes of the centre-left. The first period of the centre-left coalition (1963 to 1966) was dominated by two apparently disconnected events, whose relationship set a pattern for future development. The two were the threat of a *coup d'état* by dissident senior officers in the militarised police force, the *carabinieri,* and the nationalisation of electricity.

The problem of subversion from within the security services was particularly prevalent from 1960 to the end of the historic compromise in 1979. Individual episodes of disloyalty within the security services (merely rumoured at the time but now well-documented) were also associated through personal and organisational links with right- and left-wing terrorism of the 1970s.[26] The significance of the internal security problems is not only in the direct effect of the actions themselves, though this was severe enough – hundreds of groups active, thousands of terrorist attacks, senior political figures under constant threat, the former Prime Minister Aldo Moro kidnapped and murdered. The strategic consequences were felt much earlier than the Moro affair, with the first major episode in 1964, referred to as the 'De Lorenzo gambit', after the police chief involved, which was used by the DC and by senior administration officials to maintain the perceived threat from the Socialists within tolerable limits.[27] Irrespective of the threat posed to the stability of the Republic, De Lorenzo and his successors (from Borghese to Licio Gelli) served as a warning to potential reformers about the possible consequences of excesses of enthusiasm. A particular strand of the security gambit was the so-called 'strategy of tension', the term used to refer to the increase in civil disorder and acts of terrorism around the time of elections and government crises. Terrorism, conspiracies, scandals, plots and rumours of plots contributed to the preservation of established methods and boundaries of negotiation whenever new entrants threatened to challenge them.

The instability engendered by new entrants was not only the result of their impact on residual extreme-right officials in public administration and the military. There was also the possible destabilisation of Italy's international position within NATO and the EEC to consider, because of the responses of Italy's partners, particularly the United States and West Germany. Against the background of open concern expressed by DC ministers, by senior Armed Forces staff, and on occasions by the President of the Republic, the Socialists and later the Communists attempted to come to terms with their new role in government.

In this context, electricity nationalisation in 1964 was an issue of crucial symbolic and practical significance.[28] It reinforced the mutual suspicion between the Socialists and the traditional liberals, allowed the DC to appear as mediators between bitter antagonists, and gave the Socialists an early warning of where the boundaries lay. The base of the argument was the bitter dispute about the form of compensation to be paid in return for nationalisation of the privately owned electricity supply trusts. The Socialists sought to pay compensation directly to the shareholders, who were very numerous, while the right sought to maintain the existing electricity supply trusts in being through compensation to them as the legal previous owners. The solution was a muddled compromise, but one which ensured that the traditional families which had controlled the vast financial resources of the electricity supply trusts, families such as the Bastogi, retained their domination over the private sector capital assets of the Italian stock market at least in the short term.

The waves from this apparently isolated episode continued long after the issue was formally resolved. Not only did it bring out the De Lorenzo gambit and the intervention of the President of the Republic. Ten years later, a provocative and influential analysis by two left-wing journalists identified in this episode the political origins of the speculative and corrupt financial class who dominated the Italian stock market with their manoeuvres in the late 1960s and 1970s – the *razza padrona*, the 'boss breed' such as Sindona and Calvi.[29] Twenty-five years later the episode was still regarded by one of the chief proponents of the liberal right, Guido Carli, as a justification for abiding suspicion about the objectives of the Socialists.[30]

To the observer, the bitterness and ill-feeling might seem disproportionate to the real extent of the division. The socialists had broken the alliance with the Communists in 1953, and unequivocally turned away from their maximalist rhetoric in 1957. The centre-left governments brought not revolution but modest sporadic reform, such as compulsory secondary education (1962), regional reform (1968), the workers' charter (1970); also a greater openness to civil issues, with a referendum law and a divorce law both passed in 1970. The governments were particularly associated with the attempt to rationalise long-term government support for industry through the Giolitti plan in 1964 and then through the *Progetto Ottanta* (project 80) in 1969–

70 (see chapter 8). But the indicative planning system which was intended to be a strategic instrument of modernisation failed to deliver, and the period was one of heightened labour unrest. Some Socialists, particularly in the South and particularly through the Ministry of Public Works, showed a ready enthusiasm for DC methods of vote-winning.[31] Apart from the electoral weakness of the PSI, with only 10 per cent of the vote, the threat of authoritarian responses from outside Parliament was a major limitation, symptomatic (in different ways) of the incomplete integration of Left and Right into the political system.

In the 1970s the PSI were overshadowed by the emergence of the PCI from isolation, though their refusal to consider any coalition excluding the Communists in 1976 was a decisive factor in pushing the DC towards acceptance of the electoral realities of the day. Their strategy since 1979 has been to assert their independence of the Communists and to present themselves as the potential dominant party of the Left. By the 1980s, with the Socialist Prime Minister Bettino Craxi, the PSI was a fully functioning part of the governmental majority, differentiated from the DC not so much by policy as by its centralised and highly unified party structure, dominated by Craxi and his supporters. The Socialists have even developed their own industrial constituency, in the shape of the 'new money' of the communications and TV conglomerate of Silvio Berlusconi.

The only other governing party with a clear line on central issues of policy control has been the Republican Party. Throughout the post-war period the Republicans have been a constant component of the governing coalition, under the leadership of the former *azionista* Ugo La Malfa and then of his son Giorgio. In government the PRI have tried to stand for fiscal rectitude and sound money. In the 1960s, at the peak of the planning experiment, their interpretation of the reform was radically different from that of the PSI, in that they viewed the mechanisms as a means of bringing order to the processes of public expenditure and as a potential instrument of incomes policy.[32] This approach was the origin of disputes with the socialists in government, particularly prior to 1983. In so far as there has ever been a policy cause behind government instability, the differences between the Republicans and Socialists would have to be held to be one of the main causes. This was especially noticeable during the sixth legislature (1972–76). But it must be emphasised that the extent of this causation is limited, as policies often seem to be a pretext for government crises sought for quite other grounds. The strength of the PRI has always been in the intellectual and practical reputation of its leaders, particularly of Ugo and Giorgio La Malfa, of Giovanni Spadolini, who first broke the succession of DC Prime Ministers in 1981, and of Bruno Visentini, an industrialist and tax expert who was responsible for the major tax reforms of 1982–83. The weaknesses of the Republicans, however, are the weaknesses of all the allies of the DC – the smallness of their effective constituency, and their local involvement in the system of petty patronage whose national economic consequences their national leaders excoriate.

## Policy and the Communists

The problem of the limits of tolerable reform has been felt even more strongly by the Communists. They regarded themselves as a constitutional party, pursuing 'the Italian road to Socialism', confident in the rightness of their cause and in the consistent support of a near majority of the population in the 'red belt' areas of central Italy.[33] Until the beginning of the historic compromise period, the PCI saw themselves as the alternative government, even as the alternative state, and tried to constitute a complete replacement for the DC within the existing system. This applied in policy, in personnel, in organisation, in general objectives and values. They sought to represent actively, to provide the dynamic organising centre not for some crudely defined proletariat but for all who wished to enrol themselves under the banner of 'all progressive forces'.

The party structure was in principle Leninist, based on democratic centralism and proletarian internationalism. This meant that the membership were to be regarded as an active vanguard, subject to internal discipline exercised by the Central Committee. It also meant that links with the Soviet Union were a dominant factor in the setting of PCI foreign policy. But these two principles were diluted and eventually transformed.[34]

First, this was under pressure from the organisational demands of the mass membership. With over 2 million members from 1946 to 1956, and over 1.5 million thereafter until 1987, the PCI was never able and arguably never seriously attempted to maintain the rigorous control of debate and decision which the original democratic centralist model demanded. Second, the PCI's own strategy of political integration and cultural domination required it to open its doors to groups and individuals whose commitment was to the progressive Left rather than unambiguously to the principles of Marxism–Leninism. Third, the party rapidly became the major party of local government in central Italy, and developed a network of local administrators imbued with a strong sense of their own effectiveness and with their own practical policy concerns. The experience of Bologna and of the region of Emilia-Romagna was increasingly important to the PCI during the 1970s, as an example of the honesty and proven competence of Communist rule. Finally, the party's relationship with the trade union movement altered radically. The party had regarded CGIL as its transmission belt, an instrument of party policy, a source of recruitment and a training-ground. This became increasingly untenable from about 1969 on, with the importance of common action with the other confederations (CISL and UIL) and pressure from the factory shop-floor for active local representation. Though Communists remained numerically dominant in CGIL, the party recognised the importance of allowing CGIL to develop its own policy debate and an independent relationship with its ordinary members.[35]

But the PCI–CGIL link was critically important to both in the 1970s and 1980s. The strength of the relationship was such that, despite the conventional wisdom of party dominance, PCI policy-making and tactics sometimes appeared to be led by industrial relations issues, to the exclusion of other areas. Only foreign policy ever received the same continual attention from PCI leaders. This is scarcely surprising, since the PCI's identity and historical legitimacy rested on its dual claim to represent the working-class and to represent non-capitalist and anti-capitalist interests in Italian foreign relations. This did not necessarily make the link with CGIL an easy one, but it did offer some compensation for the isolation of the PCI. The capacity of CGIL to mobilise sectors of the industrial labour force was a visible and at times frequent reminder to employers and government of the social support for the Communists. It has been argued with some plausibility that the willingness of Ministers of Labour to negotiate nationally with CGIL acted as a compensation for the refusal to grant such a badge of respectability to the PCI.[36]

In 1977–78, the CGIL leadership backed the efforts of the PCI to moderate economic demands in return for closer co-operation with the DC government over social and industrial reform. This controversial policy has since been severely criticised as a missed opportunity for the PCI to reassert its leadership over the progressive left.[37] Instead of moderating demands, the argument ran, CGIL and the PCI could have concentrated on radical workplace reforms, in order to shift the balance of power in favour of organised labour and to affect directly the working conditions of the industrial workforce. In doing so the PCI would have brought onto one platform a wide range of left-wing activists who were increasingly disenchanted with the PCI's role in government (including groups in the DP and in the *comitati di base*). But for the PCI, the problem then was not the fragmentation of the Left – the Communists had won 34 per cent of the vote at the previous elections. The strategy of the PCI, in 1978 as in 1948, rested on its re-insertion into the mainstream of government. Its democratic legiti-macy was more in question than its leadership of the Left.

The break-up of the historic compromise coalition in 1979 sent the PCI back into isolation. It attempted belatedly to re-impose its domination of the Left with the campaign against the incomes policy reforms of 1983 and 1984, and sought to reassert itself as the 'shadow government' – albeit one whose policies lacked any institutional forum for debate and whose role looked increasingly marginal in view of the emerging alternation between the DC and the PSI, and in view of the internal difficulties of recruitment and organisation faced by CGIL.

The other issue area favoured by the PCI and emphasised by its opponents was foreign policy.[38] Communist domination of CGIL was never as such a direct justification for treating the PCI as a pariah, but its independent stand on international relations was. Traditionally, the Communists opposed Italian membership of NATO. The party was bound by personal, organisational and ideological links to the Communist Party of the Soviet Union, but its position could never be described as one of implicit subservience to Soviet interests. The PCI modulated its recognition of the leading role of the CPSU with repeated assertions of its own independence, which brought it into increasing disfavour in Moscow even if Western powers were uncon-vinced. The PCI moved slowly away from support for the Soviet Union while continuing to criticise American military involvement in Europe. The party criticised the invasion of Hungary in 1956, though not strongly enough for some of its members, but by the time of the invasion of Czechoslovakia in 1968 it had moved to a position of unequivocal disapproval of such Soviet interventionism.

In a well-publicised interview in 1975, Enrico Berlinguer, party secretary, declared that he 'felt safer on this side of the fence'.[39] This was taken as implying that the PCI was no longer opposed in principle to NATO bases in Italy, and the statement cleared away some of the misgivings other governments felt about Communist participation in governing coalitions. In 1981, Berlinguer criticised Soviet involvement in the Polish military takeover in terms strong enough to persuade Italy's sub-editors to use the term *lo strappo*, the break in relations. The

PCI finally seemed to have persuaded the foreign policy community that it was no longer tied to the interests of the Soviet Union, that its own supporters no longer looked to the Soviet Union for guidance. From this time on the main argument against the PCI was not foreign relations but its alleged commitment to radical internal change, its apparent ambiguity about the workings of liberal democracy. This criticism was used particularly by the Socialists.

At the 17th party congress in 1986, the PCI declared itself to be 'an integral part of the European Left', unequivocally in favour of European integration. For the party supporters, the evident failings of the Soviet system of government have meant that the *strappo*, though not painless, could be explained in terms of the PCI's commitment to emancipation and economic modernisation. Its radical international aspirations found a ready and less anachronistic home in support for Third World liberation movements, anti-colonialism and anti-militarism, with a distinct increase in support for the minority pacifist wing in the party.

All of these changes were part of the party's efforts to adapt its identity and to find a new role after the failure of the historic compromise strategy of coalition with the DC. In 1987, the PCI share of the vote fell to its lowest level since 1963, the sharpest falls being recorded in its industrial support in the North. The already vigorous debate over its own identity sharpened further, with proposals from its new secretary Achille Occhetto to 're-found' the party under a new name with new statutes. These were given further impetus by the collapse of the Communist regimes in Eastern Europe, and at a turbulent and difficult congress at Rimini, in February 1991, the PCI agreed to dissolve itself and to form the 'Democratic Party of the Left' (*Partito Democratico della Sinistra*). The new party is composed of the bulk of the old Communists, but aims to attract a wide range of groups on the Left, and adopted new statutes which explicitly allowed organised groups to use the party for specific causes. At the same time the party passed resolutions vigorously opposing the Gulf War and calling for the withdrawal of Italian troops. The veteran left-winger Pietro Ingrao described pacificism as 'not a tactical choice but an assertion of identity'. Occhetto refrained from endorsing the principle, but the obvious strength of the 'radical internationalists' and their importance within the majority of the new party allowed the Socialists immediately to claim that the PDS lacked the 'culture of government'. This amounted to a reiteration of the traditional veto, a restatement of the boundaries and a warning that for the time being, the PDS lay outside them.[40]

Other parties face demands from different regional interests, and have to combine particular clientelistic requirements with those of social constituencies. The Communists were almost alone among the major parties in Italy in not being predominantly a clientelistic party and in not having access to national instruments of welfare distribution. The only other parties about whom this can be said are the much smaller and more overtly ideological parties, the neo-Fascist MSI, the extreme Left DP, and the issue-based campaigning parties the Greens and the Radicals. The PCI therefore faced relatively unusual problems of having to develop national policy for several different issue-based constituencies. There is no reason to believe that the PDS will differ from the PCI in this. The PCI electorate has become increasingly heterogeneous, both because of changing patterns of employment and because of its own relative success in broadening its base. The PCI was primarily a party of government – actual, in local government, and aspirant at the national level. Associated with this was its own view of itself as a constitutional party, in fact as the party whose role it was to protect the Constitution, particularly the radical and progressive elements. But its own strategy of the Italian road to Socialism demanded that it present itself as an alternative – an alternative ideal, but also an alternative practice. The party was also the main party of protest, the party of outsiders – a role increasingly under threat from the extreme Left groups after 1969. And finally, the party's past was that of a revolutionary vanguard party, and much of its rhetoric maintained the allusions to radical change even if the strategies and policies belied the rhetoric.

As party of government, party of the Constitution, party of the alternative, party of protest, and vanguard party, the PCI had to manage extraordinary tensions – between its core industrial worker vote and the local government administrators, between the intellectuals and the professional politicians, between the middle-class support in the sub-culture of central Italy and the protest votes of the cities of the South. In view of the weakness of policy development in the other parties, and the lack of an effective forum for policy debate, the constant temptation for the PCI was to resolve the tensions by emphasising its uniqueness, the extent of the difference between PCI and DC or PSI. The problem with this approach is that it can condemn the party of the alternative, the new PDS, to remaining precisely that – the permanent alternative.

## NOTES

1 Sartori, G. 'European political parties – the case of polarised pluralism', pp. 137–176 in La Palombara, J. and Weiner, M., *Political parties and political development* (Princeton, NJ, Princeton U.P., 1966); Sartori, G., 'Il caso italiano – salvare il pluralismo e superare la polarizzazione', pp. 675–678 in *Rivista Italiana di Scienza Politica*, a.IV n.3 dicembre 1974; Sartori, G., 'Rivisitando il pluralismo polarizzato', pp. 196–223 in Cavazza, F. and Graubard, S., *Il caso italiano* (Milano, Garzanti, 1974); Sartori, G., *Parties and party systems* (Cambridge, Cambridge U.P., 1976).

2 Galli, G. (ed.) *Il comportamento elettorale degli italiani* (Bologna, Il Mulino, 1968); Galli G. and Prandi, A., *Patterns of political participation in Italy* (New Haven, Conn., Yale U.P., 1970); Galli, G., *I Partiti Politici* (Torino, UTET, 1974).

3 See map 3 on the geography of the sub-cultures at the 1963 elections. On the concept of sub-cultures, see Galli and Prandi 1970; Kertzer, D., *Comrades and Christians* (Cambridge U.P., 1980); White, C., *Patrons and partisans* (Cambridge, Cambridge U.P., 1988); more generally, Merton, R., *Social theory and social structure* (New York, Free Press, 1968).

4 The 'third Italy' debate is discussed in more detail in chapter 9.

5 Sartori 1966, pp. 143–144; but see also Somogyi *et al.* 1964, pp. 319–346.

6 Luzzatto Fegis, *Il volto sconosciuto degli italiani* (Milano, Giuffrè, various years); Eurobarometer surveys since 1963 corroborate this (EC Commission Publications Office, Luxembourg, annually).

7 Galli and Prandi 1970, p. 302.

8 Tarrow, S.G., *Between centre and periphery: grassroots politicians in France and Italy* (New Haven, Conn., Yale U.P., 1977) p. 64.

9 Parisi, A. and Pasquino, G., 'Changes in Italian electoral behaviour: the relationships between parties and voters,' *West European Politics*, vol.2 no.3 October 1979, pp. 6–30; Mannheimer, R. and Allum, P.A., 'Italy', in Crewe, I. and Denver, D., *Electoral change in Western democracies* (London, Croom Helm, 1985).

10 Sani, G., 'Political culture in Italy: continuity and change', in Almond, G.A. and Verba, S., *The civic culture revisited* (Boston, Little Brown, 1980).

11 Daalder, H., 'The Italian party system in transition: the end of polarised pluralism,' pp. 216–236 in *West European Politics*, vol.6 no.3, July 1983.

12 Ancisi, A., *La cattura del voto – sociologia del voto di preferenza* (Milano, Franco Angeli, 1976) pp. 63–64.

13 Pizzorno, A., 'I ceti medi nei meccanismi di consenso', pp. 315–338 in Cavazza and Graubard, 1974; Pizzorno, A., *I soggetti del pluralismo* (Bologna, Il Mulino, 1980).

14 Pizzorno, 1980, p. 53.

15 On the economic background to this, see Salvati, M., 'The impasse of Italian capitalism' pp. 3–33 in *New Left Review*, November 1972, no.76.

16 Berger, S. and Piore, M., *Dualism and discontinuity in industrial societies* (Cambridge, Cambridge U.P., 1980).

17 On the impact of secularisation, see Wertman, D., 'The Catholic church and Italian politics: the impact of secularisation,' pp. 87–107 in *West European Politics*, vol.5 no.2, April 1982; Furlong, P.F., 'The Vatican in

Italian Politics,' pp. 63–79 in Quartermaine L. and Pollard, J. (eds.), *Italy today – patterns of life and politics* (Exeter, Exeter University Press, 1987, 2nd edition); Furlong, P.F., 'Authority, change and conflict in Italian Catholicism' in Gannon, T. (ed.) *World Catholicism in Transition* (London, Macmillan, 1988).

18 Quoted in Galli, G., *Fanfani* (Milano, Feltrinelli, 1976) p. 60.

19 Leonardi and Wertman 1989 p. 91.

20 See for example Zuckerman, A., *The politics of faction – Christian Democrat rule in Italy* (New Haven, Conn., Yale U.P, 1979).

21 Zuckerman, 1979.

22 I discuss this in more detail in Furlong, P.F., *The Italian Christian Democrats: from Catholic movement to conservative party*, Hull Papers in Politics no. 25, 1982.

23 De Rosa, G., *Il Movimento Cattolico in Italia, dalla restaurazione all'età giolittiana* (Bari, Laterza, 1972); Jemolo 1974; Candeloro 1974.

24 Treves, G., 'The public corporation in Italy' in Friedmann, W. and Garner, J.F. (eds), *Government enterprise, a comparative study* (London, Stevens, 1970).

25 Revelli, M., 'Defeat at FIAT' pp. 96–109 in *Capital and Class*, no.16, Spring 1982.

26 On the 'strategy of tension', see Furlong, P.F., 'Political terrorism in Italy – responses reactions and immobilism', pp. 57–90 in Lodge, J. (ed.), *Terrorism – a challenge to the state* (Oxford, Martin Robertson, 1981); Meade, R.C., *Red Brigade – the story of Italian terrorism* (London, Macmillan, 1990).

27 On this episode, see Collin, R., *The De Lorenzo gambit – the Italian coup manqué of 1964* (London, Sage, 1976).

28 The economic and political background to nationalisation is discussed in Allen, K. and Stevenson, A., *An introduction to the Italian economy* (Oxford, Martin Robertson, 1974), particularly chapter 7.

29 Scalfari, E. and Turani, S., *Razza Padrona – storia della borghesia di stato* (Milano, Feltrinelli, 1975); also Panerai, P. and De Luca, M., *Il Crack – Sindona, La DC, il Vaticano e gli altri amici* (Milano, Mondadori, 1975); Cornwell, R., *God's Banker – an account of the life and death of Roberto Calvi* (London, Gollancz, 1983).

30 See Carli, G., *Pensieri di un ex-governatore* (Pordenone, Edizioni Studio Tesi, 1988).

31 Walston, J., 1988.

32 La Malfa, U., *Intervista sul non-governo* (Bari, Laterza, 1977).

33 Among the voluminous material on the Communists, for a general introduction see Sassoon, D., *The strategy of the Italian Communist party, from the resistance to the historic compromise* (London, Frances Pinter, 1981); Amyot, G., 1981.

34 Barth Urban, J., 1986.

35 Lange, P., Ross., G., and Vannicelli, M., *Unions – change and crisis* (London, Allen and Unwin, 1982); Blackmer, D. and Tarrow, S. (eds), *Communism in Italy and France* (Princeton, New Jersey, Princeton U.P. 1975); Golden, M., *Labor divided – austerity and working class politics in contemporary Italy* (London, Cornell U.P., 1988); Accornero, A. (ed.), *L'identità comunista* (Roma, Editori Riuniti, 1983).

36  Lange, P. and Regini, M. (eds), *Stato e regolazione sociale* (Bologna, Il Mulino, 1987); on the early record, La Palombara, J., *The Italian Labour movement – problems and prospects* (Ithaca, NY, Cornell U.P., 1957).

37  See particularly Golden 1988.

38  Hobsbawm, E., *The Italian road to socialism – an interview with Giorgio Napoletano*, (Westport, Conn., Hill Press, 1977).

39  Sassoon, D. (ed.), *The Italian Communists speak for themselves* (London, Spokesman Press, 1978) pp. 73–74.

40  For a detailed description of the 20th Congress, see Furlong, P.F., 'The last Congress of the PCI,' *Government and Opposition*, vol. 26 no. 2, Spring 1991, pp. 267–273.

# Part II

# The practice of policy

# Chapter 7

# A general framework, and an Italian application

## A STATIC ANALYTICAL VIEW

In chapter 1 I described how the Italian political system might be understood as a specific variant within the family of Western European policy processes, with their emphasis on structured interaction among a number of groups, bounded by institutional continuities. This interaction is determined by differing levels of resources, by variations in forms of dependence, and by the different impact of strategies, rules and processes of exchange. To summarise the discussion in the chapters which followed, in Italy this complex interaction:

a)  follows a pattern of distribution of resources broadly established in earlier regimes;
b)  is sanctioned by a constitutional system which emphasises formal law and representational pluralism;
c)  is mediated through a public administration which separates routine patronage from substantial policy;
d)  depends on the permanence in office of the governing parties to maintain the stability of the exchange values and to determine the outcomes of the barter in an orderly manner.

As a result, policy communities are the exception rather than the rule in Italian policy-making. The term 'policy community' is understood to imply a degree of cohesion and directive capacity which had usually been lacking in the Italian case. In general, the conclusion is that issue networks tend to predominate in Italian policy-making. Further than this, research has tended not to provide us with sufficient material to specify how and why the different forms of policy-making subsist, and what the different outcomes are. On the contrary, the predominance of parties has normally discouraged the adoption of models which might shift attention towards interest-group/bureaucracy interaction. When this has been the object of study, the research has usually been permeated by reference to the pervasive control of the governing parties, the weakness of the bureaucracy and the dependence of interest-groups on association with party representatives.

Despite or because of the rhetoric of its corporatist past, Italy has not developed neo-corporatist structures in its post-war government. Periodic sightings of emerging patterns of corporatist intermediation (for instance, with the wages policy agreement of 1983) have so far proved premature.[1] Italy lacks the core state structures to guide such a strong form of representation. The term 'consociational' was widely used in a pejorative sense by critics of the Italian mode of policy-making in the 1970s and early 1980s. The problems with this term are several.[2] Consociationalism has not been convincingly applied as an explanatory model outside its original homeland, the Netherlands, partly because of the difficulty of finding the equivalent degree of elite consensus over major policy within an agreed constitutional framework. In Italy the consensus is limited to a stalemate supported by a restricted range of parties, and conventionally has relied on a single dominant party to enforce the rules by which negotiation is conducted. Consociationalism has been used as a generic term of abuse to refer to the secrecy with which deals are struck and their failure to achieve substantive policy change. This alters the original content of the term, which originally applied to the capacity of the system to make genuine progress using rules accepted by all, in which no one party is predominant. As we have seen, these qualities do not apply in Italy.

The competitive pluralist model of representation is implicit in parts of the Constitution, in parliamentary regulations handed down from the Liberal state and in the practices and conventions of the state apparatus. It therefore has the undoubted advantage that it has descriptive plausibility when applied to the normative framework, even if it fails to explain fully the real distribution of power within the system. Also it vies with other forms of representation, particularly with class-based representation through the mass parties and the clientelism of the traditional administration. In all the governing parties, the distinctions between parties, interest-groups and factions are blurred, so that it is not at all obvious what type of politics is going on – individualistic support, issue-based representation, class-based representation, associational support, clientelism. Because of the factionalised party structures at regional or provincial level the associational networks may actually function as electoral machines for the politician whose patronage network dominates in the area – not for the association membership or even for the party as a whole. In some areas, again particularly in the South, preference voting has sustained the local patronage strategies of notables, who also rely on their membership of modern mass parties to give them access to office. Issue, class, association and client-group combine to put cross-pressures on the elected representatives and to confuse the political input into the policy-making process. The party-dominated pluralism succeeds in guaranteeing a modicum of stability for the ordinary processes of government, but can do little to stimulate elite consensus over the substance of collective public interest, and rests on a very low level of public satisfaction with the way democracy works in Italy. In terms of the discussion of representation at the beginning of this work, the competitive and highly pluralist pattern of representation does determine how coalitions are formed and how proposed legislation is ranked, but it does so on the basis of criteria which relate to factional objectives, not on criteria related to national aims about the stuff of modern politics elsewhere – inflation, unemployment, trade balance, social security and welfare. Its capacity to aggregate and identify the collective public interest is not strong, and the legitimacy of the representative system suffers accordingly.

Recent work has sought to widen the debate.[3] While accepting the quantitative predominance of party elites in formal decision-making processes, the more recent research leads to the conclusion that there is a fundamental distinction between partisan policy-making and substantial policy-making. Partisan policy-making means processes in which a political grouping uses formal procedures to express coalitional preferences; substantial policy-making refers to preferences of the various actors (usually having a party-political link) for specific action in a sector of public policy – pensions, taxes, energy and so on. Research by Dente and Regini found that preferences expressed in the partisan arena rarely showed the same pattern as those expressed in the substantial arena – allies and antagonists in the one were not necessarily allies and antagonists in the other. Furthermore, the pattern of alliance and antagonism within the substantial arena varied from issue to issue. The implication of this is that coalitions formed at the partisan level are not necessarily paid for directly in the currency of substantial policy. This also suggests that, within the variety of configurations available, substantial policy arenas may be characterised by sectoral rather than comprehensive decision-making, with considerable co-operation across groups who are antagonistic in the partisan arena, and by openness to the specific preferences of other actors. The comparative model based on the difference between substantive and partisan policy-making has clear affinities with the policy community and issue network literature, and helps explain some of the paradoxes of Italian policy-making – such as particularly the apparent 'politicisation' of decision-making, in the party-political sense, together with the lack of obvious pattern connecting the various sectors and issues.

An advantage of the policy community approach is that it is intuitively plausible to begin with a recognition of the first paradox of Italian politics: the domination of the political system by the same group of parties for over forty years, and the apparent lack of any significant overall patterns or strategies in policy-making during this period. Notions of political lag generally fail to address this issue, while clientelism and immobilism signify the lack of an overall national pattern, not the existence of one. Policy community and issue or policy network studies begin by accepting this superficially patternless phenomenon, and identify the mechanisms within it which actually structure the way decisions are made – in particular, resources, processes of exchange, constraints, objectives and rules. Like the pluralist theories from which they derive, policy community approaches concentrate attention on intermediate elites, on non-dominant organisations which either by selection or by their own initiative come between formal political office-holders in central government and the diverse policy interests of particular sectors.

Analysis within this framework does not presuppose any one overall pattern – it is possible to argue in different cases for different models, ranging from unregulated sectoral competition between elites, through issue networks, to incorporation into policy communities by administrative elites. In Italy, the individual explanations in specific cases of substantial policy show some areas of 'community' behaviour, but are overlaid with partisan policy-making. The partisan policy-making is much less structured than the substantial policy-making and is closer to the issue network model than to community pattern (see Table 7.1).

In the Italian case, the 'rules of the game' within which strategies are played out are characterised by the reliance on rapid switches between the formal and informal, described in chapter 4, which is a defining characteristic of Italian policy-making. Though individual policy communities may subsist in some areas where there are dominant

Table 7.1 Community and partisan policy-making

|  | Policy community ideal type | Partisan policy in Italy |
|---|---|---|
| group resources | even across restricted range of non-party groups | skewed to parties |
| relations with bureaucracy | dominated by professional associations | professional associations weak |
| state leadership capacity | authoritative | lacking authority |
| preferred strategy | consensual integration, co-operative | selective exchange, clientelist |
| objectives | group-specific | system maintenance |
| value-system | interest-based, flexible | given, non-negotiable |
| elite strategies | technocratic, dirigiste | populist, distributive |

groups able to structure the exchange, in the majority the system is one of sub-dominant players using the informal rules so as to maintain the relative imbalance of resources – in employment, in health care, in fiscal policy particularly. The automaticity of the formal procedures leads the players in the game to seek informal arrangements. These make them subordinate in specific cases to those who have the authority to waive the application of regulations, such as individual ministers, individual *assessori* in local government, or those acting for them. Power in this context is predominantly but not exclusively discretion over the application of written formal rules. The informal rules of the game, which govern the actual process of exchange, appear to place a high premium on contract-type issues typical of the market-place. The market-place to which these rules refer, however, is structured and closed, and the rules reflect this. While any attempt to identify informal unstructured and flexible guides to behaviour must be éxtremely approximate, observation suggests that the following constitute the basic rules of the game:

1 *Confidentiality of agreements* – contracts reached between parties cannot be minuted in official records of any sort, and if necessary structures may be developed within formal institutions to allow contracting parties to adjourn into restricted non-recorded committees.

2 *Reciprocity of relationships* – trust is essential between the contracting parties, particularly since the exchange may amount to no more than agreement to support now in return for unspecified support later.

3 *Conflict avoidance* – the societal basis is highly conflictual, but the policy rules exclude the possibility of zero-sum conflicts. Irreconcilable conflict between contracting parties would disturb the market and would threaten the integrity of the other rules. Orderly exchange requires acceptance of the procedures by all, and complete commitment to the process of exchange.

But the lack of electoral or other sanctions against errant behaviour makes the confidentiality, reciprocity and commitment difficult to sustain. Outside the informal and private arena of agreement, other factors intervene. Further rules are required which recognise the need for adaptability.

4 *Arbitrariness of values* – the exchange is based on subjective assessments of worth, and may change radically and rapidly.

5 *Temporaneity of alliances* – the fluidity of values and the lack of external pressure to the contrary ensure that alliances between players are rarely of long duration, and in any case are not expected to be so. It follows from this that it is difficult to reach agreement about policy changes which might be likely to have long-term or structural effects much beyond the duration of the alliance.

6 *Flexibility of membership* – exclusion from one sectoral exchange network does not entail exclusion from all others. Despite repeated efforts by one party or another to impose complete consistency of alliances, parties do in fact achieve different sectoral and territorial arrangements.[4]

It is within this context that 'clientelism' is adopted as a label to cover the obscurer parts of the policy process. Described in terms of the power–dependence framework, clientelism narrowly perceived is a set of informal bilateral relationships between a politician and a varying number of individuals. The patron has access to resources because of his or her formal office-holding. These resources are usually material, relating to state financial benefits such as pensions and allowances, or to contracts for public procurement, but may also be facilitative – as for instance when the patron may waive a particularly irksome regulation to the benefit of a client. In return, the client provides political support of a variety of types including voting. Little need be said of the strategies of the client since the client has very few options available: exit or loyalty, but no voice.[5] This is not a free-market exchange. The client cannot affect the policy, since the policy is largely incidental to the exchange. The objectives of the patron are to maximise the extent of the clientelist support and to deploy it as a resource in the range of political relationships undertaken. The strategies employed by the patron are vote-maximising, where the vote depends not on perceived competence, ideological affinity or sociological affiliation but on an instrumental relationship. Clientelism as a theory of the substantial policy process is highly unspecific as to outcome; by definition it presupposes very limited resources and strategies on the part of societal interests, and suggests a general lack of concern for the effects of the outcome on the collective interest. What it may cover is action in the partisan policy arena, where it explains at least partially the determination of policy outcomes in their effects on specific interest groups such as public employees, professional associations, and pension groups.

The policy communities on the other hand are characterised by a more equal sharing of resources, a more consensual style of management, and a high degree of institutional co-ordination. There is little evidence of these in partisan policy-making, where the exchange of political goods is at its most complex and most fluid.[6] Where there is substantial policy-making, this falls towards the community-cooption end of the spectrum, with the cooption carried out mainly by the parties – in other words, with the parties still controlling access to the specific exchanges over policy in accordance with the rules which govern both partisan and substantial policy-making. But the relationship between the partisan and substantial policy arenas is not clear, and it remains for future research to elucidate the channelling of issues into either arena.

Most non-Italian research using this analysis has emphasised the crucial role played by public administration in the processes of marshalling the interests, selecting the intermediary groups, and regulating the competitive elements. Indeed, the conformation and the processes internal to government apparatus determined to a large extent how successfully governments may achieve their objectives in interest-group management. In Italy, as we saw in Chapter 4, the interests of public administration are primarily the preservation of their corporate structure, its job security, the ease of working conditions, and particularly the rigid protection against political interference provided by the statutory procedural requirements.

Interest-group regulation is not part of the territory of public administration except under relatively rigid conditions. Such regulation is normally carried out within a bureaucratic market-place, in which professional bureaucrats act as market-makers, exercise some autonomous control over resources, and are able to play a pivotal role in substantial policy-making. But in Italy, the political parties are the market-makers. Public administration is the missing actor, silent in the debate, usually lacking any sense of its own preferences in individual sectors, and restricted by the formality and automaticity of its procedures from entering genuine negotiations with politicians and interested groups. Public administration is one of the main reasons why the structured market predicted by the pluralist approach cannot be fully applied. The above analysis would suggest that the professionalisation of public administration is a necessary condition of progress to an orderly system of interest-group regulation.

## Historical development of policy

The static framework proposed for analysis of Italy's processes of partisan and substantial decision-making suggests clearly that Italy fits into the West European pattern of pluralist intermediation, with particular variations based on the longevity of the dominant coalition, the persistence of patronage-based exchange, and the anomalous role of an unreformed public administration. The overall pattern is one of societal conflict mitigated by a selective exchange conducted by mutually dependent political organisations. What this does not tell us is how to look at chronological development of policy. We can now apply the same kind of analysis to the historical development of public policy, beginning with general observations about some common features, and identifying the Italian variant.

Macro-economic policy lies at the heart of public policy decisions, because it determines the scope and direction of government spending and because it can affect the framework of prices, labour relations, social mobility and welfare needs within which other policy operates. In comparative terms, the historical objectives of economic policy in Western Europe are usually identified as follows (not necessarily in this order of priority):[7]

1 Self-sustaining and balanced growth of national income (gross and per capita).
2 Stable prices, or at least levels of inflation in line with competitors;
3 Balance of payments equilibrium.

4 Full employment, or as close as is compatible with the proper functioning of the labour market.

These objectives were an integral part of the Keynesian post-war consensus, formed out of the experience of the depression, the war, and the rapid rebuilding of the economies of continental Europe. They implied an activist government role in the economy, and the belief that within limits the state could actually manipulate the demand side of the economy so as to correct imbalances and to mitigate the worst effects of cyclical trends. They also imply the use of what Heidenheimer refers to as the 'big levers' – monetary instruments, tax policy, government spending.[8]

In Italy, only monetary policy has been a reliable tool, the other two being ruled out as either ineffective or uncontrollable. The national objectives are not radically different, and in Italy as elsewhere they were not only an end in themselves. They were also an instrument through which the benefits of economic development could be shared throughout the population through the development of welfare policies, improved education and health, and rising real wages for all the workforce. By some very different routes, and in some cases very imperfectly and late, social policy in post-war Western Europe is characterised by the adoption in principle of universalism, in accordance with which the benefits of economic growth were considered an entitlement for the entire population to share, if necessary through direct intervention by the state.[9] The adoption of these aims and of the instruments they entailed puts economic policy at the pivot of government activity, so that choices of economic policy have direct consequences for all other aspects of policy – social security, employment, education, health, defence, industry. All of these policies may entail redistributive effects both from the direct consequences of the policies themselves (particularly if they involve transfer payments) and because of the tax and government borrowing implications. Hence, even when budget balances are not giving cause for concern, the question of levels of deficit or surplus is not only financial and macro-economic, it is also a social and political question.

With these objectives and with these tools governments are therefore committed to economic management. This applies whether they wish it or not. In developed countries, even when governments (usually led by Conservative Parties) attempt to disengage from one or other of the objectives, their own actions have an unavoidable impact, because of the size and scope of government economic activity. In some countries, Italy included, governments have at times taken on direct responsibility for growth through indicative planning and through state ownership or support of key sectors. The Italian experience of national planning lasted only from 1964 to 1972, but regional and sectoral plans have been a constant feature of government thinking, and public sector ownership has been a powerful weapon throughout the post-war period.

Governments may be driven to try to disengage from economic management for a variety of reasons. From a position far removed from classical economics, the problems inherent in government activism were predicted by the Polish economist Michal Kalecki, who in an article published in 1943 argued that governments in modern capitalist economies would be unwilling to sustain the costs of full employment despite having the means to do so. This was because of the pressures on capitalist enterprises which full employment entailed. Government spending would therefore have the function of a short-term palliative for endemic social conflict rather than long-term economic support.[10] In the 1980s, from the other side of the political spectrum, the resurgence of monetarist theories in economics led to increasing interest in the notion of the political business cycle, which was held to predict regular increases in the size of government spending in the periods immediately before major elections. The policy conclusion was a large-scale withdrawal from Keynesian policy arenas in response to the increasing costs inherent in government's welfare role. In the view of the New Right, the objectives of economic intervention resulted in government activity which, by reason both of its size and its long-term impact was profoundly dysfunctional for the underlying micro-economy.

From either end of the political spectrum, therefore, the coherence of government intervention has been questioned. There has undoubtedly been an implicit tension in the medium term between anti-inflationary objectives and the goal of near-full employment. Until the early 1970s, this was kept within manageable proportions by the sustained high growth rates and the effectiveness of the Philips curve relationship, the trade-off between wage inflation and unemployment. But even then, governments had to make difficult choices about their priorities and about the kinds of instruments they were willing to use to achieve them. The most difficult choices tended to be over incomes policies, which in the later years of the Keynesian period became an increasingly important means of keeping the relationship between wages and growth within tolerable dimensions. It follows from these points that as well as the effects referred to above, government policies have a further redistributive impact on income, because of the different impact of the inflation or unemployment burdens on different sectors of the economy – savers or consumers, wage-earners or unwaged, users of collective services or of private services. This has been particularly important in Italy, where the failure to bring government revenue and spending into balance results in high interest rates for government debt which when sustained over a number of years have structural effects on capital investment and on forms of saving.

In Italy as elsewhere, development of the strategic choices underwent a profound change in the early 1970s following the collapse of the Bretton Woods exchange rates system in 1971 and the oil price rises of 1973–74. The inflation and recession which followed brought into question the economic assumptions on which the post-war Keynesian consensus had been founded. They revealed the difficulties of increasing or even of maintaining established levels of welfare in times of wage inflation and declining real growth rates, and led to an increasing polarisation over issues of income distribution and economic growth.

The Keynesian consensus relied on the government's direction of the 'big levers' to deliver optimal resource allocation for the economy as a whole. This connection had the important political effect of promising a genuine reduction or even elimination of the bitter social conflict which had characterised economic development in Europe from the middle nineteenth century onwards. When it failed, or was superseded by new and unfavourable relationships between unemployment and inflation, the business of optimal resource allocation was no longer compatible in any relatively simple way with the reduction of social conflict. In Italy as elsewhere, the state has had to find a new role and to alter its objectives on strategic issues.

## Italy's historical variation

Most of the specific differences in Italy have already been described, and there is no need to repeat the detail here. Italy had a late and uneven industrial development which left the country deeply divided; it has bitter political divisions left unresolved, and has a public administration which identifies itself with nineteenth century models of the state. Its application of the Keynesian consensus was therefore incomplete, mainly because its control of the instruments of demand management is limited and because the political intentions behind social policy never fully adopted the universalistic principles typical (in various ways) of modern European welfare states.

The limited objectives of Italian public policy were sometimes camouflaged with the rhetoric and even some of the instruments of technocratic social democracy, for example during the planning phase in the 1960s, but this never achieved the effectiveness of the French *dirigisme* on which it was modelled. In part, as Tarrow has argued, this is because of the way in which state organisation is structured, with a highly diffuse distribution of authority ill-suited to the uniform implementation of central objectives.[11] In part also, it results from the deliberate choices of successive generations of Christian Democrat and lay politicians to use the public sector for populist, distributive purposes. In Italy, the break-up of the post-war managerialist alliances, such as they were, occurred rather earlier than elsewhere, with the outbreak of serious labour unrest in the 'hot autumn' of 1969, which coincided with Italy's first major post-war recession. From this point on, the function of the state had to change radically. The conflict between worker and employer could no longer be managed with the promise of distributive welfare funded by increased growth and mediated by the ubiquitous and accommodatory majority party. A graphic indication of the failure of the state in the 1970s came with the *scala mobile* wage indexing agreement between employers and trade unions in 1975, which was settled in bilateral negotiations between the two in defiance of the government's attempt to impose a classically Keynesian incomes policy.

From the early 1970s on, in partial corroboration of the warnings of the neglected Michal Kalecki, the pretensions of the state to manage the conflicts engendered by economic change were severely constrained, and increasingly the state was in practice if not in rhetoric limited to maintaining the equilibrium between independent social groups through its distributive policies. Since then, the function of public spending has been to guarantee as far as possible the relative position of the competing groups, without any real capacity for altering the equilibrium or directing its development. Political exchange is therefore characterised by an unstable combination of conflict and dependency.

A consequence of these changes, in dramatic contrast with the unstable equilibrium of the 1950s and 1960s, is the increasing divergence between what groups demand of the state and what the state can deliver. Underlying this is the replacement of the bipolar conflict of organised labour and relatively compact interests of the industrial owners with a multiple conflict, sometimes referred to as polycentric conflict.[12] This conflict is between the individual groups over the distribution of public resources. But it is also between the state and sectoral and regional groups, over the availability of resources and over the scope and content of reform. The state is therefore an important actor in this conflict, not only because of the pressure on public spending but also because of the widespread consensus within the political and administrative elites of the need for radical change to existing structures of control and of delivery of policy. This in turn results at least partly from the awareness of the process described above, the development of financial and practical constraints in managing the ever-expanding functions of the post-Keynesian state.

These developments can be presented in diagrammatic form. Figure 7.1 provides a chronological view of the changes in the roles of the state and its interaction with international and domestic conditions. The approach is that adopted earlier in this chapter, based on the assumption that Italy has a specific variant of general patterns of state intervention. It therefore shares with other similar countries the predominance of Keynesian objectives and instruments, their break-up and the emergence of more conflictual policy processes. In the Italian case these are exacerbated by the variety of historically specific factors, in particular the regional imbalances, the unreformed state structure and the governmental predominance of a single party. Figure 7.2 provides a brief outline of the main features of the policy process which result from this development.

## THE CONFLICT/DEPENDENCY/EXCHANGE MODEL – ITALIAN VARIANT

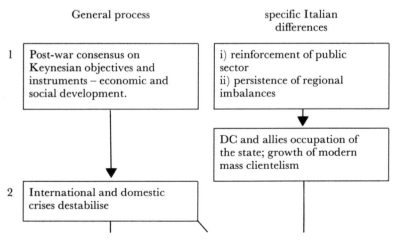

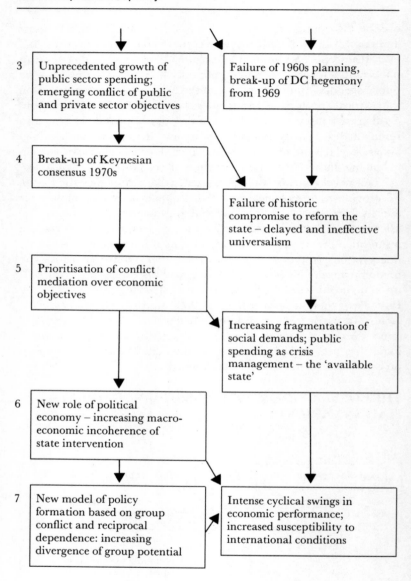

*Figure 7.1* Post-war development

POLICY PROCESS IN ITALY: POLYCENTRIC CONFLICT AND DEPENDENCE

1 Increasing societal division
2 Exclusion of weakest groups
3 Permanence of party oligopoly
4 Interdependence of parties
5 Weakness of state co-ordination
6 Urgency and complexity of reform
7 Public spending as currency of compromise with strongest groups
8 Exchange of political resources between parties to establish ranking of parties and clients

## SECTORAL CONSEQUENCES

1 TO 1983–84

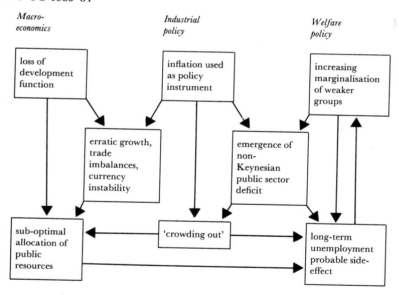

*Macro-economics*

*Industrial policy*

*Welfare policy*

loss of development function

inflation used as policy instrument

increasing marginalisation of weaker groups

erratic growth, trade imbalances, currency instability

emergence of non-Keynesian public sector deficit

sub-optimal allocation of public resources

'crowding out'

long-term unemployment probable side-effect

*Figure 7.2* A model for the 1980s, and two different outcomes (continued over page)

## 2  FROM 1984 ONWARDS

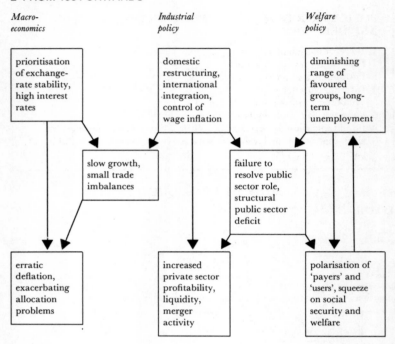

*Figure 7.2* Continued

These processes undermined the traditional function of state intervention as rational manager of the macro-economic constraints within which the economy operates. The consequences of the state's failure were at first the development of a vicious circle of erratic growth, persistent inflation and increasingly inequitable distribution of resources within society. This overlapped to some extent with the attempted reform of the state during the historic compromise period, and helps explain why the neo-corporatist restructuring attempted from 1976 to 1979 failed. The attempt to break out from the cycle was led by the state, with austerity programmes and state-directed industrial restructuring backed up by attempts to reform the public administration, and (more successfully) the radical changes to the health services and the pensions system.

The anti-inflationary objectives of the period were impeded, however, by two main factors. The first of these was the usefulness of the *scala mobile* to both sides of industry. For the employers it removed a major workplace irritant from the negotiating agenda, by ensuring that wages were subject to automatic procedures. Inflation allowed them to maintain their profit margins, though at the cost of loss of international competitiveness and increasing exchange-rate instability. For the unions, it was a highly favourable deal which seemed to enhance further their weight in national policy-making. The second difficulty was the unwillingness of all the governing parties, including those who loudly proclaimed their fiscal virtue, to desist from using the public sector as an employment exchange for patronage purposes. Factors such as the *scala mobile*, the pensions reform and the use of the Integration Fund (*Cassa Integrazione*, discussed in more detail in chapter 9) reinforced the differences between the formal labour market and the increasingly widespread informal black and grey markets. Thus the emerging integration of employers and unions into government-led structures for national economic direction was stifled by the fragmentation of the labour and patronage markets, and by political differences over the scope and purpose of state intervention.

The advent of the Craxi government in 1983 was followed by an unprecedented shift in political strategy on the part of the governing parties. Within the constraints fixed mainly by the need to maintain the employment functions of public sector ownership, the new government found itself the point of convergence of several trends. One was the extraordinary increase in the size of the public sector deficit, which is described in more detail in the next chapter. The second was the renewed confidence of Italy's private sector entrepreneurs, who had been able to shake out labour in the formal industrial sector during the recession of the early 1980s. This is described in chapter 9. There was also the confidence that the apparent decay and defeat of the Red Brigade terrorists would bring an end to the sporadic violence and sabotage which had been affecting many larger companies during the late 1970s at the height of the terrorist violence. To this was added the prospect for the Socialist Party, of which Craxi was leader, of profiting from the loss of votes of the Communists and Christian Democrats at the 1983 elections. A further stimulus to change was the increasing impact of the exchange rate mechanism of the European monetary system, appearing to enforce monetary prudence and certainly preventing any easy recourse to the weapon of devaluation to maintain competitiveness.

Perhaps surprisingly, granted Craxi's political origins, the shift after 1983 is away from state-led solutions towards restructuring led by the market – always within the limits set by the political processes on which the governing parties relied. Craxi's major successes in this context were the renegotiation and reduction of the *scala mobile* in 1983 and 1984, the tax reforms of 1983, and the reform of the Milan stock market in 1984, which resulted in a considerable increase in the inflow of funds and the value of assets quoted. There was also a partial restructuring of the state participation system which resulted in a return to profitability. The pressures for reform were added to by prospect of the single European market, enforcing further international integration on Italy's private and public sector traders. But in other sectors Craxi's government was less successful. The emergence of persistently high levels of long-term unemployment, particularly among younger entrants to the labour market, has contributed to an increasingly sharp difference in pay and prospects between those who are part of the formal employment system and those who have to survive at its margins. Also, as we see in the next chapter, the public sector deficit remains extremely difficult to control. Public spending is difficult to control in any case because of the impact of inflation and the interest-rate implications of the ERM. Its use as the currency of political compromise to mediate the increasing numbers of political claims adds to the constraints on government and reduces their control over the key levers and over policy in general.

This shows itself in three specific ways. First, rapid technological progress and unprecedented social mobility have taken their toll on the previously compact mass organisations which articulated diverse interests in relatively consistent forms. In their different ways, both the DC and the PCI felt the force of these social changes which fragmented and undermined their social support. In retrospect, the historic compromise period when they were in coalition together represents a late and unexploited opportunity for the two mass political parties to reform the state into a modern instrument of political organisation.

Second, it is not just the state which is at the mercy of a multitude of sectoral interests. Employers, trade union confederations and the major pillars of civil society which provided their power of social mobilisation have had increasing difficulty in guaranteeing any but the most short-term of political bargains, whether over government coalition strategy or over substantial policy reform. In the 1980s, none of the major interest groups or their political agents have been representative enough to make the political exchanges work beyond the immediate political horizon. It is in the face of this increasing crisis of representation that the 'new social movements' of the 1970s have fragmented into a variety of competing special interests. In the process, established political parties have come under challenge from environmental, civil liberties, and regional organised groups able to mount significant electoral challenges.[13]

Third, the gradual loss of control by the established groups shows itself in the effective relinquishing of state authority to the more compact and powerful of the economic interests, particularly the big multi-national conglomerates – a re-emergence of the tradition of 'sub-government'. In mediating the competing demands of the FIAT group, Ferruzzi, the De Benedetti and Berlusconi groups, the Italian state is having to deal with successful modern commercial enterprises whose cultural and administrative resources are much superior in quality to its own.[14] The loss of control also shows itself in the way in which organised illegality is confronted. In the 1970s the state had to face widespread political terrorism, which it eventually defeated by giving controversial and unprecedented powers to a special police organisation. In rather different ways, the struggle against the Sicilian mafia and the Neapolitan camorra demonstrate the same constraints and the same strategy of circumventing the rigours of the law through special mandate.[15]

The central organisation of the state is increasingly in conflict with the professional and client groups involved in its major welfare and service functions, but it lacks the organisational, revenue or moral autonomy to ensure its predominance. It is not only that the fragmented interest groups are in conflict with one another and dependent on the state; the state itself is internally divided, and is dependent on particular groups within and outside its own structures. Some of these divisions are ideologically based, and relate to the long-standing disagreements within political elites dealt with earlier. But other divisions result from the peculiar position of the public administration and enlarged public sector, which makes them both deliverer and recipient of resources. When the state is itself a client, engaged in the market for employment and corporate privileges, reform of the structures achieves an intimidating complexity. Elites apprised of the need for reform have to bargain with their own managers, administrators and clerical staff, to exchange limitations on reform in return for co-operation in reducing demand, collaboration in managing supply of services more rationally, partial reductions in employee privileges, and in some cases in return simply for better information and more adequate reporting of results.[16] Increasingly the state directs its resources in favour of the strongest sectoral and regional groups, that is, those groups who have most to exchange in the new market of public policy.

This process is challenged, however, by the threat of international competition and integration, by the fractious and newly confident interests of large private sector capital, and by the divisions between what Ferrera has referred to as the 'welfare' and 'producer' constituency – between those who are net recipients of social security and welfare, and those who are net contributors.[17] Thus, in managing the inherent tensions between anti-inflation and anti-unemployment policy, the state's scope for choice is ever more restricted by the incoherence and irrationality of its own intervention. In the next two chapters, we look at some of the ways this works out in particular sectors. In the final chapter we address the general questions of how the system maintains itself and what the prospects for development are.

## NOTES

1 Dal Co, M. and Perulli, P., 'The trilateral agreement of 1983: social pact or political truce?' pp. 157–170 in Jacobi, O., Jessop, B., Kastendiek, H. and Regini, M. (eds), *Economic crisis, trade unions and the state* (London, Croom Helm, 1986); Regini, M., 'Social pacts in Italy' in Scholten, I. (ed.), *Political stability and neo-corporatism* (London, Sage, 1987); Regini, M., 'The crisis of representation in class-oriented unions' in Clegg, S., Dow, G. and Boreham, P. (eds), *The state, class and the recession* (London, Croom Helm, 1983).

2 Lijphart, A., *The politics of accommodation* (Berkeley, Calif., University of California Press, 1975, 2nd edition).

3 See for example Lange, P. and Regini, M., 'Regolazione sociale e politiche pubbliche: schemi analitici per lo studio del caso italiano' pp. 97–121 in *Stato e Mercato* no.19, April 1987; Lange, P. and Regini, M., *Stato e Regolazione Sociale* (Bologna, Il Mulino, 1987).

4 Persistent examples of this are the attempts by one of the major governing parties, usually the DC, to enforce the coalition arrangement operative in the national government as a formula for all possible local governments. In this they are generally supported by the minor governing parties, particularly the PSDI, who tend to lose office locally when heterogeneity of alliances is allowed to flourish.

5 Hirschman's categorisation of voter strategies, in Hirschman, A.O., *Exit voice and loyalty* (Cambridge, Mass., Harvard U.P., 1979).

6 Examples of industrial policy communities are discussed in chapter 9.

7 Heidenheimer *et al.* 1983, pp.122–167

8 Heidenheimer *et al.* 1983, p.125 ff.

9 Flora and Heidenheimer 1981; also Flora *et al.* 1986, vol.1.

10 Kalecki, M., 'Political aspects of full employment,' *Political Quarterly*, vol.14 1943; see also Sawyer, M., *The economics of Michal Kalecki* (London, Macmillan, 1985); Feiwel, G.R., *The intellectual capital of Michal Kalecki* (Knoxville, University of Tennessee Press, 1975).

11 Tarrow, S.G., 1977.

12 Brunetta, R., *Spesa Pubblica e Conflitto* (Bologna, Il Mulino, 1987).

13 Pinto 1981.

14 The relationship of private industry to government is also considered in ch.9. Little detailed information is available on the workings of the major conglomerates, but a thorough account of the Montedison empire is given in Marchi, A. and Marchionetti, E., *Montedison 1966–1989* (Milano, Franco Angeli, 1992); see also Friedman, A., *Agnelli and the network of power* (London, Harrap, 1988); Peruzzi, C., *Il caso Ferruzzi* (Milano, Edizioni del Sole – 24 Ore, 1987).

15 On the Mafia, see Arlacchi, P., *Mafia peasants and great estates* (Cambridge, Cambridge University Press, 1983); *Mafia e Potere Politico – relazione di minoranza e proposte unitarie della commissione parlamentare d'inchiesta sulla mafia* (Roma, Editori Riuniti, 1976); Chubb, 1982.

16 An example from the Health Service is described in Ferrera, M., *Reforming the Reform – the Italian Servizio Sanitario Nazionale in the 1980s*, Centro de Estudios Avanzados en Ciencias Sociales, Instituto Juan March Madrid, Estudios Working Papers no.13, January 1991.

17 Ferrera, 1984, p.461 ff.

# Chapter 8

# Economic policy
## Decisions and benefits

## INTRODUCTION

Realistic budgets are an expression of practical politics. The allocation of resources necessarily reflects the distribution of power. Budgeting is so basic it must reflect the norms by which men live in a particular political culture – for it is through the choices inherent in limited resources that consensus is established and conflict is generated. The authority of government is made manifest by its ability not only to make a budget but also to make it stick. Public policymaking in action – which programs to benefit whom will be established or maintained at what levels of support? – is epitomized through the budget.[1]

Wildavsky asserts bluntly the central role of budgeting in the understanding of politics. Budgets tell us how the most basic decisions are made, who benefits from them, and on what values political activity is predicated. Since Wildavsky wrote, financial mechanisms have assumed even greater practical and symbolic importance because of the impact of monetarism and the rise of the new Right. But even before this, as we saw in chapter 7, budgets occupied an important function in demand management and in the conduct of economic policy. In Italy, the failure of successive governments to control the budget deficit thus reflects multiple failures of values, of institutional competence, of political authority and of distributional policy.

Wildavsky identifies two dominant variables which determine the characteristic forms of budgetary behaviour. They are wealth and predictability. Most advanced industrial societies, he argues, have budgetary systems which are on the whole both rich and certain. Wealth provides long-term stability, allowing the country to absorb short-term instabilities without having continually to re-argue the spending decisions of previous years; administrative certainty means that political decisions are understood to refer to real events, so that the budget can be used as a real instrument of resource allocation. In these terms, Italy falls into the category of 'rich and relatively uncertain.' Resources are available to meet rolling annual expenditure, and the bulk of the expenditure is committed formally to such programmes. But the political instability, the lack of effective costing and control measures, and the vulnerability to pressures from political brokers mean that expectations about revenue and expenditure are not stable enough for long-term decisions about resource allocation to be taken with confidence about outcomes. This leads to uncertainty over programme revenues, and concentration on those areas which are most easily manipulated for short-term exchange purposes: social security, public sector employment, fiscal exemptions, and subsidies of various kinds to commercial and industrial activities. So in this sense budgets are subject to partisan policy-making, led by ministries in the manner described in chapter 5. Ministers and to a lesser extent parliamentarians determine the distribution of public resources to a large number of separate groups which operate within diffuse issue networks. They achieve political support for their favoured groups through the multitude of informal individual bargains struck within the formal institutions.

But, at the same time, government spending, taxation and borrowing policy have direct consequences for macro-economic management. Decisions about budgets make a difference to the growth and stability of the economy. Ministers, senior officials and parliamentarians not only engage in political brokerage, they also choose between inflation and unemployment, try to avoid balance of payments deficits, adjust interest rates. These decisions are substantial policy-making, and in Italy they are governed by a relatively rigid set of norms, operated by a long-established and small set of institutional actors, a policy community composed of ministers and officials in the Treasury, with senior officials in the Bank of Italy, with chairmen of the major state-owned banks, and with senior parliamentarians in the budget committees. When the previous chapter referred to the break-up of the post-war consensus, one of the elements in this was the increasing difficulty of preventing the macro-economic choices from being contaminated by the brokerage inherent in the budget procedures. This chapter looks at how the relationship between Treasury, spending ministries and Parliament leads to uncertainty over budget outcomes, and what the consequences are.

## THE ADMINISTRATIVE CONTROL OF PUBLIC EXPENDITURE

Other major factors referred to by Wildavsky which enter into the budget procedure are the relationships between institutions and the values of the elites. These converge around the issues of trust, formality and proportionality. Systems characterised by low levels of trust typically develop multiple layers of control. If, as is likely, they are also highly conflictual, there will be emphasis on formal procedures to contain and resolve disputes; and a consequence of the low trust/ high conflict system is that decisions about merits are extremely difficult to make. Such systems therefore tend to be wedded to proportionality – 'equal shares for all' is the norm. This is a summary of one part of Wildavsky's argument.[2] He does not refer to Italy at all in this context, but the syndrome described above applies with almost startling accuracy to the Italian case: low trust, high conflict, formal procedures evaded by political exemption, agreement on the principle of something for everyone. The Italian term is *lottizzazione*, described already in the party-political context in chapter 6.[3]

The framework of rules for state revenue and expenditure is made up of several historical layers. The basic ethos of financial administration was that of a classical Liberal state. This gave priority to the regulatory functions of the state, to its absolute claims within a restricted sphere of action, and to the uniformity of the rule of law, with political responsibility sitting uneasily astride these.[4] In the early decades of the Liberal state, there was little reason to treat the state's finances as radically different from those of private companies, though of course the methods of collecting revenue and spending funds raised important political principles. As a result of this analogy with the private sector, the state's budgets were not viewed as a means by which the Parliament could amend the weight and pace of financial functions, but rather as a means by which the state reported on the legality and financial propriety of its management. If the major functions of the state were related to the maintenance of order, to the raising of armed forces, to the pursuit of foreign policy aims, it is scarcely surprising that the budget was not seen as a political instrument in its own right.

The basic framework for the conduct of the state's finances is now provided by the De Stefani law of 1923, already referred to in chapter 4. The De Stefani law was not a major reform of principle, but rather consolidated the practices which had built up over the previous fifty years. These reflect very strongly the regulatory view of the state: this is not the accounting system of a state involved in providing services, in making cash transfers to citizens for welfare, in managing large manufacturing companies. On the contrary, the entire structure of principle underlying the budgetary system of the state emphasises the limited nature of the state's operations and the irrelevance of decisions of substance to the procedures of control. The state most appropriate to these procedures is not a manager of complex operations but a dispenser of cash for a limited range of purposes such as supply needs and salaries to employees.

The crucial innovation of De Stefani was to impose a formal uniformity on previously diverse practices, and to bring this system of spending under the control of the General Accountancy Office – the *Ragioneria Generale dello Stato* (RGS). This was achieved by making the central accountancy offices within each ministry directly dependent on the RGS, which under De Stefani formed part of the Ministry of Finance, but which as we have seen came under the control of the Treasury in 1944. The ministerial accountancy offices known individually as the *Ragionerie Centrali* are in effect outposts of the *Ragioneria Generale*, with important functions of control. The De Stefani law makes a clear distinction of principle between the accountancy function and the administrative function. It is the administrative function which regulates the decisions of substance about spending, in accordance with individual spending laws. Formally speaking, these two functions of the spending process precede and are separate from the budgetary phase.

The complexity of the operations obscures the abstract distinction between accountancy and administration, so that the two functions are difficult to separate in practice. The strength of the control exercised by the central accountancy offices in each ministry was obviously enhanced by the De Stefani law, since in normal routine it allowed them to oversee the most important phases of administrative procedure. In the absence of genuine controls of substance over the effectiveness of spending, the accountancy function has come to overshadow the administrative. But the detailed regulations relating to the formal legality of spending are generally found to be difficult to adhere to strictly, and even before 1923 their inflexibility and rigour had been contributory factors in the growth of the large para-state sector. As we saw in chapter 4, this was made up of public sector organisations deliberately established in a quasi-independent status so as to avoid the difficulties of ministerial operations. Even within the ministries, there has been constant pressure to allow derogations from the standard procedures in order to expedite business.

The De Stefani 1923 law, which also reorganised the pay and conditions of the bureaucracy, has been added to and amended on several occasions. In 1939, the power of the *Ragioneria Generale* was extended further to authorise it to control not only the spending phases but also the preparation of legislation. With this reform, the development of the financial control reached its logical conclusion, and it became possible after the war for the General Accountancy Office, by now situated in the Treasury, to determine the pace and direction of spending through all its phases. The main objection to this has not been that the principle of central control is wrong, but that there is no effective political control over the Treasury so as to maintain a counterbalance to the zealous and undiscriminating parsimony of the *Ragioneria Generale*. Because it makes no judgements on merits, the control system drives the budget process firmly towards proportionality in distribution. The persistence of low trust/ high formality procedures and the failure to establish a proper role for acceptable political compromise has driven the political function to evade the procedures by informal face-to-face understandings over increasingly minor budgetary exchanges, which (as we saw in chapter 7) place a high premium on reciprocity and conflict avoidance – enforcing trust where confidence is limited, and rewarding the willingness to compromise. For the same reason, the General Accountancy Office in the Treasury has tended not to have a clear policy on overall macroeconomic objectives despite its pivotal position.[5] In substantial policy-making, Government policy has been driven to a much greater extent by the procedural and formal concerns of the accountancy office, except where the Bank of Italy has been able to fill the vacuum with its own priorities and technical expertise.

The main work of the RGS is to monitor and direct the actual flow of government spending and government revenue. The branch offices of the RGS in the provinces and in the ministries are responsible for allocating the budget authorisations to the appropriate spending organisations within the various parts of the enlarged public sector. As well as allocating specific authority under the individual budget headings, the RGS also has to authorise explicitly every commitment to pay and every actual payment, to ensure that they are formally correct and are in accordance with the spending legislation.

A further check is provided from outside the ministerial ambit by the Court of Accounts (*Corte dei Conti*, CdC). This institution, which dates from 1862, is an independent body with consultative, juridical and monitoring functions. As well as handling all cases of financial litigation involving the state, it has general responsibility for ensuring that executive action remains within the limits of competence fixed by the law. It is therefore both judge and inspector. The Court of Accounts usually has officers permanently allocated to individual ministries who work in the ministry itself, and whose function is preventative and consultative. The close working relationship between these auditors and the ministry is a crucial means of minimising errors by the ministry and of helping officials to expedite business. But it has also been argued that the auditors may become accomplices in helping the ministry avoid proper control of financial decisions – gamekeepers turned poachers, in effect.[6]

Inspection of executive acts by the Court of Accounts is usually prior to the act, and no actual payment can be made without a counter-check from the Court itself. Though the Court claims to deal with most authorisations within a week, its critics allege that it may take considerably longer. The Court also makes detailed annual reports to Parliament, which often provide trenchant criticism of Government budgetary methods, particular targets being waste, delay and lack of effective political control. Though widely respected for its expertise, it has been no more successful than others in achieving improvement. The Court can prosecute and can impose fines, but it cannot conduct efficiency audits on how money has actually been spent. As well as the RGS and the Court of Accounts, other institutions may be involved in monitoring executive action – sometimes on the same issues, prior authorisation may also be required from the Ministry of the Budget, the Council of  State, the Government Advocate's Office and the Higher Council for Public Works. Once final authorisation is received from the Court of Accounts, the appropriate payment order is issued by the Bank of Italy, subject of course to the Bank's own internal controls.

This multi-layered, detailed and pervasive control helps to explain the paradox that as well as persistent budgetary deficits there are also extraordinary delays in government spending on specific projects. These delays, frequently noted in Court of Accounts' reports to Parliament, achieved a degree of notoriety in the 1960s and 1970s. The results are not trivial. The gap between decision and spending may be so great on occasions that counter-cyclical measures, particularly in public investment, are rendered ineffective for their original objective. The fact that these effects are uncertain seriously exacerbates the problem, and curtails the scope of substantial policy-making.[7] A spectacular example of government failure to act promptly were the relief measures after the Val Belice earthquake in Sicily in 1968, where large sums of money remained unspent ten years after the original legislation. The lessons were not learnt, because very similar problems showed themselves in the aftermath of the 1980 earthquake in the hinterland of the South.[8] But the difficulty is also felt at the individual level: a substantial proportion of any Senator's or deputy's constituency correspondence relates to requests from individuals for help in dealing with financial claims on the state, requests which are then passed on to the ministry concerned in the form of written questions. Failure to respond to these promptly and adequately is a constant source of complaint from parliamentarians.

The administrative system of control of public expenditure gives considerable influence to the RGS, an influence which for a variety of reasons seems to be exercised mainly to restrict spending absolutely rather than to ensure the efficient use of public funds. Furthermore, the RGS, the CdC and the other monitoring bodies do not operate by imposing a particular view of what the objectives of spending ought to be. They constitute a series of vetoes which can be used to prevent or delay spending, but there is no evidence that they possess any established institutional policies in favour of particular substantive objectives. Not even within the Treasury as a whole is there clear evidence of a departmental view about the proper aims of governmental policy, such as might provide continuity in a system characterised by governmental instability. As we saw in chapter 4, some individual spending ministries do appear to have their own positive objectives, particularly those whose relationship with client groups is long-lasting and undisturbed. The only exception among those institutions of state that have a major financial role is the Bank of Italy, which has consistently pursued policies aimed at exchange rate stability and low domestic price inflation, at the expense if necessary of government objectives for growth and unemployment.

## THE ANNUAL BUDGET

The normative framework for the budget is provided by Article 81 of the Constitution, together with law no.468 of 1978, which introduced a major reform; further reforms were added by law no.362 of 1988.[9] Article 81 is worth quoting in its entirety:

> The Houses vote on the budgets and the expenditure accounts submitted by the Government each year.

The law may authorise the Government for a maximum period not exceeding four months to use the budget before its approval.

No new taxes or new expenditure can be established by the law approving the budget.

In all other laws implying new or additional expenditures the means for covering them must be set forth.

Clauses 3 and 4 of this article were inserted at the behest of the Liberals in the constituent Assembly and particularly of Luigi Einaudi, then Treasury Minister, a Piedmontese with past ministerial experience in the Liberal state, who represented a powerful and determined free-market lobby. The article was also supported by influential economists within the Christian Democrats such as Ezio Vanoni, who represented the closest approximation within the DC to the social market strategies of the West German Christian Democrats.

This article means in effect that the budget law was not intended to be used as a mechanism for adjusting spending or taxation in accordance with macro-economic objectives. At a stroke, a crucial instrument of Keynesian fine-tuning was ruled out of bounds: the article appears to prevent the use of the budget to co-ordinate spending and taxation for the coming year in a single exercise. Also, it appears to prohibit entirely all long-term deficit financing: this was certainly how it was read by the frugal and cautious Einaudi. The first of these effects, the ban on the use of the budget to provide political direction for the economy, has proved difficult to overcome, and there is no doubt that even under the most energetic and competent managers Italy's macro-economic policy has tended towards the piecemeal and sporadic. The second, the prevention of deficit financing, has been the object of the successful attentions of constitutional lawyers and politicians, who have outflanked the defences put up by the old guard. Their main route has been the inclusion of medium- and long-term debt within the 'means for covering' (clause 4), a practice received with outrage by the Liberals.

Law 468 of 1978 attempted to resolve the problem of clause 3 of article 81 with an unusual attempt at radical reform. Law 468 made the budget approval process include a separate law, the Financial Law, which actually does have the function of changing revenue and expenditure law. The budget process itself, alone before 1978 and with the Financial Law after then, consists of the submission of an appropriations budget (*bilancio di competenza*) which in effect lays down the limits within which the government can undertake financial commitments, always in accordance with existing expenditure laws; it also provides an estimate of the potential amount the government can raise in taxation in the coming year, again in accordance with existing legislation. It therefore provides a legal ceiling to government financial activities during the year, and authorises spending and collection of revenues within the limits which it establishes. The difficulty with the appropriations budget is that, though it enables the RGS and the Court of Accounts to check for legal correctness prior to spending, it does not allow for parliamentary control of the development of actual spending. Law 468 therefore obliges the government to submit a cash budget as well (*bilancio di cassa*), which with the other documents provides a more realistic forecast of the growth of spending and revenue in the context of national and international trends. The cash budget is usually quite significantly lower than the appropriations budget. Law 468 also obliges the Treasury to give Parliament quarterly reports on the progress of spending and revenue, on the basis of figures provided by the RGS.

Because it is based on existing legislation, the budget itself, excluding the Financial Law, gives Parliament and government very little scope for actual decision-taking, but usually amounts to a consolidation of many spending laws of different degrees of importance and complexity. In some cases the sums entered under the different headings are the original nominal valuations contained in the legislation; in others, compulsory expenditure carried on from year to year changes in line with specific economic variables such as interest rates or cost of living indices. Where nominal valuations are used, the amounts entered in the annual budget are necessarily based on prices and forecasts current at the time the law was passed. The budget provides several small budget headings to allow adjustment to be made for inflation, but these are limited in scope. If the original law contained multi-year allocations which inflation has reduced significantly, the appropriate procedure (in conformity with the De Stefani law and with article 81) is to pass a new spending law revising the original allocations.

A large part of the budget is in fact made up of pre-determined multi-year expenditure, over which there is little room for adjustment. For the rigid element in the budget, it is possible for the Treasury to adjust the annual appropriation under particular headings, but not to adjust the limits to actual total spending, which are of course fixed by the original spending laws. The fixed element in the annual state budget varies annually, but is usually estimated at between 83 per cent and 88 per cent of the total.

In the pre-1978 regime the remainder, over which a degree of flexibility of allocation can be found, was largely composed of the section known as 'global funds', which consisted of funds set aside to cover spending bills expected to become law in the next year. The global funds occupied a crucial role in the system. Whereas virement between the different headings for the committed part of the budget was virtually impossible, financial cover within the global funds section could be transferred from the intended bill if for some reason it failed to make parliamentary progress. Also, new bills could be financed from offsetting savings if such could be found within the global funds section. The global funds section does not appear to have been adjusted yearly for fine-tuning purposes, to expand or deflate the economy. Its function was narrowly conceived as providing cover for planned spending, the amounts for which were determined by other criteria. After 1978, the global funds were abolished and replaced by a special funds section, which was intended to be more tightly controlled by the RGS.

Law 468, then, did not sweep away the established budgetary process. It had three main objectives. First, it added to the legislative instruments contained in the budget, with the aim of making it a genuine instrument of macro-economic policy. This was at a time when Keynesian fine-tuning in Italy and elsewhere was becoming increasingly problematic and subject to the criticisms of monetarists. Second, it sought to widen the scope of the budget in order to bring under Treasury control areas of the public sector previously excluded from the budget. Third, it attempted to curtail the increasing budgetary deficits by altering those mechanisms held most responsible.

The first of these objectives was intended to be met with the introduction of the *legge finanziaria*, the Finance bill, which enabled Parliament to consider changes to taxation and expenditure at the same time as the budget. To clarify the macro-economic implications of the budget, the Treasury was obliged for the first time to present specific aggregate figures on its proposed credit and financing operations, and to provide detailed quarterly reports to Parliament. With the same purpose it introduced a statutory timetable for budget to be considered in Parliament. Debate begins in September of each year and is scheduled to finish by the end of December, in order to meet the beginning of the new financial year in January. The Budget and its associated instruments were given a favoured place in the timetable, with provisions that other legislation could be considered by the

Assembly during this period only with the unanimous approval of the Group leaders' conference. Like other laws, the budget has to pass through virtually identical procedures in both houses, and if necessary to shuttle between them after amendment. This requirement, which results from the Constitutional parity of the Senate and the Chamber of Deputies, was not changed by law 468. If there is serious delay in one house, particularly at a late stage in proceedings, the timetable can quickly become unachievable.

The second major reform contained in law 468 together with other reforms of the same period was to provide clear definitions of the scope of the public sector. These brought into Treasury and parliamentary control a wide range of activity left out previously. This had the additional benefit of bringing Italian figures more into line with OECD and IMF definitions. The traditional budget had covered the ministries and some operations directly associated with them such as the Fund for the South, the Savings and Loans fund (*Cassa Depositi e Prestiti*) and the Central Statistical Office (ISTAT). It therefore left out the independent financial operations of local government, of the social security agencies, of the *Aziende Autonome* such as the railways, telephones and postal service, and of the hospitals and municipal enterprises. By 1979, these had all been roped into the budget, in some cases defined as 'state sector', in others 'public sector' and in others the 'enlarged public sector'. The size and diversity of the public sector operations mean that some areas are still excluded – most notably, the state-owned subsidiaries of the state participation companies, and the special credit institutes.

The preparation of the budget lies in the hands of the ubiquitous RGS. Government financial years run from January to December. Early in the year, and certainly before March, the Treasury and Budget ministers jointly submit a general report on the economic situation of the country to the inter-ministerial committee for economic planning (CIPE), a cabinet committee with statutory responsibility for national economic policy which is chaired by the Minister for the Budget. CIPE approves general guidelines to be followed in drawing up the detailed draft appropriations, and these are then sent by the RGS to its offices in the ministries. These branch offices, the *ragionerie centrali*, are responsible for ensuring that the ministries to which they are attached follow the guidelines and the timetable. In due course, the ministries send their draft appropriations to the RGS, which may require the ministries to make changes. These negotiations between the ministries and the RGS do not appear to have a strong political input, at least in the strategic sense: Ministers do not get involved in detail at this stage. The procedure does provide the Treasury with the opportunity to make detailed adjustment of the priorities of government spending having regard for the general guidelines, for which the Treasury itself is partly responsible. The drafting process also allows ministries to exercise some selectivity about the legislative timetable. The draft budget has to be agreed with the Treasury minister and with the Budget minister; the pivotal role in the procedure is carried out by the Treasury, since it is the Treasury which negotiates bilaterally with the senior officers of individual ministries, and it is the Treasury draft which is submitted to ministers. Despite occasional efforts to activate CIPE by enthusiastic Budget ministers, there is little evidence that CIPE has ever been able to impose a collegiate political view on the budgetary process. Last of all, the budget is discussed in Cabinet, and is presented to Parliament by the end of September.

Longer-term economic planning is largely the responsibility of the Budget Minister. The Budget Ministry, which is separate from the Treasury, was established in 1947 and considerably reinforced in 1967, when it was given the function of formulating multi-year indicative national plans. Partly because of changes in the political and economic climate, the Ministry of the Budget and Economic Planning (to give it its full title) was never able to bring the idea of a national plan to fruition. It now finds itself struggling for resources and for a role between the Treasury, which controls spending, and the Finance Ministry, which deals with the collection of state revenue. Its formal position in the budgetary process is a residue of the ambitions and objectives of the reform-minded centre-left governments of the 1960s. The Budget Ministry's formal approval is required for large spending bills, but it lacks the resources or political authority to impose an independent view. Though it is certainly possible for an activist minister to use the Budget Ministry to publicise his or her view of desirable objectives and current problems, it cannot be described as a ministry capable of imposing long-term order and coherence on the budgetary system. At the same time, institutional inertia in the administrative structure makes it difficult to dispose of redundant ministries (of which there are other examples) or to rationalise functions. The Budget Ministry was intended to be the rationalising centre of the policy process. Though it does not fulfil this function, it appears unlikely either that it will be strengthened or that it will be replaced by something more effective.

As well as the appropriations and cash budgets approved by the Treasury and Budget Ministers, the government also has to provide a statement of account, duly checked and authorised by the Court of Accounts. This amounts to a full analytical account of the previous year's revenue and expenditure operations by individual ministries, and by some agencies not included in the budget. It also provides balance sheet summaries of assets and liabilities. Associated with these documents, the government publishes a Preliminary Note describing the framework and assumptions for the budget, and containing the actual bill by which the budget is approved by Parliament.

In many respects, these procedures prior to 1978 were reminiscent of a company report to shareholders rather than a part of national macro-economic decision-making. They amount to a report on the conduct and outcomes of the government's financial policies, and a description of what programmes are planned for the future. Despite the inadequacy of the instruments, parliamentarians did actually attempt to use the old machinery to influence real choices in the macro-economic field, but found themselves increasingly frustrated by the normative framework. It was partly their pressure, together with the change in governing coalition in 1976, which produced the 1978 law. Only after 1978, with the addition of the Financial Law and the other changes, did the budgetary process begin to lend itself to genuine debate and decision over political economy. But the other objectives of the reform were less successful, particularly where they required a positive change of technique from the ministries or a willingness on the part of Parliament to refrain from putting a multitude of small amendments. Neither of these conditions has been visible. As a result, one of the most noticeable effects of law 468 was that, despite the formal timetable, delays in the budgetary process became more frequent. In the first decade after the reform, the budget was approved on time only in 1983 and 1984, two years of unusual government stability. In all other years, political and administrative difficulties forced the government to seek provisional authorisation while the procedures ground their way through the Chamber and the Senate. An extreme case was 1986, when the budget approval was granted six months late and ended with a government crisis. The problems usually centred on the new Finance bill, which became a battleground for amendments and shuttled between the two Houses apparently without regard for the formal timetable. Some of these amendments were major political changes entailed by compromise between government and opposition, but many were minor additions prompted by particular interests on the government back-benches. Further reforms were introduced in 1988 (laws 262 and 400) to improve costings and to reinforce Prime Ministerial control of spending bills, but the immediate indications were that the 1988 reforms, like those of 1978, depended on radical changes of culture and of procedure elsewhere in the budgetary system, and that these were not forthcoming.

Thus the budget procedure is highly incremental. It has to work within a legal framework which keeps conflict at bay by imposing many formal procedures on the allocation and spending mechanisms. In their turn, these procedures are circumvented by informal agreements, in the ministries and in Parliament, through which substantial decisions are made. The system is driven by the need to use budgetary accounts for many minor processes of exchange. The combination of formality and informality in different phases makes spending allocations both difficult to change and imprecise in their effects. The 1978 reforms enhanced the political input into the budget, and made the mechanisms more open. But they did not reform the routine practice of public administration and did not alter the balance of political interests involved. Without fundamental change on these two fronts, the budget cannot develop into an effective instrument of long-term fiscal and monetary management. It is scarcely surprising that the budget deficit fails to respond to the increasingly urgent demands for macro-economic management.

## THE PROBLEM OF THE BUDGET DEFICIT

### Tables 8.1–8.4 Government finances

*Table 8.1* Current income, general government (%GDP at current market prices)

|         | 1960 | 1965 | 1970 | 1975 | 1980 | 1985 | 1989 |
|---------|------|------|------|------|------|------|------|
| Germany | 35.1 | 35.7 | 38.3 | 43.4 | 45.4 | 46.4 | 45.2 |
| France  | 34.9 | 38.4 | 39.0 | 41.2 | 46.1 | 49.3 | 48.6 |
| Italy   | 28.8 | 30.1 | 30.4 | 27.4 | 33.1 | 38.1 | 40.7 |
| Spain   | n.a. | n.a. | 22.5 | 24.8 | 30.2 | 35.1 | 39.0 |
| UK      | 30.1 | 34.1 | 40.5 | 39.6 | 39.7 | 41.6 | 38.9 |
| EC12    | n.a. | n.a. | n.a. | n.a. | 40.9 | 43.8 | 43.6 |

*Table 8.2* Total expenditure, general government (%GDP at current market prices)

|  | 1960 | 1965 | 1970 | 1975 | 1980 | 1985 | 1989 |
|---|---|---|---|---|---|---|---|
| Germany | 32.5 | 36.7 | 38.7 | 49.0 | 48.3 | 47.5 | 46.5 |
| France | 34.6 | 38.4 | 38.9 | 43.5 | 46.1 | 52.0 | 50.4 |
| Italy | 30.1 | 34.3 | 34.2 | 37.5 | 41.6 | 50.6 | 50.7 |
| Spain | n.a. | n.a. | 21.7 | 24.6 | 32.9 | 42.1 | 41.9 |
| UK | 32.4 | 36.2 | 39.2 | 44.1 | 43.0 | 44.3 | 39.1 |
| EC12 | n.a. | n.a. | n.a. | n.a. | n.a. | 49.0 | 47.0 |

*Table 8.3* Net lending or borrowing, general government (%GDP at current market prices)

|  | 1960 | 1965 | 1970 | 1975 | 1980 | 1985 | 1989 |
|---|---|---|---|---|---|---|---|
| Germany | 3.0 | −0.6 | 0.2 | −5.6 | −2.9 | −1.1 | −1.3 |
| France | 0.9 | 0.7 | 0.9 | −2.2 | 0.0 | −2.8 | −1.8 |
| Italy | −0.9 | −3.8 | −3.1 | −10.1 | −8.5 | −12.5 | −10.0 |
| Spain | n.a. | n.a. | 0.7 | 0.0 | −2.6 | −7.0 | −2.9 |
| UK | −1.0 | −2.0 | 3.0 | −4.5 | −3.4 | −3.9 | −0.1 |
| EC12 | n.a. | n.a. | n.a. | n.a. | n.a. | −5.2 | −3.5 |

*Table 8.4* Long-term interest rates (%)

|  | 1960 | 1965 | 1970 | 1975 | 1980 | 1985 | 1989 |
|---|---|---|---|---|---|---|---|
| Germany | 6.3 | 7.1 | 8.3 | 8.5 | 8.5 | 6.9 | 6.1 |
| France | 5.7 | 6.2 | 8.6 | 10.5 | 13.1 | 10.9 | 9.0 |
| Italy | 5.3 | 6.9 | 9.0 | 11.5 | 16.1 | 14.3 | 12.1 |
| Spain | n.a | n.a | n.a | n.a | 16.0 | 13.4 | 11.8 |
| UK | 5.4 | 6.6 | 9.3 | 14.5 | 13.9 | 10.6 | 9.4 |
| EC12 | n.a | 6.6 | 8.7 | 11.0 | 13.0 | 10.9 | 9.3 |

Tables 8.1 to 8.4 give a comparative view of the components of the budgetary deficit.[10] For the sake of clarity, the countries quoted are those closest to Italy in size and (excluding Spain) in general level of economic development. In terms of total public expenditure, Italy is not particularly out of line with other EC countries. It usually has a higher level of public expenditure than any of its close comparators, though other smaller countries have much higher levels (Holland and Denmark, not in the tables, have 57.6 per cent and 59.8 per cent for 1989 respectively). Italy stands out, however, in three ways. Of all EC

countries, only Belgium has a higher proportion of public expenditure committed to meet monetary liabilities (interest payments and maturity payments). Second, only Greece and Italy have the unwelcome combination of relatively low revenue and relatively high expenditure, which pushes their borrowing regularly into double figures as a proportion of GDP. Third, as Table 8.4 indicates, Italy has persistently had higher interest rates than the other large developed economies of the EC. Of all EC countries, only Greece has maintained higher levels over long periods. Among the 'big five' of the EC, Italy's 'low tax, high spend' budget is unique. Italy's budgetary problems are not simply those of a spendthrift government unable or unwilling to control public spending. The problem of uncontrolled expenditure is exacerbated by the weakness of the taxation system and the consistently high level of interest rates.

The difficulty of control begins with the ineffectiveness of the constitutional and legislative provisions. As we have seen, Article 81 of the Constitution demands specific financial cover for all spending bills. In practice, the pressure on spending is such that a variety of expedients has developed to ensure that Article 81 is not observed in spirit, and sometimes not even in the letter. The existence of this general formal obstacle to spending, ineffective as it may be, has discouraged the development of detailed instruments of financial control. The accounting, monitoring and reporting techniques within Parliament and the administration remain largely unreformed from their original 1923 De Stefani form, and have been added to rather than remodelled by the 1978 and 1988 changes.

One of the most important expedients within Parliament is the sophisticated use of what used to be referred to as the 'global funds' section of the budget, the section of the budget allocated to spending bills for the coming year. This practice involves the identification of particular accounts within the global funds which have not been exhausted in the period since the budget was passed and which are unlikely to be used in the financial year for their declared purpose. With the help and tacit approval of the RGS, the funds in the accounts are then used to provide a legal cover for parliamentary bills which otherwise might be bereft of finance. The practice is frequently used for private members' bills and occasionally for government bills. It is obviously not conducive to effective financial management, and suggests a failure to tailor objectives to available resources. However, the systematic nature of the abuse seems to indicate that a further problem is the reluctance to acknowledge objectives, an unwillingness to subject them to normal public scrutiny. It is alleged sometimes that ministries deliberately create these under-used accounts, the purpose being to provide themselves with some flexible means of satisfying client groups.[11]

Though considerable concern is voiced at this practice, there is no evidence to suggest that it is responsible for the greater proportion of the deficits, since the accounts concerned are not usually sizeable.[12] To take typical examples, in 1979, Parliament approved a contribution of 250 million lire to the International Labour Organisation to be paid from a fund allocated to war damage and national civil emergency; in the same year, a Bill to provide support for disabled police was funded from money allocated to pay for the general census (3 billion lire for one year only); in 1980, funds originally destined to pay honoraria to marriage guidance counsellors in family law cases were used to provide an increase in the number of prison guards recruited (8.9 billion lire per year indefinitely). In the 1980s, particularly favourite accounts for 'plundering' seemed to be the account for research into geothermal energy and the account for projects aimed at preventing soil erosion.[13]

Such practices skirt the borders of legality, since they amount to virement, which is only allowable in very specific cases. Even more dubious are the practices of funding a specific Bill through a specific increase in government debt, which seems to evade the intentions of the 1978 reform, and the practice of leaving a Bill entirely without costing or financing. In such cases the President of the Republic can refuse to counter-sign the bill and can send it back to Parliament. Their predecessors did not exercise this responsibility, but both Alessandro Pertini and Francesco Cossiga have done so, Cossiga with increasing frequency. The traditional reluctance to use this authority on every possible occasion results in part from their awareness of the likely consequences on the general business of Parliament.

Within Parliament, control should be exercised by the Permanent Committees for the Budget (CP 5 in both chambers). These have to approve all spending Bills originating in other committees, and have the right to impose amendments. But until 1986, the budget committees lacked direct access to information from the RGS, and they still lack the research and technical assistance to monitor legislation properly.

All Permanent Committees in Parliament have to cope with bills presented to them incomplete or unclear. This applies to Government Bills as well as to private members' Bills. The debates of the committees clearly indicate that their members are aware of the problems of improper costings and lack of financial cover. But there would be immense practical difficulties for the committees if they were to try to carry out drafting work which should have been done by the ministry or the proposer. Also, the members feel a responsibility to the interests of the sectors within their legislative remit. They are therefore reluctant to take on the task of imposing financial rigour on their own sectors unless they are sure that all others are doing likewise.

The responsibility of the administration lies particularly in its failure to provide reliable costings, either in ordinary draft legislation presented to Parliament or in the Finance Bill. Techniques for costing appear to be primitive, and the control exercised by the Treasury or the Prime Minister's Office is haphazard. Draft Bills appear in front of Parliament often in a highly approximate form. Even when there is clear and convincing identification of the resource implications of the original draft, ministers are rarely able to provide information on the cost of proposed amendments put by backbenchers, though the procedures give these a considerable chance of success. Ministers are usually loth to explain costs in detail to Parliament, and do not respond readily to questions about the financing of government bills. Little effort is made to monitor the aggregate impact of individual provisions, and commitment to multi-year spending programmes may be made without clear specification of the likely costs in future years. Underlying this is the weakness of the internal structures of the ministries at the rudimentary business of identifying attainable objectives and linking them both to responsible officials and to available resources. It is not surprising if Parliament has to step into what amounts to a policy vacuum to make up for the defects of the administrative apparatus. Nor is it surprising if the legislature is not equal to the task, in view of its own lack of resources.

One clear consequence of the budgetary processes is some increase in the power of the Treasury, since the central control of reduction in spending lies in its hands. For example, in 1986 the total projected deficit (PSBR) was 159,394 billion lire (cash) for the enlarged public sector, though the actual deficit appearing in Article 1 of the Finance bill was 139,277 billion lire, a deficit *di competenza* (in appropriations). The higher sum is an elaboration of this together with further actual commitments in the Budget Bill. But the target PSBR was neither of these; the target declared by the Treasury in the associated report and in the Treasury Minister's speech in the opening debate was 110,000 billion. This divergence of estimates frequently occurs, and remains in the two bills in their final forms. No clear indication is given as to how the target is to be reached, but by convention the Treasury Minister finds reductions in payments at his discretion, though he has never in recent years been able to find sufficient to meet the target. For the most part, the reductions come from the capital account, and particularly from the capital expenditure account for the regions. These tend to be the easiest to cut politically, because they do not have an impact on services or transfer payments which is directly visible. They are easiest to cut technically in a appropriations-based system because they normally apply to generic finite projects rather than to continuous specific commitments. Reducing capital investment funds does not usually require any further legislative action, whereas reducing other accounts might involve complex legislation to change particular welfare entitlements or might require staffing cuts in the public sector. In 1986, out of a total budget of about 535,000 billion lire, about 425,000 billion was already committed, not available for reductions. In the face of persistent cost overruns on current account and increasing proportions allocated to debt charges, the Treasury needs some room to adjust the spending, and the capital account provides this safety valve. In addition, it is argued that the inaccuracy of the budget figures is not accidental. Opposition backbenchers allege that the Treasury repeatedly understates both the spending and the revenue side. This is either incompetence or deliberate massaging of the figures; in either case, argues the opposition, the result is to allow the Treasury Minister funds and areas of cuts at his discretion, subject to the usual discussions with the group leaders and secretaries of the parties.

The problem of budgetary deficits is made more obvious by the budgetary reforms. These reveal the mechanisms without resolving the problems. They reveal the incapacity of the Treasury to control fully the increase in planned expenditure by the spending departments as declared in the annual budget. The proportion of the budget committed to automatic transfer payments ought to make this section a target for reform if the deficit is seriously to be tackled, but efforts at curtailing the high-spending accounts have proved ineffective so far – an example being the failure of the attempt in 1983 by Gianni De Michelis, then Minister of Labour, to reform the management structure of the largest social security agency INPS and to cash-limit its expenditure. Spending departments have great difficulty in keeping within their declared budget ceilings, and merely legislating in the budget has been insufficient. A consequence of this is that the precise size of actual budget deficits is not known until some time after the spending year. The first stage of the budget deficit appears in advance of spending, when towards the end of year $x - 1$ it transpires that total planned government expenditure in year $x$ may exceed total government planned revenue in year x by a greater amount than last year's projected deficit (that is the equivalent figures projected for the year just finishing, $x - 1$). The actual results of year $x$'s financial management will not be known in detail until the budgetary process two years hence, $x + 2$, and this provides the second stage of the deficit, when it is discovered that the actual deficit reported to Parliament is even worse than the planned deficit. Hence when the Socialist Treasury Minister Giuliano Amato attempted his 'orbit of re-entry' plan in 1987, one of his first targets was to keep the actual deficit as close as possible to the projected deficit.[14]

As part of the Budget, the 1978 reform also introduced a multi-year (3 or 5 year) budget which projects current and planned spending into the future and which among other things fixes a limit to recourse to market for credit for each of the years. This is tied to article one of the Finance Bill, also introduced by law 468, which specifies the maximum level of deficit for the year, and which was intended to act as an aggregate ceiling for the rest of the Finance Bill. This has not proved effective because the practice has been to leave article one until all other amendments to the Bill have been approved. The ceiling therefore has become descriptive rather than prescriptive.

## THE DEFICIT IN CONTEXT

### The partisan effects

To critics on the Right, the deficit which has been the dominant feature of the landscape in the 1980s results from the explosion of social security and other welfare payments, in particular the cost of the short-term unemployment benefit (*cassa integrazione*) the health service and other services now devolved to regional authorities. Those on the Left argue that the prior problem is the interest rate component of the debt. To take 1986 again, in that year over 70,00 billion was allocated to debt charges. Since the target deficit was set by the Treasury at 110 billion lire, it is not difficult to make a plausible argument that the reduction in interest rates would not only stimulate growth and therefore increase tax revenue, it would also substantially reduce the deficit. The main beneficiaries of persistently high interest rates are the net savers in the economy, normally the higher income groups. However, the Italian economy shows a comparatively high propensity to save, and the practice of saving in local banks and in the state-run *Cassa Depositi e Prestiti* is widespread.[15] It is therefore difficult to make out a substantial case that high interest rates following high government debt amount to a large redistribution of income towards the better-off. The problem of weakness of tax revenue remains. As Table 8.1 indicates, Italy does not have a high level of tax burden compared with other EC countries. Partly this is because tax evasion appears to be embedded in the economic culture, and affects particularly the labour market and the retail trade. The black market in services and in cheap labour for small industry is now acknowledged to amount to about 30 per cent of the total value added in firms with under 20 employees, and about 8 per cent of GDP.[16] Labour in such sectors is highly casual, paying no income tax and having no recognition of statutory rights. Though the black and grey markets have always been present, they became especially widespread in the 1970s, when employers appeared to respond to the enhanced job security of the Workers Charter of 1970 by moving out of the conventional market in search of the traditional flexibility of labour. That they were able to do so reflects the underlying slack in the labour market which has been an almost constant feature of Italian post-war economic development. Employers using black market labour pay no social security contributions and hide the company or personal income which accrues.

Partly also the weakness results from the repeated failure to modernise the tax collection system, despite several attempts at computerisation which have so far failed to become fully effective. This encourages evasion, in the sense that it encourages individuals and firms to flout the system by declaring flagrantly unrealistic amounts of income with little fear of discovery. There is also a political responsibility, both in the failure to reform the Ministry of Finance and in the maintenance of a complex set of exemptions and special regulations favouring particular sectors – one example being agriculture, where farmers owning their own land are taxed on valuations of assets which date from before the Second World War. Another sector which has tended to escape the system is investment in equities. Though income from bank deposits has been taxed for some time, dividends and capital gains have only recently been brought into the system and there is still considerable resistance from this politically sensitive sector.

The increase in government revenue which dates particularly from the early 1980s follows the efforts to resolve some of these problems in the Visentini reforms of 1982–83 (see Table 8.1). These extended the deductions system to cover the self-employed more effectively, and strengthened the collection procedures for value-added tax. But the reforms were strongly contested by the groups most affected, who were largely the same in both cases, and who formed an important part of the political constituencies of the DC and of the Social Democrats. They also required the reform of the tax inspectorate, which has only been partially carried out. The increase also reflects the impact of long-term inflation on tax thresholds ('fiscal drag'), and the willingness of the conservative governments of the 1980s to increase indirect taxation and charges for services rather than direct taxation. Both of these changes affect lower-income groups disproportionately, but these are less politically sensitive than the self-employed groups affected by the Visentini reforms, and the changes are less visible. Partly to compensate for the unequal collection system and for the fiscal drag, in January 1989 the DC Prime Minister Ciriaco De Mita reached an agreement with the trade unions over the indexation of tax thresholds. But the agreement was also designed to meet purely short-term needs, since it came immediately before what was promising to be an extremely difficult DC Party Congress. The deal reminded all concerned of De Mita's trade union origins and was intended to reinforce his support on the Left of the DC. Such countervailing pressures make tax policy a frequent casualty of government inconsistency. In this not untypical case, the Prime Minister's party position was too weak for him to be able to withstand a series of attacks from his colleagues, who were particularly unhappy about the fact that he was also party secretary. Inside and outside the party, his rivals attacked the agreement for its effects on the budget deficit. De Mita lost the party secretaryship at the Congress and the Prime Ministership soon after. Again quite typically, this was also associated with increasing concern over the scandal of the misuse of earthquake funds in southern Italy.[17]

## The substantial policy effects

In the first half of the 1970s, government borrowing needs were largely met with monetary financing (the share of the debt financed by the central bank and therefore matched by a creation of monetary base), so that the share of the public debt held by the Bank of Italy rose from 25 per cent in 1970 to 40 per cent in 1976 (the highest level recorded). After this, monetary financing fell sharply so that the share of public debt held by the Bank of Italy decreased to 22 per cent at the end of 1979, and to 17 per cent by the end of 1983. Initially, the growth in the interest-bearing part of the debt came from purchases of securities by the banking system, stimulated by the ceiling on bank lending in the 1970s plus the compulsory security investment requirement; when these were lifted in 1978, it came from purchases of securities by savers, with dis-intermediation of the banking system, encouraged by the wider differential between the yields on securities and those on bank deposits, and by the tax exemption on securities. In simple terms, after a period of direct financing by the Bank of Italy, the PSBR was predominantly unfunded (met by the banking system) until 1978, and therefore entailed an increase in the money supply. Since then, PSBR has been mainly funded (met by the non-bank sector) and has had a much reduced effect on the money supply.[18] The tax exemption on securities is criticised by the Left as having gone too far, in the sense that it does little for the small investor who is already well covered by the tax system, and favours the large investors whose tax position is much more ambiguous. However, the method of financing leads to higher interest rates overall and, according to the left-wing parties, to the alleged unwelcome redistribution of income, to high costs for productive investment, and to downward pressure on the other components of PSBR. Actually the change in the method of financing from central bank to non-bank investors is less dramatic than might appear, and reflects the ill-health of the securities market in the early to mid-1970s. It also is reinforced by the so-called 'divorce' between the Bank of Italy and the Treasury in 1981, after which the Bank was released from its obligation to act as lender of last resort to the Government. Within the general constraints of the market, the Government has generally favoured medium- to long-term securities, index-linked if necessary, because of the high costs of repeated short-term issues. This is also favoured politically as it has a helpful cosmetic effect on the annual Budget.[19]

All of this has important implications for Italy's external position. Once Italy was in the EMS (admittedly within relatively broad bands) devaluing the lire to maintain growth at the cost of inflation was not a ready option. In the early 1980s, the lire devalued several times within the ERM, mainly against the Dmark and with the French franc.[20]

These adjustments were clearly competitive, aiming at keeping the lire in line with French rates. The French economy has tended to be regarded as providing a benchmark for Italian economic performance because of its similarities in size and structure. After this early period of adjustment, the ERM became more rigid. Devaluations of the weaker currencies were declared by their newly virtuous central bankers to be bad practice. Interest rates thus became a central part of domestic policy. In Italy, this meant governments could no longer hope to finance the PSBR by expanding the money supply while at the same time maintaining rigid technical constraints on the banking system and artifically low interest rates. For most of the 1980s there was thus a two-fold reason for keeping interest rates high – to bear down on inflation and to fund the PSBR. In consequence, policy-makers have had to find other ways of achieving the priority objective of macro-economic strategy, consistent high growth rates (see Tables 8.5 to 8.8).

## Tables 8.5–8.9 Basic macro-economic indicators

*Table 8.5* Size of economies (gross domestic product at current market prices (purchasing power standard, EC12))

|         | 1960  | 1965  | 1970  | 1975   | 1980   | 1985   | 1989   |
|---------|-------|-------|-------|--------|--------|--------|--------|
| Germany | 63.4  | 99.3  | 151.2 | 272.7  | 556.1  | 885.1  | 1162.3 |
| France  | 45.0  | 73.6  | 118.7 | 235.1  | 478.1  | 772.9  | 1006.2 |
| Italy   | 44.4  | 70.7  | 118.8 | 217.9  | 455.4  | 740.8  | 974.1  |
| Spain   | 17.5  | 32.5  | 54.6  | 114.3  | 218.1  | 350.6  | 490.1  |
| UK      | 65.2  | 94.3  | 132.4 | 239.7  | 450.2  | 739.8  | 1020.9 |
| EC12    | 270.9 | 427.0 | 666.5 | 1254.7 | 2514.0 | 4056.9 | 5380.3 |

*Table 8.6* Growth rates (average annual percentage change in gross domestic product at constant market prices (national currency))

|         | 1961–64 | 1965–69 | 1970–74 | 1975–79 | 1980–84 | 1985–89 |
|---------|---------|---------|---------|---------|---------|---------|
| Germany | 4.7     | 4.3     | 3.4     | 2.8     | 1.1     | 2.5     |
| France  | n.a.    | 5.2     | 5.1     | 3.0     | 1.5     | 2.4     |
| Italy   | 5.7     | 5.8     | 4.2     | 2.4     | 1.8     | 3.1     |
| Spain   | 7.2     | 6.7     | 5.9     | 1.6     | 1.2     | 3.9     |
| UK      | 2.7     | 2.5     | 2.8     | 2.0     | 0.7     | 3.6     |
| EC12    | 5.2     | 4.6     | 4.1     | 2.5     | 1.2     | 2.9     |

Table 8.7 Inflation (average annual percentage inflation)

|         | 1960–64 | 1965–69 | 1970–74 | 1975–79 | 1980–84 | 1985–89 |
|---------|---------|---------|---------|---------|---------|---------|
| Germany | 3.7     | 2.9     | 6.9     | 4.3     | 3.7     | 2.3     |
| France  | 4.2     | 4.2     | 7.3     | 10.5    | 10.4    | 3.6     |
| Italy   | 5.9     | 3.0     | 10.1    | 16.9    | 16.6    | 6.2     |
| Spain   | 4.5     | 6.9     | 10.3    | 18.8    | 12.5    | 6.7     |
| UK      | 2.5     | 4.4     | 9.4     | 16.3    | 9.6     | 5.1     |
| EC12    | 4.3     | 4.0     | 8.5     | 12.1    | 9.9     | 4.6     |

Table 8.8 Unemployment (% civilian labour force, end year)

|         | 1960 | 1965 | 1970 | 1975 | 1980 | 1985 | 1989 |
|---------|------|------|------|------|------|------|------|
| Germany | 1.0  | 0.6  | 0.6  | 4.1  | 3.4  | 8.4  | 8.2  |
| France  | 0.7  | 0.7  | 1.3  | 3.9  | 6.4  | 10.5 | 10.8 |
| Italy   | 7.2  | 5.7  | 4.4  | 5.3  | 7.2  | 12.9 | 14.5 |
| Spain   | n.a. | n.a. | 1.2  | 1.9  | 11.8 | 21.4 | 19.6 |
| UK      | 1.6  | 1.4  | 2.5  | 3.6  | 6.0  | 12.0 | 7.2  |
| EC12    | n.a. | n.a. | n.a. | 3.9  | 6.1  | 11.8 | 10.9 |

Table 8.9 Trade balance (average annual external surplus or deficit, current account (%GDP))

|         | 1960–64 | 1965–69 | 1970–74 | 1975–79 | 1980–84 | 1985–89 |
|---------|---------|---------|---------|---------|---------|---------|
| Germany | 0.6     | 1.0     | 1.2     | 0.7     | 0.0     | 3.8     |
| France  | 0.9     | −0.1    | −0.3    | 0.1     | −0.9    | 0.1     |
| Italy   | 0.5     | 3.0     | −0.3    | 0.7     | −1.3    | −0.2    |
| Spain   | 0.6     | −1.5    | 0.3     | −1.4    | −1.5    | 0.5     |
| UK      | −0.3    | −0.3    | −0.6    | −0.7    | 1.1     | −1.5    |
| EC12    | 0.3     | 0.5     | 0.2     | 0.0     | −0.4    | 0.9     |

In the 1980s the balance of payments constraint did not appear a matter of undue concern to policy-makers (see Table 8.9). Italy was in current account external surplus for only two periods in the 1980s – in all four quarters of 1983 and in the last three quarters of 1986. A small deficit on the trade account appeared to be regarded as an inevitable side effect of the pursuit of growth, and one that in the long-term did not threaten Italy's economic stability. In 1975 and 1976 Italy found out to its cost what the consequence of external deficit could be – specifically, intervention by the IMF.[21] But one of the effects of membership of the EMS was paradoxically to reduce the salience of balance of payments difficulties in the eyes of investors. In the Italian case there was a distinct 'coat-tails' effect, as investors were convinced that the need to shadow Europe's stronger currencies would keep interest rates high and would deter irresponsible over-rapid expansion of the economy. The restrictive monetary policy of high interest rates and direct constraints on banking credit was combined, as we have seen, with a relatively loose fiscal policy, as if the authorities were pressing on the brake and on the accelerator at the same time. Certainly for most of the 1980s internal demand was buoyant, for whatever reason, increasing the need for anti-inflationary measures. The high PSBR reflected conscious strategic decisions by successive governments to sustain services and transfer payments. These served both as currency within the short-term political market and as a crude means of stimulating growth rates in the face of generally difficult international trading conditions. Thus to a certain extent partisan and substantial policy-making converged, though whether this was towards the appropriate strategy is another matter. The effect of EMS membership appears to have been to allow Italy to sustain balance of payments deficits for considerable periods by convincing investors that devaluation was not an available option. The constant pressures for high interest rates from all these sources left the monetary authorities with limited room for manoeuvre should they wish to use interest rate policy for other objectives.

For a period in the middle of 1989, a perverse effect of ERM membership began to be felt, adding to the problems of monetary management. With inflation still at relatively high levels compared with Italy's main competitors, domestic objectives required the persistence of high interest rates to curtail demand. But Italy's relatively high interest rates together with the security of the ERM encouraged foreign investors into the lira. As a result, the lira was pushed up to the ceiling of its ERM bands, and the authorities were compelled to lower interest rates. The political instability of the 1990s removed the unusual conditions which had produced this, and Italy's problem reverted to the more conventional one of having to use high interest rates to sustain the lira during lengthy periods of recession. It was this tightrope act that failed in September 1992, with the speculative attacks resulting in the devaluation of the lira and its exit, at least temporarily, from the ERM. This provides a stark example of the way the ERM, together with removal of exchange controls, forces the weaker economies into monetary policy convergence with the stronger (particularly towards the lower interest rates of the West

German regime) even though domestic demand considerations suggest otherwise. Hence one of the objectives of the EMS is achieved, convergence of monetary policy, at the expense of another, namely convergence of inflation rates. Speculators correctly identified that these kinds of tensions are sustainable in the long-term. Inside or outside the ERM, Italy's macro-economic policy-makers are under increasing pressure to reduce the public sector deficit as another means of dampening demand and of bringing interest rates down. Lower interest rates would have a beneficial effect on the debt-servicing element of the general government borrowing requirement, but to get the deficit down would require not only interest-rate reductions but also difficult decisions over substantive public expenditure. Savers who benefit from high real interest rates would suffer, but so would recipients of the government transfer payments. The spiral of increases in public debt and interest burden now tends to be self-sustaining, since the yield on government debt exceeds the growth in income from which the debt repayments have to be met.

The problem of the budget deficit is its impact on private sector savings, and thence on real interest rates, private investment and eventually the external account, and secondly that it adds to the stock of public debt, increasing the service costs and reducing budget flexibility. Finally, and most important, the deficit is perceived as a constraint on progress towards the central objectives of long-term policy, which have been faster growth without increased inflation in order to achieve sustained improvement in employment. This conflicts, however, with short-term interests which entail inflationary pressures — both from the interest-rate spiral and from the need to maintain government spending. Inflation in this context must therefore be seen as a consequence of the need to sustain demand in the economy in the short term. But strong domestic growth risks fuelling internal demand inflation further. The contradiction within macro-economic policy hinges on the need to break out from the position in which Italy can only have growth at the price both of higher real interest rates and higher unemployment.

These conflicts are partly institutionalised. Parliament, Treasury and the Bank of Italy dispute the right to control macro-economic policy but in doing so are also giving voice to powerful lobbies whose interests diverge — political parties seeking client satisfaction, Bank officials making themselves the voice of 'sound money' and institutional savers, ministry officials seeking to maintain their corporate authority and privileges by mediating between the political forces. Other conflicts may be found in the different sectors to a greater or lesser extent, depending on the degree of penetration by the dominant parties and the interests which they represent. In practice, as the analysis in chapter 7 suggests, the conflict is structural, and can only be resolved by structural reform.

## NOTES

1 Wildavsky, A., *Budgeting – a comparative theory of budgetary processes* (Boston, Little, Brown and Co., 1975) pp.xii–xiii.
2 Wildavsky 1975, p.14.
3 See ch.6.
4 Onida, V., 'The historical and constitutional foundations of the budgetary system in Italy', pp.215–236 in Coombes, D. (ed.), *The power of the purse* (London, George Allen and Unwin, 1976); Cassese, S., 'Special problems of budgetary decision making in Italy', pp.254–267 in Coombes 1976.
5 Gambale, S., *Struttura e ruolo del bilancio dello stato in Italia* (Bologna, Il Mulino, 1980), chapters 5 and 6; Cassese 1983, chapters 9 and 10; Ferraresi 1980, chapter 6.
6 Cassese 1978, pp.15–85; see also Perez, R., *Le procedure finanziarie dello stato* (Milano, Franco Angeli, 1980) ch.1.
7 On the problems of the 'tempi tecnici', see for example the interview with the Accountant General Giovanni Ruggeri 'Come fatica lo Stato ad investire – parla il Ragioniere dello Stato,' pp.1–2 in *Il Messagero*, 14 febbraio 1985; more generally, Gambale 1980, chapters 3 and 4; Perez 1980, chapter 4.
8 Angotti, T., 'Playing politics with disaster – the earthquakes of Friuli and Belice', pp.327–331 in *International Journal of Urban and Regional Research*, vol.1 no.2 January 1978. Further examples are given in Cassese 1978, ch.4.
9 The discussion which follows is based on my own research in the Chamber of Deputies, and on Brunetta, R., *Spesa pubblica e conflitto* (Bologna, Il Mulino, 1987); Cavazzuti, F., *Debito pubblico ricchezza privata* (Bologna, Il Mulino, 1986); Gambale 1980; Perez 1980.
10 On the problem of the budgetary deficit, see *Review of Economic Conditions in Italy*, May–August 1989, particularly Valiani, R., 'What solutions are there to Italy's public debt?' pp.75–95; also *Monetary Trends*, no.39, June 1989; Carli 1988, pp.119–132.
11 For example, Bassanini, F.,and Visco, V., 'Ecco perche il bilancio è fuori controllo', p.5 in *La Repubblica*, 20 marzo 1985.
12 Sources for these data are the *Atti Parlamentari*, Commissioni Permanenti, Discussioni, various years.
13 Nominal currency rates for 1981, monthly average: £ sterling = 2284 lire; US\$ = 1138 lire. 1 billion lire = *c*.£437,828 or \$878,734.
14 *The Economist* – Survey, the Italian Economy, 27 February 1989.
15 *Monetary trends* 1989; *Review of economic conditions in Italy* 1985, p.80ff.
16 A detailed statistical explanation of these figures is given in *Annuario Statistico Italiano 1979*; for an English-language review of the problem as a

whole, see Contini, B., 'The irregular economy of Italy – a survey of contributions', pp.237–250 in Feize, E. (ed.), *The underground economies – tax evasion and information distortion* (Cambridge, Cambridge University Press, 1989); see also Sylos-Labini, P., 'L'evasione fiscale autorizzata', pp.9–11 in *Mondoperaio*, no.12 1984.

17 On De Mita's role in this, see Locatelli, G., *Irpiniagate – Ciriaco De Mita da Nusco a palazzo Chigi* (Rome, Newton Compton Editore, 1989).

18 Sources for this discussion are the invaluable Annual Reports of the Bank of Italy, together with *Monetary Trends*, *BNL Quarterly Review*, and *Review of Economic Conditions*, passim.

19 Addis, E., 'Banca d'Italia e politica monetaria: la riallocazione del potere fra Stato Mercato e Banca centrale', pp.73–96 in *Stato e Mercato* no.19, aprile 1987.

20 For further details see Furlong, P.F., 'Economic recession and political underdevelopment in Italy', pp.142–171 in Cox, A.W. (ed.) *State responses to the recession in Europe* (London, Macmillan, 1985).

21 Goodman argues that Italy was treated favourably by the IMF particularly because of West German concern about the electoral successes of the PCI: Goodman, J.E., 'Monetary policy in France Italy and Germany', pp.171–201 in Guernieri, P. and Padoan, P. (eds), *The political economy of European integration* (London, Harvester/Wheatsheaf, 1989).

# Chapter 9

# Industrial policy
## Communities and networks

---

## A GENERAL VIEW OF INDUSTRIAL POLICY PROCESSES

Industrial policy is particularly significant in Italian public policy for several reasons. Firstly, since 1870 political elites have linked industrialisation with the development of the nation as an independent entity, because they have identified industrial growth as an instrument of national self-determination. Industrial growth was important because it was believed to ensure that Italy enjoyed a reasonable degree of economic independence in the supply of critical products, whether these were military or civil, whether they served secondary industrial needs or supplied food and other goods for private consumption. Italy is poorly supplied with most of the essential raw materials of industrial production, having only limited domestic resources of iron ore, bauxite and phosphates. It has very small domestic deposits of coal and gas, and has generally had to meet over 70 per cent of its energy needs from imported oil and gas. Though Italy has traditionally had a large agricultural sector, now much reduced in employment size, it has not been self-sufficient in food, and its capacity to export manufactured goods has been seen as critical to its economic and social stability.

What Italy has had, however, is a long tradition of trade within Europe and the Mediterranean, skilled and educated financial and commercial elites, and an enduring surplus of labour. This surplus has generally been seen as both a resource and a problem, because of the potential for social disorder which large numbers of unemployed may generate, as well as for humanitarian reasons. From its origins as a unified country, there has been a widespread consensus that Italy needed a broad independent industrial base to mitigate the effects of its natural constraints, to employ its given advantages to best effect, and to provide a genuine material identity to the geographical expression.

Secondly, in Italy as elsewhere, industrial growth has been seen over the last 150 years as the essential route to economic development and thence to improved standards of living for the population as a whole. But the form of industrial development was a subject of considerable political conflict, because of its impact on wider issues in society as whole. It related directly to income distribution, authority relationships, public order, political participation and, most important in this context, access to public goods. Liberals, Fascists, Christian Democrats and Socialists differed radically from one another over the pace and direction of industrial change. All may have agreed that industrial growth was essential, but its organisation and control have been the source of bitter conflict.

In Italy, those who regard social welfare as a function of the free market have tended to identify industrial policy as all government policy in so far as it affects the business environment. The term can therefore be used to refer to social security policy, labour regulation, public works on infrastructure, and to fiscal and monetary policy. By the same token, it can also mean 'deregulation', the removal of state restrictions on commerce and production. Those who view direct government intervention more positively have a narrower version of the term, and tend to use it to refer specifically to active government policies aimed at stimulating development in particular sectors, usually though not necessarily through financial support of various sorts. Industrial policy in this sense is in principle selective, and in its more radical versions favours indicative planning by government to coordinate government action and business activity.

Thirdly, industrial growth was important to enable Italy to compete successfully on world markets and to stand comparison with its European neighbours. Associated with this is the widespread belief that as an 'industrial latecomer' Italy has special problems which require individual policies and which may result in Italy following a highly individualistic path. Italian political and economic elites have felt constrained by Italy's apparent failure to develop what they regard as its full economic potential, a constraint made increasingly visible by the pace of integration in Europe. This sentiment is heightened by the vast cultural heritage of which Italy disposes and by its continuing capacity to lead international trends in architecture, literature, clothing fashion, and design of manufactured goods. It used to be said of the Federal Republic of Germany that it was 'economic giant, political dwarf'. Of Italy in the postwar period, it could be said it was

Table 9.1 Interest organisation in industrial policy

|  | policy community | issue network | interest group |
|---|---|---|---|
| primary examples in industrial policy | Fund for the South, state participation | small firms, artisans | large private sector firms |
| external differentiation | exclusive professionalism | extended professional links | multi-professional |
| internal cohesion | complete coverage of practitioners, common style | disaggregated decisions, moderate territorial differentiation | high territoriality, diverse values |
| common interest | continuous, multi-issue | discontinuous, incomplete issue coverage | single-issue, temporary alliances |
| administrative strategy | incorporation | unstructured consultation, discrete bargaining | regulation, isolation |

'cultural giant, political dwarf', and if this was so it had something to do with the delays and imbalances in Italy's economic development.

## COMMUNITIES AND NETWORKS IN INDUSTRIAL POLICY

These themes of national identity, political stability, popular welfare and international integration were accentuated in the post-war period, as we saw in the earlier chapters. Because of the domestic and external pressures, industrial policy, which was in any case already salient, changed and expanded in an environment controlled directly by the political parties. Once again we find in this sector as in others a fluid mix of partisan and substantial policy, combinations of independent interest groups, issue networks bound together by short-term exchange, and policy communities acting as coherent guardians of a sectoral interest. The differentiation between the three types of interest articulation, and the application here, can be summarised schematically (see Table 9.1).

Because of the fluidity of the relationships, industrial policy has been fragmented across sectors, discontinuous, and dependent on the specific relationships which key groups established with the parties and with the central bureaucracy. In general, the most successful groups were those who established patronage relations with the parties that were sufficiently strong to survive changes of government and ministerial impermanence, such as the small farmers' organisation *Coldiretti*. But within the general predominance of clientele relations, a variety of policy-making types can be found. In some sectors, such as petrochemicals and steel, there developed exclusive, specialised and coherent elite groups, made up of managers, interest-groups and political factions who over a period of about thirty years were able to exercise significant control over their area of interest. These groups were differentiated from one another, were sometimes in conflict with one another over scarce resources, and like all such had to operate within the exchange-based environment of patron–client networks. In the terms used in chapter 7, partisan policy-making set the framework. Nevertheless, substantial policy-making is possible within restricted areas where such groups can emerge. These groups were sufficiently cohesive and influential for us to be able to describe them as forming individual policy communities.

To render matters more complex, some of the important industrial interests are able to achieve significant influence without developing close elite relationships. Examples of these are the sector of small and medium firms mainly located in the Centre and in the North-East, and the private sector interests concentrated in the industrial-finance groups of the Lombardy–Piedmont area. What prevents us describing these two categories as policy communities is the overall lack of internal organisation and to a lesser extent of specialisation. Small firms have in their own way been favoured recipients of public largesse, but this has been the result of their ideological resonance and patronage uses at the local and national level rather than of their cohesive political influence. In this sector, partisan policy has predominated to the exclusion of more stable, less politicised relationships. The large private sector companies are an entirely different question, since their relationship with the state has been determined on the one hand by the deep fracture between them and the post-war ruling parties, and on the other hand by the strategic role played by them in the processes of economic development. The result of this combination has been to ensure that the relationship is one of mistrustful but distant regulation by the state and studied detachment on the part of the large private oligopolies, against a counterpoint of ironic and occasionally despairing criticism of the state by their leaders. In general comparative terms, the policy groups in the small and medium enterprise sector could be said to form issue networks, whereas the large private sector firms have had a relatively loose pressure-group relationship with the state.

Apart from education, which we do not have space to consider here, the main areas characterised by the relatively intense politico-administrative relationship described as policy communities have been the Southern Development policy elites and the heavy industrial sectors dominated by state-owned companies.

These industrial policy communities were differentiated from excluded groups in the same sectors by the privileged political nature of their access to resources, and from dominant groups in different sectors by the specific expertises and interests which they represented. The extent of their specialisation is clear: the fragmented nature of Italian interest group organisation has encouraged the development of narrow sectoral associations, sometimes loosely organised into weak inter-sectoral groups such as *Intersind* (the organisation of public sector employers) or *Confcommercio* (representing the numerous small retailers), but in any case enjoying considerable autonomy of relationship with individual ministries or public sector agencies. Their internal organisation was maintained by their close relationship with the political parties and with the public authorities, which ensured the long-term survival of conventional norms and established channels of communication, as well as of shared objectives.

The policy communities in southern development and in public sector heavy industry were held together by a fundamental consensus over the distribution of resources and over the appropriate roles for the various members. Within the policy community, the role of broker and arbiter was played by the Christian Democrats, whose overall control over the allocation of resources enabled them to enforce agreements and to maintain the shifts in the balances of power within acceptable limits. As we saw in chapter 5, this did not require the DC always to occupy the ministries of state participation and industry, but they have always had at least a junior ministerial presence in them. The public sector groups are organised through the major public sector holding companies IRI, ENI, and EFIM. They had solid links with the political apparatus through the Fanfani and Dorotei factions in the DC, and later through the technocratic wing of the Socialist Party. Their main relationship with the state administration is through the Ministry of State Participation. Formally, these conglomerates are part of the state, but their subsidiaries may be publicly quoted companies whose major or indeed only shareholder is the state. Their structure is that of large holding companies which own other subsidiary holding companies, and the input of the state is predominantly through the 'peak' companies. In principle, they are supposed to operate with full managerial autonomy in accordance with commercial criteria. Nevertheless, their size and the strategic nature of their holdings tends to put them directly in the political arena. These groups tend to be differentiated from one another by industrial sector – steel, chemicals, construction, telecommunications. They have their own employers' organisation, *Intersind*. The dominant trade union in these sectors has been the metalworkers federations, the *metalmeccanici* or FLM, who for much of the period have operated with a high degree of unity across the three main trade union confederations CGIL, CISL and UIL.

The Southern Development community have generally worked closely with the public sector organisations, but are structurally differentiated from them by their electoral weight and their different expertise. This community could almost be said to be brought into being with the establishment of the Fund for the South (*Cassa per il Mezzogiorno*) in 1950. This was given special responsibilities and large sums of money for more than thirty years, during the course of which it developed both considerable technical expertise in large-scale public works and a large patronage-based clientele. As befits a powerful lobby-cum-service organisation, the *Cassa* has generally had direct access to ministerial authority through the Minister with special responsibility for the South, a ministry without portfolio which nevertheless has usually been given to senior DC figures, as we saw in chapter 5.

The private sector groupings in industry are less internally differentiated and are made up of the large traditional oligopolistic companies dominating their individual sectors – FIAT for the automobile industry, Pirelli for tyres and rubber, Olivetti for office and electronic equipment, Ferruzzi for food processing. Montedison in petrochemicals and chemicals is a separate case, as it has been operating in sectors close to those of ENI, the state-owned public sector conglomerate. Montedison is therefore an exception to the normal pattern, as its relationships with other large companies have generally been highly competitive. It is also unusual in that its ownership has been shared between the public and private sector for most of the time, though it is now firmly in the hands of the private sector conglomerate Ferruzzi. These groups have dominated the employers' confederation

*Confindustria* for the entire post-war period, albeit with differing strategies at times. Their links with political society have tended to be weak, as their traditional parties the Liberals and Republicans have too small a vote to exercise major influence, though the Republicans have a considerable reputation as the natural home for progressive technocrats. Until the mid-1970s they generally had no natural allies within the DC. [1]

This has not necessarily made relationships with the DC conflictual (except as mentioned above in the case of Montedison). On the contrary, there tended to be a tacit division of labour within the Italian economy, accepted by both major sets of employers, public and private, within industry. The lack of political base for the private sector was partially compensated by the strength of their links with key actors in administration. La Palombara's now classic analysis emphasises the importance of their relationship with the Ministry of Industry. [2] This was certainly been very fruitful for them, not only in enabling them to have an early input into legislation which might affect their interests, but also in legitimating and enhancing their claim to represent Italy's national interest in these issues. But this relationship, referred to by La Palombara as the *clientela* relationship, did not survive the intense politicisation of all ministries which took place as the DC gradually extended their scope and reinforced their permanence in office during the 1950s and 1960s. The division of roles between the DC and the large private sector left the latter with their traditional privileged relationship with the Northern finance community. That this was partly owned by the public sector was not directly relevant. The major national banks were owned by the public sector conglomerate IRI, and the Bank of Italy which regulates the financial community is nominally under public control. Nevertheless, it is clear that the extent of political control over these institutions has generally been limited. The priorities of the Bank of Italy for currency stability and good order in the marketplace have led it to work closely with the private sector industrialists, particularly through the influential public sector investment bank *Mediobanca* and particularly when Guido Carli was Governor of the Bank of Italy (1960–1975). [3] In Italian policy-making, legislation may or may not be ineffective; direct responsibility for credit provides a more certain impact, albeit within a environment whose general conditions were determined by political groups alien to the Northern liberals.

The period since 1983 saw a major shift in the conflict exchange strategies, as we saw in chapter 7. This affected industrial policy particularly, showing itself in a general decline in the capacities of the Southern Development groups and the public sector organisations. The decline is the result of diminishing public resources, the increasing conflicts between the two favoured groups, the break-up of the old consensus over the division of roles in industrial policy and the failure to replace it with new agreements which can maintain existing distributions of resources. It also results from the strength of other actors. Particularly important in this context is the much-analysed phenomenon of the 'third Italy', the networks of small enterprises in Central and North-Eastern Italy which underwent rapid growth in the 1970s and early 1980s and whose successes do not seem directly and intentionally the result of government action. In so far as it follows public policy at all, the success of the small enterprise sector seems to be associated among other factors with the limited but active development of industrial policy by the regional governments established in 1970. In general terms, these changes suggest the break-up of established complex policy communities in industrial policy (the Southern and public sector elites), a new political activism on the part of the large private sector companies (the *Confindustria group*), and the emergence of a powerful new actor previously dependent on patronage (the small and medium enterprises of the 'third Italy'). The previous structured set of relationships has been replaced by a much more conflictual and more pattern of issue networks. As a result, strategies which divided the resources and responsibilities between and within the public and private sector by agreed partition are no longer viable. In industrial policy, the capacity of the DC to maintain the existing processes of exchange, to guard the boundaries and to enforce agreements, has been undermined, to the extent that in this critical issue area, consensus has been lost and the balance of power among the various actors is highly fluid.

## EARLY POST-WAR POLICY TO 1969

The two major tendencies in industrial policy, understood either as all government activity or as strategically directed intervention as described earlier in this chapter (p. 232) were associated with minority parties in government coalitions, namely the Liberals and Republicans on the one hand and the Socialists on the other. The direction of policy in the first two decades after the war tended to follow, in very broad terms, whichever of these two was relatively predominant in the government coalition formula at the time – the

Liberals dominating the first period up to 1958, and the Socialists increasingly influential thereafter. As is usual, both sides claimed to be representing national interests while pursuing sectoral concerns. The groups most advantaged by the Liberal policies tended to be the established private sector industries of the North, who were best placed to profit from the opening up of European trade and from the removal of restrictive regulations dating from the Fascist period, and who also saw Italy's low labour costs as a historic opportunity for export-led growth at a time of rapid international expansion. The Socialists were particularly concerned to improve historically low wages and poor working conditions in the Northern factories, but they were also intent on resolving the problem of unemployment and land hunger in the South. There was therefore plenty of room for disagreement between the Liberals and Socialists. For many years after the expulsion of the Socialists and Communists from government in May 1947, the PLI and the PSI were incompatible, and they were not to find themselves supporting the same government again together until the national solidarity phase of 1976–79. But the practice of policy was always mitigated by the requirements of the Christian Democrats, who have never identified themselves unequivocally with either of these two approaches.

The DC supported in general terms the principles of Catholic social doctrine enunciated in the papal encyclical *Quadragesimo Anno*, but particularly the principle of subsidiarity, which declares that collective action should always be undertaken by the most local level of organisation possible. This enabled them to pronounce their opposition to any policy smacking of the overweening absolute state (such as centralised planning) while at the same time acknowledging the need for government action in specific sectors. Ideologically then, the DC was disposed to mix, to mitigate, to dilute the purer doctrines of the minority parties. This also suited its electoral and organisational needs, as we described in chapter 6, so that it could extend its appeal towards the lay conservative middle classes while at the same time maintaining a firm grip on its provincial Catholic vote.

The Catholic vote identified particularly with two sectors of the economy and with two regions: in sectoral terms, the artisan class in small industry, and the peasant owner-farmer, and in regional terms, the North-East (particularly the Veneto) and the Southern hinterland. The policy can thus be explained as a convergence of ideal and material interests, which also had the advantage that the strategy did not require the DC to impose a coherent authoritative view of appropriate objectives. Despite being the majority party, the DC did not see its function as identifying and pursuing an exclusive definition of national interest; on the contrary, its organic view of society and its own broad electoral base encouraged it to adapt to the views of others. DC priorities in substantial and in partisan policy-making converged around the pursuit of employment and stable growth, which in turn led to its insistence not on particular sectors or types of development but on its own control over the distribution of key managerial positions. These proved to be the most important bargaining counters not just in industrial policy but in politics as a whole (as chapter 6 describes). It is this which explains the opposition of the DC to privatisation, which it sees not in terms of specific objectives for industrial efficiency but as a loss of the strategic political levers with which it has dominated the processes of exchange.

The policy conformation as it developed in the 50s and 60s may be summarised as shown in Table 9.2.

Italy emerged from the war relatively underdeveloped, with 44 per cent of active population engaged in agriculture in 1946. Also the traditional North–South dualism which partly mirrored the agricultural cleavages was compounded by further divisions. Most salient of these were those between the public and private sector, between the traditional liberal economic elites and the emerging Catholic majority, and between the large number of small artisan industrial firms and the few industrial giants, both in the public and private sector. Initially it appeared it might be possible to return to a pre-Fascist political economy. The Liberal Party re-entered the governing coalition from May 1947 on. Through the Liberal Treasury minister Luigi Einaudi, the established oligopolistic interests of the North were able to ensure that reconstruction began under free-trade auspices, with the rapid lifting of foreign exchange controls, the selective removal of tariff barriers to foreign goods particularly manufacturing equipment and heavy machinery, and the abolition of price and supply controls in some sectors particularly foodstuffs. But for several reasons this line did not persist in its most rigorous form.

First, it was soon clear that reconstruction financed partly by Marshall Aid demanded some direct intervention by the state to ensure the rebuilding and expansion of social and industrial infra-structure, in transport and communications particularly. The instrument for such intervention was already to hand, in the shape of the public sector holding companies inherited from the Fascist regimes. Some consideration was given to dismantling these structures,

*Table 9.2* Parties and policy in industry

|  | Christian Democrats | Liberals | Socialists |
|---|---|---|---|
| resources | validation by Church and US; sole Catholic and main conservative party | traditional oligopolistic wealth, technical expertise. | intellectual and TU support; second largest coalition party; small minority vote |
| objectives | independent organisation, stable majority, social balance. | return to pre-Fascist forms, limited state budgets; economic stability | extension of political participation, employment growth |
| preferred industrial strategy | inclusive patronage, organic growth, international integration | disengagement of state; export-led growth | indicative planning; Southern development |
| value system | anti-Communist, commitment to distributive equity, socially religious conservative | anti-Communist, socially lay-conservative | pro-Communist, socially progressive |
| level of dependence | relatively low, dominant actor in coalition | high; economic influence, political subordination | moderate, scope for substantial policy, partisan constraints. |

but the option was not an obvious one and the main proponents (*Confindustria* and the Einaudi group) lacked the political influence to push through such drastic action. In 1947, IRI's central role in postwar reconstruction was reinforced by its takeover of a major shipbuilding works in Genoa through a newly-created subsidiary *Finmeccanica*. IRI's formal position was resolved by a 1948 law which enhanced its managerial independence and the potential scope of its activities. In 1951, a report by Ugo La Malfa, a junior minister and future leader of the Republicans, called for the rationalisation of state holdings, the establishment of a separate ministry of state participation, and direct accounting to Parliament for the sector. In 1953 a second major conglomerate known as ENI was put together at the behest of the DC entrepreneur Enrico Mattei from the variety of industrial companies in the petrochemical sector which had accumulated during the Fascist period.

The Ministry of State Participation was set up in 1956. During the 1950s both IRI and ENI expanded rapidly. Their function was not to supplant the large private sector industries but rather to provide indigenous support for the manufacturing base in key sectors, such as in non-specialised mass steel products through the IRI holding company *Finsider*. To the private-sector Liberals, the state participation sector was a second best solution to the problem of ensuring sufficient finance for strategically important sectors. To the DC it provided a pragmatic solution to particular industrial deficiencies without having to resort to long-term planning mechanisms and without having to integrate the management within the cumbersome legal structures of the state. The expansion of the state participation sector based on state ownership of share capital also promised to provide the majority party with extensive and relatively unaccountable control over nominations to senior management positions and over mass employment.

Second, the problem of the South presented itself in a dramatic manner from 1948 to 1950, with land occupations and widespread public disorder in the face of the failure of the government to implement land reform and investment promised earlier. The outbreak of civil disorder on a wide scale was particularly threatening because of the potential use to be made of such mobilisation by the Communists. Aside from questions of equity, which certainly played their part, the short-term political problems also provided the Christian Democrats with opportunities to develop an independent state-sponsored power base. In 1950 another state-controlled investment organisation was set up, the Fund for the South (*Cassa per il Mezzogiorno*, known as the *Cassa*). Associated with this was a limited programme of land reform, but the main function of the *Cassa* was to channel state funds into the provision of industrial and agricultural infrastructure. Here once again we can perceive a compromise between the willingness of the DC to intervene in industrial development and the concerns of the Liberals and Republicans over the health of public finance and over the principle of state support. For the first decade after the war, the restriction of the *Cassa* to public works was based on the belief that the industrial activity would develop spontaneously in the South if only its traditional weakness in infrastructure could be overcome. The emphasis on reducing the costs to Southern industrialists by improving road and rail networks, providing electrification, irrigation, adequate communication links and storage facilities, was acceptable in these terms. It was also acceptable because it provided an immediate and welcome boost in demand for the large-scale construction works whose suppliers were predominantly Northern, both public and private sector.

Changes in Southern policy match accurately the swings within the DC as well as the changing coalition environment. The initial dominance of the *Fanfaniani* in the 1950s attracted considerable undifferentiated support within the party, both because it appealed to the Catholic cultural origins of many post-war adherents and because it provided a means of building up the new party through the use of state intervention. Fanfani's first ministerial briefs were in agriculture and in public works. He and his faction used the first of these to develop policies for the small farmers in the *Coldiretti* association. Among the most active areas of policy for the DC-led governments of the 1950s were financial and technical agricultural schemes, particularly in the South. These tied the peasants into state-supported and state-run organisations – technical assistance schemes, infra-structural development, purchasing associations, many under the umbrella organisation *Federconsorzi*, and the heavily subsidised pension schemes.[4] The other main target of the activist *Fanfaniani* was the accommodation crisis in the expanding cities of the North, and they contributed with others to the establishment of large state-supported housing associations, chief among them Ina-Casa. The overall rationale for the policy adopted in the South was to use infrastructural assistance of different kinds to lower costs to entrepreneurs and to stimulate direct investment, a rationale which fitted well with the neo-Liberal macro-economic strategy of the period, even if the neo-Liberals were less than content with some of the instruments used. Underlying these policies was the presupposition, supported by influential advice from American economists, that the problem of under-employment in the South could only be resolved by a large-scale movement off the land into more efficient labour intensive industry either in the South itself or in the Northern industrial areas.

A third element in the patchwork of state intervention was the spread of policies aimed at providing direct support for small industry. If any single policy can be associated directly and unequivocally with the Christian Democrats, this would be it. Support for the small entrepreneur, for the local family retailer, for the family firm, was a constant theme of DC documents from 1943 on. It was a theme which was entirely congruent with their localistic vision of society as an organic entity of interdependent units. It was also a policy which met their need to develop a counterweight to the power of big business, whose record was considered somewhat tainted by their support for or at best failure to oppose Mussolini. But it was typical of the emerging DC style that intervention mechanisms grew slowly and without apparent design. In 1947 a special credit institute, *Artigiancassa*, was empowered and funded to provide investment for the sector. Difficulties over the scale and types of funding and criteria for distribution resulted in law 949/1952, which gave the co-ordination of funding for the entire sector of small and medium enterprises to *Mediobanca*, already emerging as the trusted vehicle for DC financial support to key sectors.

The main instruments for support were partial tax exemptions, subsidised loans, and loan guarantees, and the most important criterion for eligibility was firm size. This was made yet more complex with the so-called 'Artisan Statute', law 860/1956, which drew together the various provisions. In what was to become a pattern for such legislation, the law repeated the 1952 criterion that the scheme applied only to firms with less than ten employees, but then proceeded to refer to a variety of exceptional circumstances in ambiguous terms. For example, partnerships and limited companies up to certain sizes are eligible 'so long as members are personally involved in the work and as long as such work has a pre-eminent role over capital.' The Artisan Charter did not specify eligibility by craft, skill, occupation or sector. As Weiss argues, its effect was to open up the category to a very wide variety of manufacturing and commercial activities. The social security and tax exemptions it offered, as well as the access to subsidised loans, made it a very desirable proposition. It followed from this that control of qualification was a useful instrument for aspiring local politicians, since apart from size the main qualification was registration with the local chamber of commerce.[5]

From 1951 to 1963 Italy's GDP grew at an average annual rate of over 5 per cent. The investment base provided by industrial policy in its various forms undoubtedly contributed to this, even if indirectly, but it would be wrong to attribute the success of the 'economic miracle' solely or even predominantly to the existence of an aggressive independent and expansionist public sector, even when coupled with support for public works in the South and with subsidies to small enterprises. The steady and rapid growth of the period was much more marked in the North than in the South, and relied on particularly favourable international and domestic circumstances. The form it took exacerbated existing imbalances and made it difficult for such growth to be achieved again over such a long period. The 'economic miracle' was largely export-led, and relied on buoyant international demand together with the availability of a ready supply of cheap non-unionised labour. The relative weakness of internal demand helped ensure that balance of payments problems did not arise to curtail the expansionary fiscal policies of the central authorities or to dampen buoyant business expectations.

The period was marked by a shift of income away from wages towards profits and by a high rate of industrial investment both in the public sector and in the private sector. As predicted, it was also marked by a vast internal migration of labour from the subsistence farming of the South to the cities of the North. The fact that these were increasingly crowded and ill-equipped was a consequence of the failure of state expenditure on social investment to keep pace with investment in other sectors. In this period Italy could be said to have mitigated its 'peasant question' mainly by transferring the problem to the cities and developing an 'urban question' in the process.

From the mid-1950s on, and with increasing pace after 1959, the favoured position of the Liberals as representatives of the private sector was undermined by their further electoral decline and by their incapacity to adapt to the new implicit partition between public and private sector. By the end of the 1950s, influential private-sector industrialists such as Gianni Agnelli and Leopoldi Pirelli were voicing their willingness to accept closer relations between the DC and the Socialists in government, always subject to US agreement. Other groups in the private sector were intransigently opposed, particularly the Montedison group associated with the electricity supply trusts, who not surprisingly feared nationalisation. The increasing influence of the Socialists was felt also in the willingness of left-wing factions in the DC to consider more radical solutions to the problem of the South. In this context the state participation system emerged as an important instrument of direct intervention. Already law 646/1950, which established the *Cassa*, had laid down that 60 per cent of new public sector investment had to be in the South. This, however, had proved ineffective, not least because the state participation companies lacked specific authority to depart from standard commercial criteria, without which southern investment was unlikely. Law 634/1957 provided clearer grounds on which such investment decisions could be made, and extended the obligation to the private sector also, at a lower rate of 40 per cent of new investment.

These provisions were a recognition of the failure of the Liberal approach to stimulate self-sustaining growth in the South, but they suggested an unrealistic optimism over the capacity of legislation radically to alter entrepreneurial behaviour by command alone, without direction and financial support from the state. IRI and ENI had actually begun to expand their activities in the South from 1957 onwards. In 1962, an amendment to the 1950 law extended eligibility for Southern subsidies from small and medium enterprises to larger companies. In 1959 in the Saraceno plan a full-scale co-ordinated attempt was made to intervene through direct investment by the state. This was associated with the DC economist Pasquale Saraceno, who identified an approach to industrialisation in the South based on concentration of large industry in favoured areas so as to stimulate demand for industrial goods within the regions concerned. The plan identified eight industrial 'poles', around which large-scale public and private sector factories were to be sited. Private sector companies were encouraged to invest by the availability of long 'tax holidays' on profits as well as subsidised credit, capital grants and exemptions from social security payments. The package was extremely costly, but was regarded as a 'once-only' effort to raise investment in the South rapidly to acceptable levels. This involved the use of state-owned industry to establish and to build up the industrial poles in the selected areas, including for example a new steel mill at Taranto, modern chemical works at Bari and at Syracuse, and other very large mass-production factories elsewhere, which together became known as the 'cathedrals in the desert'.

Saraceno had earlier developed a model of financing for public sector companies which in theory enabled them to take account of social costs. Government requirements which fall outside the normal range of commercial judgement on the part of state holding companies are known in this model as *oneri impropri*, literally improper burdens. This term was not meant to suggest (at least initially) that there was an element of impropriety, only that the requirements were imposed from outside. In a well-ordered relationship between state and public sector company, it ought to be possible for the state to quantify the opportunity cost imposed on the company by the state's requirements, and to compensate it accordingly. The difficulty has tended to be that even if the commercial strategy of the company was clearly identified, the state has generally lacked the capacity to provide the detailed long-term alternative to it. As a result, when the state has required IRI, ENI and EFIM to undertake less profitable investment or to maintain unprofitable factories, usually for reasons of employment, the financial implications have been unclear and the compensation from the state short-term and ill-considered.[6]

The second phase of investment after 1959 therefore showed a much greater interest in direct planned state investment in industry, and reflected a shift of power within the DC towards the more secular technocratic orientation of the Moro faction (associated in particular with the Saraceno plan of 1959). The failure of the liberal interventions in the 50s encouraged left-wing factions in the DC, particularly *Base* and the Moro group, but also the *Fanfaniani*, to welcome socialist proposals for more coherent planned approaches. These were associated with the Giolitti plan, named after the Socialist Budget minister in the first centre-left government after the 1963 elections. The more ambitious macro-economic elements of the Giolitti plan excited considerable controversy and remained unimplemented, but the 1960s did see a considerable attempt to integrate Southern development into a national framework. The investment provided major employment opportunities for the population and symbolised a positive commitment on the part of the state, but despite the intentions of Saraceno and Giolitti the South continued to show only limited capacity to support indigenous industrial development.[7]

In a more general sense these efforts contributed to the economic integration of Italy by extending the power of important national interest groups to areas from which they had previously been excluded – particularly the technocratic public sector managers and the large trade unions, both of whom developed new constituencies and reinforced their links with the political parties through the process of rapid development and implementation of public sector industrial policy. For the trade unions the post-war growth in numbers of jobs and the state-funded expansion offered the opportunity to pay more attention to employment issues and to overcome the earlier party-political divisions to a limited extent. The public sector conglomerates also developed internal cohesion, identity and dynamism. In the 1960s particularly, the public sector managers provided Italy with tech-nocratic elites, whose function, partly self-ascribed, was to make up for the locational and financial disequilibria associated with the workings of the private sector. During what I have described as the Liberal period, the public sector conglomerates could be said to have been substitute capitalists, aiming to take economic development to the regions and sectors which the nominal capitalists did not reach. The transition to progressive industrial policy associated with the centre-left coalition governments enhanced their role and their status. Its evident ambiguities and limitations could suggest, without excessive flippancy, that after the capitalism without capitalists of the 1950s Italy moved in the 1960s to a period of socialists without socialism. The public sector management style of the period, dynamic, entre-preneurial, politically sophisticated and socially aware, was a model much admired and studied outside Italy.[8] The industrial policy of the time was dominated by agreement of substance about strategic objectives led by the public sector, including collaboration with the peak trade union organisations, and with interchangeability of membership between the political representatives and the senior managers. The governing parties also profited directly, since the construction contracts and mass recruitment of labour for building and for operating the factories enabled them to develop sophisticated patronage networks, strengthening the implicit consensus around Christian Democrat methods, and ensuring that the aims of policy remained within the overall framework of DC control.

## THE DECLINE AND BREAK-UP OF THE POLICY GROUPS

The problems referred to above contributed to the disintegration of the industrial policy consensus after 1969, but an important part was also played by the changing international environment and by the party-political changes. Industrial policy was a core part of the overall strategic management of development by the DC and its allies. Its objectives of growth, employment and social stability depended on a precarious equilibrium not only among the competing groups but also in Italy's international relationships. The exchange rate turbulence and increased energy costs of the early 1970s exacerbated Italy's worsening trading position. Internally, the equilibrium had been upset by the industrial unrest which culminated in the 'hot autumn' of 1969. This had three important long-term consequences for industrial policy. Firstly, after initial trade union difficulties in controlling the shop-floor revolt, the movement came under increasing union direc-tion and resulted in the reinforcement of trade union organisation in the large factories of the North and its extension to areas from which it had previously been absent. Unions also discovered wide areas of potential co-operation among themselves. They began to claim a voice nationally and locally with increasing success, thereby threatening both the traditional mediation of the governing parties and the domination of the Left by the Communist Party. Secondly, the wage gains of the 1969–72 period dealt a severe blow to the competitive advantage based on Italy's low labour costs, since they brought Italy onto levels comparable with its main West European trading partners. As we saw in chapter 8, this shift was reinforced by the wage indexation agreement of 1975 known as the *scala mobile*. This was much more evident in the North and Centre than in the South, so a side-effect was to sustain and even to encourage investment in the South when investment elsewhere was falling. Finally, the hot autumn resulted in a considerable improvement in the statutory employment conditions for labour in large-scale industry, particularly over redundancy and pension rights. These were codified in the Worker's Statute of 1970. Partly in response to the increased rigidity in the labour market which these changes led to, governments became more involved in industrial relations both in national negotiations with unions and employers, and in the enhancement of provisions for temporary lay-offs of labour. The most important scheme by which governments attempted to mitigate some of the effects of the new balance of power was the *cassa integrazione*. This is a fund subsidised by the state which enables registered employers to lay off workers temporarily at close to normal earnings levels. The *cassa integrazione* was intended to apply for the first six months of redundancy only, as purely temporary measure. In practice, this time limit was generally ignored, and the *cassa integrazione* became a substitute for more formal structured redundancy measures – a further example of temporary solutions achieving permanency. Another effect of the difficulties of the period was the very rapid growth in the size of the informal labour market, associated with the increase in the numbers of small firms and the rigidities of the official labour market.[9]

Industrial policy in the 1970s shows clearly the efforts of government to use the state to maintain the advantages of the strongest groups, rather than to restructure towards sectors nominally given priority such as research and development and high technology investment. Support for the South was maintained and enhanced in law 183/1976, which acknowledged the role of the newly established regional governments in economic development without, however, providing a genuine transfer of power from the *Cassa per il mezzogiorno* to the regions. The industrial salvage role of the public sector was formalised in law 184/1971, which established a new publicly owned conglomerate GEPI, supported by the existing state-owned companies, with the specific purpose of intervening in support of loss-making private-sector companies. Measures such as this illustrate graphically the close practical relationship between public and private sector, in which despite the constant overt bickering between the two sectors the state has been expected to step in at critical times and support industries regarded as politically sensitive, or to assist in the restructuring plans of the big private companies by acting as 'buyer of last resort.'

One episode which demonstrated vividly the problems of the public sector was the troubled lifespan of the EGAM conglomerate. This was first instituted formally in 1958 as the metallurgy and mining holding company. It did not function fully until 1973, and then soon lost its first chairman Mario Einaudi in a scandal over misuse of company funds for political purposes. EGAM accumulated a very large operating deficit in a brief period of time and was wound up in 1977. An instructive aspect of its career, apart from its political patronage uses and its commercial weakness, is that its subsidiaries were not generally wound up, but were distributed as unwelcome non-paying guests to the other rather healthier public sector conglomerates. Though the state had a battery of legislation at its disposal, its mechanisms of political control rested on the Ministry of State Participation, which was rarely able to exercise political direction over its charges either in good times or in bad. As a result, the cohesive and determined managers of the established conglomerates IRI and ENI were able to assume a considerable degree of political independence, both for patronage purposes and for the objectives of industrial strategy. Their domination in key areas such as steel has been well-documented,[10] and it resulted in intense counter-cyclical measures to sustain employment and growth against international trends.

The brief period of PCI support for the government resulted in another attempt to draw together the disparate strands of industrial strategy with law 675/1977, on industrial restructuring. This was intended to provide a national framework for industrial policy within which sectoral and regional actors could pursue specific objectives. The law was heralded at the time as a major innovation which would overcome the fragmentation of the various sectoral activities.

One of the major objectives was support for small and medium industry, to which was added the aim of promotion of high-technology development, and again the long-term objectives were largely overrun by the need to support unprofitable but politically sensitive traditional industries. In 1983 the then Minister for Industry Filippo Pandolfi declared that his major aim was to rewrite the existing laws on industrial policy in order to redirect support towards national objectives such as export promotion. The difficult economic climate of the 1980s has seen the restructuring and partial privatisation of some public sector industry, and the development of aggressive multinational private sector conglomerates to challenge the predominance in industrial policy of the established interests of FIAT and Pirelli.

These saw for the first time a definite impetus to put parts of the public sector back in private hands. The most spectacular example was the sale of the state-owned car manufacturer Alfa Romeo to FIAT in a controversial and difficult agreement. This was part of the move by the socialists to establish an independent political consitutency for themselves. It also relates to the financial and operating problems of the state sector at a time when the public sector deficit is a particularly sensitive political issue. These problems did much to damage the professional reputation of the public sector managers and in the process weakened their political influence. In 1989 the Socialist Treasury Minister Giuliano Amato pushed through a major law preparing the public sector for privatisation. The difficulty with this process is partly that of finding buyers, particularly since the government has shown a strong preference for domestic industrial interests. But it is also that there are strong political interests within the DC which seek to maintain the state's role as a provider of employment and as a champion of national objectives.[11] A further problem is that increasingly Italy's use of state funds has been criticised by the European Commission as anti-competitive. In this instance two traditional DC policies – state involvement in industry and vocal support for European integration – come into conflict. Finally, the private sector industrialists have become increasingly active politically, willing to seek partners outside their traditional range, impatient of the inefficiencies and distortions which they perceive in government policy as a whole. Industrial policy has therefore become increasingly an arena of conflict, in which there is no obvious majority coalition.

The role of industrial policy in Italy's successful maintenance of growth is difficult to assess. One authoritative researcher characterised policy as 'defensive', and argued that its success in pursuing regional development and export promotion was not matched by equivalent successes in restructuring unprofitable enterprises or promoting high technology development.[12] Indeed, one of Italy's best known successes in industrial development is the so-called 'third Italy' already referred to in this chapter. Made up of networks of small enterprises operating under the umbrella of common credit, marketing and distribution services,[13] these owe little directly to national policy, and appear to be much more the result of traditional artisan flexibility supported by loose but strongly localised networks in regional and local government. The 'third Italy' is particularly a characteristic pattern of economic activity in the two regions of the centre and North-east, Emilia-Romagna and the Veneto. It has been associated both with decentralising strategies by large employers and with flexible specialisation by existing small and medium enterprises. Support by national government, which is piecemeal and channelled through regional government, is a critical means of ensuring access to investment credit lines. It is, however, only one factor, and is part of a context in which there is a high degree of congruence between the aims of industrial development and the existing social and political structures. Such congruence is not widespread, and particularly is not found in the Southern development. The greatest successes of Southern development have been the result of determined and cohesive managerial elites applying solutions from the outside; such efforts are difficult to sustain over long periods, and are untypical of the general pattern of public policy-making in these sectors. Furthermore, the political consensus which gave rise to the development of the political and managerial elites in Southern policy and in the public sector has broken up. The context of industrial policy at the end of the 1980s was predominantly short-term political brokerage rather than consistent sectoral planning. In this sense it reflects the increasingly conflictual patterns of policy-making overall which have been associated with the decline of the DC dominance of the exchange processes and the decay of the conventions by which they operated.

## NOTES

1 The private sector has been comparatively neglected in studies of Italian industry until recently. See particularly Friedman, A., 1988; Scalfari and Turani, 1974; Marchi, A., and Marchionetti, R., 1992; Peruzzi, 1987; more generally, Bianchi, C. and Casarosa, C., *The recent performance of the Italian economy – market outcomes and state policy* (Milano, Franco Angeli, 1991).

2 La Palombara, J., *Interest groups in Italian politics* (Princeton, NJ, Princeton U.P., 1964); but also Ranci, P., 'Italy: the weak state' in Duchene F. and Shepherd, G. (eds) *Managing industrial change in Western Europe* (London, Pinter, 1987); Prodi, R., 'L'intermediazione politica nell'economia', pp. 369–379 in Cavazza and Graubard 1974.

3 For Carli's views on industrial and economic policy during these years, see Carli 1988.

4 On DC Southern policy, see Allum, P.A., 'Thirty years of southern policy in Italy', *Political Quarterly* 1981; Graziano, A., 'The Mezzogiorno in the Italian economy' *Cambridge Journal of Economics* 1978; Rossi-Doria, M., *Dieci anni di politica agraria nel Mezzogiorno* (Bari, Laterza, 1972).

5 Weiss, L., *Creating capitalism – the state and small business since 1945* (Oxford, Basil Blackwell, 1988).

6 Treves, 1970.

7 Lo Cicero, M., 'Development finance: market and planning' in *Mezzogiorno d'Europa* no.1, January/March 1984; Martinelli, F., 'Public policy and industrial development in southern Italy: anatomy of a dependent industry' in *International Journal of Urban and Regional Research*, vol. 9, pp. 47–81.

8 See for example Holland, S., *The state as entrepreneur* (London, Weidenfeld and Nicolson, 1972).

9 Contini, 1989.

10 Eisenhammer, J., 'The politics of the state steel industry', pp.39–61 in Quartermaine, L.,1987; Merloni, F. and Ronzani, S., 'The local implementation of the national strategy – the case of steel in the 1970s', paper presented at the ECPR workshop 'The local management of national industrial problems'. ECPR Joint workshop sessions 1984.

11 Bianchi, P., 'Privatisation of industry: the Alfa Romeo case', pp.109–125 in Nanetti, R. *et al.*, *Italian politics – a review*, vol.2 (London, Pinter Press, 1988); Forte, F., 'L'impresa pubblica/privata, grande/piccola', pp.339–368 in Cavazza and Graubard 1974.

12 Del Monte, 1980 p.163–4.; Farini, R. and Schiantarelli, F., 'Italy', pp.97–118 in *Journal of Public Policy* vol.3 no.3 1983.

13 The concept is originally developed by Bagnasco, A., *Tre Italie* (Bologna, il Mulino, 1977); see also Brusco, S., 'The Emilian model; productive decentralisation and social integration', *Cambridge Journal of Economics* vol.6 no.2 1982; Weiss, L., 1988.

# Chapter 10

# Conclusion
## Challenges to representation

### AUTHENTIC CRISIS?

In this chapter I return to the themes laid out in chapter 1 and outline the forces for change. In one sense, the beginning of the 1990s is precisely the wrong time to be writing about the development of political processes in Italy. Forty years of 'hyper-stability' (to use Sartori's term) are giving way to unguided change. After several decades of 'make do and mend', in which crisis has frequently been declared and just as frequently proved illusory, the forty-year pattern appears finally to be breaking down at the beginning of the 1990s. What this chapter seeks to do is to identify the major new challenges to the prevailing distribution of power, to locate them within the existing structures, and to assess the possibilities for substantive change in policy on important issues.

A period of dramatic electoral and organisational change culminated (at least temporarily) in an unprecedented loss of votes by the DC in the elections of April 1992, a loss which was greatest in the areas where they had previously been strongest, namely the Catholic North-east. In the areas of Lombardy and Veneto, the separatist parties won sufficient seats to make themselves the fourth largest grouping, on a radical platform of tax revolt and public order issues. The government coalition which followed contained the usual parties, but was reliant on outside support. Despite the personal reputation of the Prime Minister Giuliano Amato, it lacked even the usual initial modicum of authority. At the same time, magistrates in Milan and elsewhere began to unravel extraordinary networks of corruption involving senior politicians, and in so doing struck a further blow at the authority of the governing parties, whose methods were revealed to be based on sustained and widespread abuse of public office for party ends. As the economy moved deeper into recession in the summer of 1992, the lira fell prey to national and international doubts about the capacity of the economy to sustain the costs of ERM membership and of convergence towards monetary union within the EC. This not only pushed the lira out of the ERM, it also demanded a fundamental change of policy from the new government. The crisis of the parties became the point of convergence of a dual challenge, from the Italy of the provinces and from the international economic community.

This is a crisis of representation in the most general sense, in that it threatens to break the link between authoritative political decisions and those affected by them. The crisis invests the capacity of the political forces to respond to the ever-widening break between state and society, and within society. This shows itself in many ways. Among the most important of these is the failure to satisfy sectoral demands by any means other than short-term patronage agreements funded by public expenditure. Genuine representation is replaced by the transmission of interests whose selection from this point of view is arbitrary. The resulting agreements lack popular support, but the system has in the past shown itself too weak to take more effective action to reform economic policy, since this might risk provoking the veto of one of the many special interests whose association with factions in the governing coalition can be critical to its survival. At its core, the crisis is a major conflict between those who are most effectively represented by the political parties and those who are both under-represented and proportionately bearing a higher tax burden.

As we have seen throughout this study, the breakdown of representation also affects Italy's cultural and geographical identity, as well as more prosaically the national institutional mechanisms. The political crisis then is not merely the old conflict between contending political forms. That conflict was resolved in a particular way over a long period of societal change and political mobilisation, resulting in a rigid framework for exchange of political goods between interdependent but conflicting actors. Conflicts between how people ought to be represented have been treated as subject to the same bargaining as arguments about substantial allocation of resources. This helps explain the intense pluralism in the forms of representation, and the capacity of the system to mediate many different societal groups. The precarious equilibrium of social and political forces on which this relied has broken down, as the old mass parties and their mass organisations dissolve into more unstable forms. This is a crisis of national institutions, but as well as its national origins, it has occurred under pressure from a variety of local and international challenges. These we now look at, and then conclude with a general review of the prospects for future development.

## LOCAL CHALLENGES

In modern civil society, a single individual may be a member of several organised groups, both formal and informal, each of which may give the individual a different point of access and a different form of representation. The three most obvious types of group in modern Italy are the local political party, the trade union or professional association, and the family. As well as these, there are voluntary associations involved in charitable or leisure activities, local and national pressure groups campaigning on single issues, and territorial associations amalgamating elements from all of these, such as the Chambers of Commerce and the Chambers of Labour. This last category has usually been regarded as of secondary importance, partly because of its numerical weakness, and partly because of dependence on the political parties and their subsidiary organisations. The bond with the political parties is a mix of ideology and pragmatism. Rhetoric apart, the nation has only had a distant call on the individual's grudging efforts, backed by a centralised administrative apparatus regarded as corrupt and arbitrary. Traditionally, the focus of loyalty has been family relationships first, and after them, relationships which can extend or at least mimic family links. The home locality has a strong call even for migrant families, a call supported by enduring family ties to the area of origin and rooted in centuries of historical divisions. This loyalty may include the small economic enterprises active in the local community – indeed, the capacity of the small firms to survive and to thrive depends on the intensely local nature of the support networks which provide finance, services and a path through bureaucratic regulations. But the loyalty does not generally stretch to the large-scale national firms. The political organisation reflects this dichotomy, with the larger firms expecting to exert pressure directly at senior government levels, which have traditionally been closed to the regionally based associations of smaller firms.

As we saw in chapters 2 and 4, the response of the Liberal state to the intensity of local political culture was to attempt to impose central control through legal forms and through administrative ubiquity, centred on the prefect and the province. Though the prefectoral and provincial apparatuses have withered, other forms of control have arisen. The novelty and the strength of the post-war mass parties lay, among other things in their capacity to use the local ties to form political organisations, developing eventually into the complex networks which channel social demands throughout the administrative and political institutions.

These also have changed. The regional reforms of the 1970s altered profoundly the way the state dealt with the periphery. But they did so in a typically Italian way, overlaying the old institutions with new ones, blurring responsibilities and leaving critical issues to the mercies of continuing political bargains. The main change undoubtedly has been that centre–periphery relations are now intensely political, where previously they were subject to pervasive and rigid legal regulation. A new set of regional political groups has developed, which has been able to establish important roles for itself, particularly in the areas of territorial regulation, industrial credit and health provision. Though limited, these local government responsibilities all imply extensive scope for local political decision-making. Furthermore, the constitution permits regional governments to establish their own administrations independently of central government. Particularly in the North and Centre, where party control was stable, some used this to develop technocratic management styles utterly different from the ossified rites of central government. A corollary of this is that often the administrative personnel are politically homogeneous with the elected representatives, forming a regional political elite of considerable potential.

These alternative elites have been among the most aggressive in their relations with the central government, and have successfully established for themselves a national voice through organisations such as the National Conference of Regional Presidents, and claims on the allocation of funds and responsibilities. The relationship has been conflictual but has remained within the boundaries set by national party politics. In this sense, the regional governments, directly elected and politically homogeneous, fit the multiple conflict pattern described in chapter 7, and are among the strong groups increasingly favoured by the beleaguered national authority. The dangers of this integration are now being seen. Where the state is weak, the target for discontent is not the government as such but the parties and social organisations held directly responsible. The failure of the state at the end of the 1980s brought into question the parties and trade unions – not only the governing parties, but all associated with them. The involvement of all in the continuous bargaining which kept the system going rendered all vulnerable when the costs could no longer be sustained. This included the regional political elites, who reflected more directly than the central apparatus of the state the origins the aspirations and the methods of the post-war parties because they were more directly the creation of the post-war republic. Though the revolt at the end of the 1980s against the state was a revolt of the regions, the existing regional elites could not voice the radical local discontents. They were only of use in extracting resources from a benign central patron, not in challenging the assumptions of the share-out. Their reputation for modern management (where it existed, mainly in the North and Centre) served as no defence, merely demonstrating that technocracy can serve disreputable purposes. Their direct involvement in the corruption of public sector contracts contaminated central government as well as regional administration. Their regional base helped little either: their implication in the perceived sins of central government was too great, and the regions which they served were too much the artificial creations of governments.

It is not surprising that the challenge to the system comes not in the form of a new mass national party but as a regional anti-party. But the potentiality of the electoral revolt should not be over-stated; what the *Lega Lombarda* opposes is reasonably clear, but what it stands for has yet to be determined. The localisms on which it relies are not deep-rooted loyalties to a region. They are based on a common strong sense of belonging to a city or town and to its hinterland. This may imply strong rivalry with cities and towns nearby. The Lombardy to which the *Lega* refers is its own cultural amalgam, which has yet to prove a political capacity beyond that of uniting many different local loyalties against a common central enemy. This is true of the *Lega Nord*, the Northern league of which it is the dominant component. Its authoritarian leader Mario Bossi has been able to tap rich seams of fiscal resentment, in a manner reminiscent of the *Poujadist* surge in the French Fourth Republic. Its themes are those common to populist right-wing parties in Europe – public order, immigration, exploitation by central bureaucracy, covert racism. In this case these are exacerbated by the powerful positive appeal to generic local loyalties, an appeal which the national parties used as a prop for the patronage system and which they now find turned against them.

The novelty of the new separatist parties does not lie particularly in the vigour with which they espouse radical change; post-war Italy has a long tradition of such movements, some of which pursued terrorist strategies, some street protest and some the parliamentary route. What is new is that they are mobilising the Northern components of the sensitive electorate whose acquiescence was essential to the early success of the DC and thereby of the post-war Republic (see chapter 6, pp.144–145). As we saw in chapter 6, the urban provincial self-employed have been treated with particular favour by the dominant political parties. In part this is because of their numerical strength, in part because of their alleged propensity to seek authoritarian solutions. The resurgence of their traditional themes at the beginning of the 1990s indicates the failure of the DC strategy, which relied on the incentives of economic growth and the threat of Communist government to integrate them into Italian liberal democracy. They benefited more tangibly than any other group from Italy's economic successes. But now, in times of recession and with the Communist threat dissipated, they object to the adverse consequences of the bargain in terms of redistribution of tax revenues towards the poorer regions. The threat of secession which they represent is in some senses no more than an extreme version of the traditional refusal of significant vested interests to accept their allotted share of the costs of national economic development. In this sense it is therefore a conventional revolt, even if a dangerous one also.

## THE INTERNATIONAL ARENA

For four decades the domestic market in political goods has been sustained by the international structures within which Italy has had to work, or at least by domestic interpretations of the constraints. In foreign policy, Italy was the compliant friend of the United States, ardent vocal supporter of European integration, and a loyal if not central member of NATO. A muted counterpoint to this theme could occasionally be heard, in the form of Italy's efforts to find an independent energy policy in the 1950s and 1960s, and in occasional efforts to establish special relationships with Arab countries (but much less successfully, for example, than Spain, whose foreign policy had some significant similarities). Notwithstanding these relatively cautious forays, it is not unfair to say that a genuine home-grown foreign policy was difficult to identify. Towards the end of the 1970s this began to change dramatically, as Italy developed a more active foreign policy.

There were several reasons for this. In part, it reflected the political and economic instability of the Southern Mediterranean and the Middle East region, particularly in regard to Italy's former colony and long-term sparring-partner Libya. It expressed itself in a spate of disputes with Libya about treatment of emigrants, about trading relations and about military and commercial access to the island of Malta. Also it was the result of increased Soviet interest in a Mediterranean role for its Black Sea fleet, which it built up considerably at the end of the 1970s. These developments did not threaten Italy's established status as 'Nato's Bulgaria'. But the slow pace of European integration and the weakness of the European response to the turbulence of the 1970s certainly did cause Italian policy-makers to consider their scope for independent action within the Mediterranean region. This was associated with increased pressure from Italy's private sector industrialists. Their support for integration into the Western alliance had been critical to the domestic success of this policy. That it entailed a passive government strategy in foreign affairs was not of immediate concern, since the domestic multi-nationals were well able to conduct their own relations with foreign governments. The oil shocks of 1973 and 1979, the currency instability of the mid-1970s, the world recessions of the period and declining domestic profits caused the public and private sector industrialists to become more active in seeking foreign partners and to require more of their government. Symbolic of this was the sale of 15 per cent of FIAT shares in 1976 to the Libyan state holding-company (a share later bought back in better times). Italy's commercial links with its traditional partners in the Near East began to expand further, particularly in petrochemicals and defence industries and through the public sector corporations. Politicians could be found in the mainstream parties to give voice to the 'Mediterranean temptation', or even to what was sometimes referred to as the 'Habsburg dimension' – Italy's relations with the countries of central-southern Europe. Libyan retaliation against Italy for the US bombing of Tripoli in 1986, though ineffective, was an unwelcome reminder of the extent to which Italy had concentrated its military efforts on the North-East border with Yugoslavia and Austria to the detriment of its Mediterranean capability.

These were, however, muted counterpoints to the predominant theme of integration and foreign policy stability. The end of the post-war division of Europe affected Italy directly, and not only in foreign policy. The instability engendered by the changes of the late 1980s made new demands on a political elite unused to dynamic foreign policy. One immediate and untypical response was an initiative in 1989 by the Foreign Minister Gianni De Michelis to establish Italian leadership of a Central–Southern European bloc – the 'Pentagonal group' including Italy, Yugoslavia, Austria, Czechoslovakia and

Hungary. The instability of some of the countries concerned soon made this enterprising effort by De Michelis appear rather premature. The break-up of Yugoslavia was dealt with by Italy within the framework of the intergovernmental co-operation procedures of the European Community, and did not therefore result in autonomous policy initiatives on its part.

The increased pace of trade integration after 1986 together with the emerging EC divisions between North and South found Italy lagging in the first case and torn between camps in the second. As one of the largest economies of the new Community, Italy might have been expected to take a lead in several sectors of integration policy – the size of its public sector, the strength of its small enterprises, the persistence of internal regional disparities, the size of its agricultural sector, all provided Italy with issues and potential allies. That it failed to develop a new role for itself must be attributed to some extent to the scepticism of Italy's European partners about Italy's capacity to implement the required reforms and to their concern over government instability, but it also reflected the lack of salience of such issues in the domestic political market. European integration is a totem around which all can gather, not an item of currency in decision-making. Also, though Italy is not especially favoured by the Common Agricultural Policy, it has consistently been the largest net gainer from European Community structural funds in the 1980s. Any increase in support to other Southern European countries would either be from existing EC funds, in which case Italy's share of structural funds would probably diminish, or would require an increase in the contributions from the largest states, in which case Italy would have to pay more to the Community coffers. The dilemma is enhanced by the fact that EC structural support for Italy goes overwhelmingly to the South, making it a sensitive issue for the Northern Leagues.

Annual reports from the European Commission on the implementation of Single Market directives repeatedly showed Italy to be lagging behind. In a relatively rare example of successful institutional change, this was resolved in 1990 by the development of new institutional mechanisms in Parliament to speed up the processes, and by 1992 Italy was no longer Europe's most notorious miscreant in these matters. But the institutional changes in Parliament were not typical of the political processes as a whole. Unlike some other member states, Italy did not tend to use EC policy as a justification for unpopular measures at home. Clear examples of Italy's unwillingness to use the 1992 project to force unwelcome restructuring on its industrial base were its conflict with the European Commission over steel capacity and its persistent use of state subsidies to support the recurrent costs of public sector manufacturing in the South. As we saw in chapter 8, the exchange rate mechanism of the European monetary system combined with domestic objectives to produce very high interest rates. In 1992, Italy's failure to sustain the lira within the ERM was a severe blow to its European credentials, but it enabled the Amato government to reduce interest rates and to set realistic targets both for the reduction of PSBR and for the stimulation of growth.

In domestic policy the major effect of these changes was to remove the veto on the entry of the second largest party into government, partly because of their internal responses to the upheavals in the USSR, and partly because of the reduced salience of the specific foreign policy issue. The new PDS does not appear as threatening as the old PCI, and the Soviet Union no longer divides and disrupts internal compromise. However, the conditions under which the veto ceased to be used were extremely unfavourable. As we saw in chapter 6, in the 1970s the PCI leadership had argued that it would be undesirable for it to join a weak government at a time of crisis. For its part, the price for its agreement to join a government has always included coalition commitment to structural reforms. The failure of the historic compromise from 1976 to 1979 confirmed this principle. As a result, when in the summer of 1992 the traditional governing parties evinced a willingness to include the PDS in coalition negotiations, this was not met with immediate enthusiasm by the former Communists. The notional acceptability of the PDS did not result in more stable government but merely added a further variable to a complex equation. The effect of international changes was to exacerbate rather than to alleviate internal conflict, both by requiring unaccustomed responsiveness from governments and by removing the frameworks which had previously restrained domestic political argument within manageable limits.

## SURVIVAL AND CHANGE IN ITALIAN POLITICS

The result of these combined challenges is an authentic crisis at the heart of the political institutions, affecting their most basic operations. The system is governed by a complicated process of exchange, and is acknowledged by participants to be so. This helps explain what the processes of policy-making are, but it does not explain how the system as a whole maintains itself. In general, including the processes of barter, the political system is sustained by the functionality of its own operations. Chapter 1 identified the process of representation as central to the 'efficient secret' of Italian politics. This was broken down into three related functions: leadership, participation and legitimation. These functions, put more simply, relate to how political decisions are applied, how solidarity is maintained within groups and within the system, and how political consent is sustained by collective values. It is these which are now in crisis.

One of the problems with the conventional piecemeal approach to policy is that the logic connecting these processes is incomprehensible to most. Quite how Italy sustains itself in bad times and flourishes periodically can appear an affront to reason. The transaction costs of the exchange are very high – so high that on occasions they seem to threaten the entire fabric, and certainly high enough to outweigh the putative benefits on most rational calculations. Second, actors in the process describe themselves as engaged in an exchange but act as if some kinds of exchange were simply not available (particularly those involving the non-governing parties in strategic choices). What determines these boundaries of the exchange process? Why has the market usually ceased to function beyond certain pre-determined limits? Third, the terms of trade are very uncertain, so uncertain that they make calculation very difficult. For most group actors, support of various kinds does not have a fixed value in the system. The only major exception to this is the value of the ministries in the process of cabinet formation. Otherwise, benefits are uncertain, because of the complexity of the transactions, and because most individuals do not act directly in the market but depend on brokers who may be at several removes: hence the description of public policy in an earlier chapter as a 'managed lottery'. It is not surprising that the overall functionality of the political processes is more or less opaque to most observers.

This is a particular case of general problem familiar to political analysis.[1] A general formulation of the problem would have to ask a question such as 'How do institutions generate sufficient collective action to maintain themselves?'. Groups and institutions may subsist despite their failure to achieve for their members material benefits proportionate to the costs incurred. Such groups are referred to as 'latent groups'. This phenomenon, the persistence of apparently unsuccessful forms of social organisation, is an important one, and particularly in the Italian context, where the costs of participation are often very high indeed and the benefits speculative.

Latent groups are characterised by weak leadership (that is, an authority structure unable to impose effective sanctions), and a lack of individual selective benefits available to participants. They should therefore be capable of only short-term and relatively ineffective action. Yet political processes, particularly the Italian, teem with groups which on these grounds ought to be categorised as latent but which actually operate continuously and to some collective effect. It is usually argued that they should succumb to the joint effect of the free-rider and inconsequentiality syndromes. Each individual knows that his or her own contribution is of small consequence, and can hope to take a free-ride on the contributions of others without endangering the success of the project; and each individual knows that others are subject to the same temptation, that their contribution may not be forthcoming and that his or her own efforts may therefore be wasted.[2] Such groups, lacking the prerequisites of strong leadership and selective benefits to individuals, ought to fail in the face of the unwarranted and disproportionate amount of trust required for them to take collective action. In the Italian case they ought all to be deterred by the costs involved, by the limited prospects of success for all but a limited few, and by the uncertainty surrounding the process of exchange.

In a more general sense, it would not be exaggerating greatly to say that the entire political system in Italy might be seen as an 'latent group', in that it lacks a generally effective regulatory framework and is disproportionately costly to its members. Members can quit their 'latent groups' – the paradigm case of a latent group is a spontaneous localised pressure group, in which participation is entirely voluntary. But most citizens do not quit the states of which they are members, and those that do usually do so only to pass directly to another by immigration. States are compulsory: the option of exit from member-ship of any state whatsoever is available to very few. What citizens may have is the option of thorough reform of a system commonly acknowledged to be in need of considerable mending. This option has been frequently considered in Italian post-war politics and rejected with equal frequency. In this sense, the Italian political institutions share important features with the latent groups.

Repeated efforts at reform over forty years have foundered, some like the Bozzi commission never resulting in legislation, others never being implemented, still others being assimilated into the pre-existing arrangements. Why do any but the restricted group at the centre participate so doggedly in a pattern of public policy determination (extreme partisan pluralism mixed with clientelism) which entails such high individual and collective costs? Why do politicians join again in governmental coalitions exactly the same as those whose record allegedly led to the unavoidable collapse of previous governments? Why has systematic reform proved so difficult to achieve? What makes the factions, pressure groups, occupational associations and minor parties cleave so strongly to the present system, whose need for reform is widely admitted? Finally, what difference to the distribution of power and process of exchange does a shock like the rapid electoral change of the early 1990s make?

The problem of the 'efficient secret' of Italian policy-making requires us to consider specifically how the functions of leadership, participation and legitimation combine to sustain the system as a whole. Functionalist explanations of collective behaviour imply that patterns of behaviour or of institutional organisation survive because they work – that is, they serve a particular purpose, logic or function within the system as a whole, where the whole is understood as a dependent variable made up of individuals, of groups and of institutional organisations.[3] This seems to reverse the proper causality, and in fact functionalism has frequently been criticised for circularity of argument. Institutional patterns are explained by their function within the system, but the institutional patterns are also responsible for the function – survival depends on function depends on survival. Functionalism is also criticised for omitting the critical element of human intentionality, for which it is alleged to substitute an implicit institutional intentionality, as if social institutions could somehow choose which patterns would succeed independently of their component groups or individual members.[4] However, functional analysis does match our perceptions that institutions make a difference to the way problems are handled. Institutions and organisations do appear to develop a logic of their own and can have interests and capacities as independent variables. The functionalist analysis has the advantage that without necessarily excluding human intentions, it enables us to locate self-sustaining processes and unintended consequences which are an important feature of institutional patterns of structure and operations. In this sense, much social science explanation is implicitly functional in its assumptions and in its terminology.

The logic behind such explanation needs clarifying. One way in which this might be expressed characterises the process as a circular interaction between the function, the group and the institution:[5]

*An institutional or behavioural pattern, X, is explained by its function, Y, for a group, Z, if and only if*
1   *Y is an effect of X;*
2   *Y is beneficial for Z;*
3   *Y is unintended by actions producing X;*
4   *Y or the causal relation between X and Y is unrecognised by actors in Z; and*
5   *Y maintains X through its impact on Z.*

The formulation rests on two connected functions – weak exercise of political authority (cycle A, leadership) and the maintenance of stable clear organisational boundaries (cycle B, integration), both of which are widespread characteristics of Italian public institutions. Cycle C refers to the belief structures by which the system is legitimated. The original formulation (by Mary Douglas) was developed for North American political systems. In the argument below, I have adapted the terminology of the functions and institutional patterns to fit the Italian experience. As above, $X$ stands for the institutional pattern of behaviour, $Y$ for the function, and $Z$ for the group (in this case the collectivity).

*Cycle A ( authority, decision-making, sanctions )*
1   *Y ( weak leadership ) is an effect of X ( a credible threat on the part of some members of Z to withdraw co-operation ); this applies at the factional level in political parties and in interest groups, and at the governmental level on the part of specific institutional interests.*
2   *Y is useful to Z because it enables rational powerful institutional actors to resist unwelcome demands on resources controlled by them ( public and private ).*
3   *Y is unintended and is not overtly recognised as an effect of X; nobody wants weak leadership as such, and when recognised it is usually attributed to policy differences or indirectly to clientelism.*
4   *Y maintains X by preventing the development of an effective regulatory framework.*

This cycle explains why genuinely common goals are very difficult to achieve in the Italian political context. Key resource holders may use the threat to withdraw co-operation to prevent the costs of membership increasing beyond the expected benefits to them. Members who need the collectivity for material support are vulnerable to those who could continue their operations outside the effective reach of public institutions. As we have seen, there are many such potential secessionists in private and public enterprise in Italy, and some indeed have already reduced their participation in the collectivity to a minimum, in the face of efforts by the state at various times to increase the proportion of costs born by those who control investment, jobs and welfare. As Douglas says, 'Consequently the affairs of the latent group will tend to be conducted by veto and backed by threats of withdrawal.'[6] The first part of this proposition, management by veto, is a commonplace of Italian political analysis. Until the rise of the separatist Leagues, the second element (threat of withdrawal) was rarely acknowledged, though its link with veto power is an accepted feature of sociological analysis.[7]

The second part of the overall explanation refers to the internal cohesion of the group.

*Cycle B (membership, boundaries, integration within groups)*

*1  Y (stable clear organisational boundaries) are an effect of X (virtual compulsory participation and solidarity within groups); it is a commonplace of Italian politics that belonging to an influential network is essential. Obedience to its internal support mechanisms follows membership.*

*2  Y is beneficial for Z (society as a whole, made up of the multitude of groups) because it consolidates membership.*

*3  Y is unintended and unrecognised as an effect of X; the stability and sharpness of the divisions is attributed to ideological conflict originating in the Cold War.*

*4  Y helps maintain X (by controlling free-riders and providing minimum standards for recognition).*

This cycle explains why the groups stay together despite the lack of clear commensurate material rewards. The risks of remaining outside are great, and it is notoriously difficult to assess how success has been achieved. For many, membership may provide little definitely attributable benefit, but non-membership brings the uncertainty inherent in exclusion.

What explains the settling of the boundaries between the institutionalised networks, and what explains the reluctance to redraw them? It is widely acknowledged that the costs of leaving the settled boundaries in their unreformed state are very high, but reform appears very difficult to achieve. A rational choice for individuals might be to seek collective agreement about reform, whose costs to the individual, though speculative, would not appear to match present levels of dissatisfaction. But this choice is not taken. The functionalist approach, having explained the weakness of sanctions and the strength of the boundaries, asks what are the cognitive elements which support and legitimate the institutional arrangements. The critical feature in this context is not the positive acceptance of values but the perception of threat, amounting at times to pervasive conspiracy theories.

*Cycle C (culture, legitimation, communication)*

*1   Y (a shared belief in external and internal danger) is an effect of X (mutual suspicion and accusations of complicity in past failures).*

*2   Y is beneficial for Z – it keeps the community together, and legitimates solidarity within certain limits prescribed by the extent of the danger.*

*3   Y is unintended; it is recognised by participants but its links with X are not widely acknowledged.*

*4   Y, the shared belief in danger, maintains X, the mutual suspicion.*

The causal link back from *Y* to *X* is indirect, dependent on the other cycles. Cycle A ensures that at best there is only limited agreement about sanctions against informal deviation and still less about positive policy. But Cycle B makes exit from existing groups costly, encouraging would-be secessionists to stay within their networks. The traditional perception of the system as fragile and vulnerable imposes a minimum internal discipline. But precisely because of the supposed fragility, political argument has to be indirect. Policy matters have been difficult to discuss directly because the debate may quickly turn to issues of legitimacy and constitutional propriety. Debate skirts the difficult, potentially destabilising but central issues of ineffective authority and radical reform, and may readily revert to coded accusations of untrustworthiness and potential betrayal. The belief in external and internal danger, together with 'rules of the game' about secrecy and conflict avoidance, legitimates the convention of conducting political debate as if in a complex interconnecting set of coded languages.[8] A summary of the analysis is given in Table 10.1.

The external and internal dangers resulted first from the Cold War, then terrorism and subversion, then the galloping budget deficit, always laced with financial scandals and the potential disrepute of clientelist practice, supported by a cynical mass opinion and a political class characterised by extreme caution. Only as the external and internal dangers recede has the political class developed sufficient confidence to consider radical institutional reform, helped by the decline of the founding generations and the emergence of politicians whose formative years were not spent under Fascism.

This pattern offers a way out of the unfortunate cyclical processes which have governed Italy. As the political elites become more confident, the mutual suspicion may lose its force. This in turn may encourage the development of effective sanctions and incentives supporting the exercise of authority. The functional logic not only explains why the system survives in its unprofitable form, it also

*Table 10.1* Functional cycles: a summary

|  | political authority (Cycle A) | boundaries, intra-group trust (Cycle B) | legitimation (Cycle C) |
|---|---|---|---|
| institutional pattern | persistent credible threat to withdraw from the inter-group co-operation | mass participation, internal solidarity | mutual suspicion, accusations of past complicity |
| function | weak leadership, enabling powerful groups to resist unwelcome demands | stable clear boundaries, consolidating membership | shared belief in internal and external threats, providing minimum collective solidarity |
| group | political parties and pressure groups | sub-cultures, political parties and pressure groups | society as a whole |

suggests that there is genuine potential to break out from the minimalist functionality which it now has.

It is in this context that particular significance attaches to the election turmoil from 1989 onwards. This apparently contingent response of the electorate makes the favourable break-out described above very difficult to achieve. This study has assumed the continuation in some form of the conditions which held for 45 years after the war, but this is an assumption which may be tested in the 1990s. The effect of the domestic and international divisions was to sustain a system characterised by intense mutual suspicion (Cycle C), by a similarly intense need to cooperate (Cycle B), and by the weakness of political authority within groups and in the institutions as a whole (Cycle A). So much explains broadly the operations of the organised groups and institutions. Underlying this institutional behaviour was on the one hand the Cold War division, and on the other hand the solid unvarying response of the electorate, which in a liberal democracy such as the Italian provides the critical if unsubtle condition for the maintenance of the institutional environment. The electorate shared to a greater or lesser extent the perceptions and anxieties of the governing groups, or at least showed themselves willing to tolerate these in sufficiently large numbers to legitimate the way the groups operated. Both these empirical conditions no longer apply.

It would be extremely unwise to attempt to speculate about the outcomes of the institutional crises of the early 1990s. What can be said with confidence is that they are the direct result of the electoral changes, which are themselves a response to changing perceptions about domestic and international conditions and about Italy's role within them. If Cycle A implied a serious weakness of political authority, it was partly compensated by the extraordinary cohesion and organisational stability of organised groups suggested by Cycle B. These two sets of conditions have changed with increasing pace, but retain sufficient of their grip on the electorate and on the elites for the logic overall still to hold for Cycles A and B. The area in which most change has occurred is precisely in Cycle C, where the logic is most susceptible to outside influences.

For better or worse, the opportunity now presents itself to seek to redraw the established institutional boundaries so as to include as appropriate those traditional groups previously excluded and the new groups whose rise has contributed to the decay of the old constraints. The existence of the old boundaries was one of the most important ways in which the political system distributed limited public goods to a large clientele without alienating entirely those who were not full participants. It is from this process of integration and fragmentation that the predominance of the conflict/dependency/exchange model originates. The electoral changes do not remove the conflict, and in the short term they may make the mutual dependency even greater. But the opening up of the system brings in groups whose view of the exchange process is radically different, and who in their different ways do not share the predispositions of the governing parties about the traditional medium of the barter. What the system therefore shows is a greater propensity to move from partisan exchange to substantive exchange – from barter based on the material benefits of office to compromise over policy. This could allow the policy differences described earlier in this work to achieve greater prominence. On the other hand, the emergence of the regional separatists could be seen as symptomatic of the strength of traditional territorial ties and the continued virulence of the strain of suspicion and mistrust in Italian political culture – cycles B and C above. If this were to prove predominant, the external divisions of the Cold War would be replaced by the internal divisions over identity and allocation of resources. But the functional consequences in this case would be different, since the regional political culture does not replicate the weak authority of the national state (our original cycle A). On the contrary, it could be seen as an attempt to activate the threat of secession implicit in the refusal to accept overarching collective authority.

The consequences then according to this analysis could be either benign for the future of the national state or extremely dangerous for it. If the conventional mistrust is merely transferred from the international to the domestic arena, it is unlikely that the conventional structures of solidarity, participation and membership which are already much altered in any case, could sustain political representation and other national political processes in the long term. If, on the other hand, the national political culture changes sufficiently for the traditional elites to be able to impose unwelcome solutions through the exercise of political authority, the functional cycles above could be replaced by altogether more positive processes of decision, participation and legitimation. In either case, Italy now faces major choices about representation and reform.

## NOTES

1 See for example Olson, M., *The logic of collective action* (Cambridge, Mass., Harvard U.P., 1971).
2 Olson 1971, pp.5–52.
3 For a critical review of functionalism, see Dowse, R.E., 'A functionalist's logic', pp.607–622 in *World Politics*, vol.18 1965–66; more generally, Easton, D., *Varieties of political theory* (Englewood Cliffs, NJ, Prentice Hall, 1966).
4 Dowse 1966, pp.607–622.
5 Douglas, M., *How institutions think* (London, Routledge, 1987) p.33; see also Elster, J., *Logic and society* (Chichester, Wiley, 1978).
6 Douglas 1987, p.38.
7 On veto power, see Douglas' comments (1987, pp.38–40); but also Merton 1968; Lipset, S.M., *Political man – the social bases of political action* (New York, Doubleday 1960).
8 Douglas 1987, pp.45–53.

# Select Bibliography

Aberbach, J.D., Putnam, R.D. and Rockman, B.A., *Bureaucrats and politicians in Western democracies* (London, Harvard U.P., 1981)

Accornero, A. (ed.), *L'identità communista* (Roma, Editori Riuniti, 1983).

Adams, P. and Barile, P., *The Government of Republican Italy* (Boston, Houghton Mifflin, 1966).

Adams, P. and Barile, P., 'The implementation of the Italian constitution', *American Political Science Review*, March 1953.

Addis, E., 'Banca d'Italia e politica monetaria: la riallocazione del potere fra Stato Mercato e Banca centrale', pp.73–96 in *Stato e Mercato* no.19 aprile 1987

Alford, R.R. and Friedland, R., *Powers of theory* (Cambridge, Cambridge U.P., 1985)

Allen, K. and Stevenson, A., *An introduction to the Italian economy* (Oxford, Martin Robertson, 1974)

Allum, P.A., *Politics and society in post-war Naples* (Cambridge, Cambridge U.P., 1973).

Allum, P.A., 'Thirty years of southern policy in Italy', *Political Quarterly* 1981.

Amato, G., *Economia, politica e istituzioni in Italia* (Bologna, Il Mulino, 1976).

Ammassari, P., Garzonio dell'Orto, F. and Ferraresi, F., *Il burocrate di fronte alla burocrazia* (ISAP Archivio 1968, Milano, Giuffrè, 1969).

Amyot, G., *The Italian Communist Party* (London, Croom Helm, 1981).

Ancisi, A., *La cattura del voto – sociologia del voto di preferenza* (Milano, Franco Angeli, 1976).

Anderson, E.N. and Anderson P.R., *Political institutions and social change in continental Europe in the nineteenth century* (Berkeley, University of California Press, 1967).

Andreotti, G., *Intervista su De Gasperi* (Bari, Laterza, 1977).

Angotti, T., 'Playing politics with disaster – the earthquakes of Friuli and Belice', pp.327–331 in *International Journal of Urban and Regional Research*, vol.1 no.2 January 1978.

Arlacchi, P., *Mafia peasants and great estates* (Cambridge, Cambridge University Press, 1983).

Ascoli, U. (ed.), *Welfare state all'italiana* (Bari, Laterza, 1984).

Baget-Bozzo, G., *Il partito cristiano al potere, la DC di De Gasperi e di Dossetti* (Firenze, Vallecchi, 1974).

Bagnasco, A., *Tre Italie* (Bologna, Il Mulino, 1977).

Balducci, M., 'Fonction publique en transition: le cas italien', pp.322–330 in *Revue Internationale des Sciences Administratives*, no.3–4, 1982.

Barbera, A. Barcellona, P., Bonifacio, F.P., Ferrara, G. and Manzella, A. *Il Parlamento tra crisi e riforma* (Milano, Franco Angeli, 1985).

Barbera, A. and Bassanini, F. (eds), *I nuovi poteri delle regioni e degli enti locali* (Bologna, Il Mulino, 1978).

Barcellona, P., Barbera, A., Modica, E. and Ingrao, P. *Riforme istituzionali e riforme della politica* (Roma, Claudio Salemi (ed.) Sezione formazione e scuole di partito del PCI, 1983).

Barth Urban, J., *Moscow and the Italian Communist Party* (London, I.B.Tauris, 1986).

Bassanini, F. and Visco, V., 'Ecco perche il bilancio è fuori controllo', p.5 in *La Repubblica* 20 marzo 1985.

Battaglia, R., *Storia della resistenza italiana* (Torino, Einaudi, 1964).

Bellamy, R., *Modern Italian social theory* (London, Polity Press, 1987).

Benson, J.K., 'Networks and policy sectors: a framework for extending interorganisational analysis', in Rogers, D. and Whitten, D., (eds), *Interorganisational coordination* (Iowa, Iowa State University Press, 1982).

Berger, S. and Piore, M., *Dualism and discontinuity in industrial societies* (Cambridge, Cambridge U.P., 1980).

Berti, G., 'La riforma dello stato', pp.447–492 in Graziano, L. and Tarrow, S.G., *La crisi italiana* (Torino, Einaudi, 1979).

Berti, G., 'La politique de choix des fonctionnaires en Italie', pp.137–147 in Debrasch, C., *La fonction publique en Europe* (Paris, Editions du CNRS, 1981).

Bianchi, G., *L'Italia dei ministeri: lo sfascio guidato* (Roma, Editori Riuniti, 1981).

Bianchi, C., and Casarosa, C., *The recent performance of the Italian economy – market outcomes and state policy* (Milano, Franco Angeli, 1991).

Bianchi, P., 'Privatisation of industry: the Alfa Romeo case', pp.109–125 in Nanetti, R. *et al.*, *Italian Politics – a review*, vol.2 (London, Pinter Press, 1988).

Bibes, G., *Le système politique italien* (Paris, P.U.F., 1974).

Birch, A.H., *Representative and responsible government* (London, Allen and Unwin, 1972).

Blackmer, D. and Tarrow, S. (eds), *Communism in Italy and France* (Princeton, New Jersey, Princeton U.P. 1975).

Bobbio, N., *Stato, governo, società* (Torino, Einaudi, 1985).

Bobbio, N., 'Gramsci and the concept of civil society', pp.139–161 in Bobbio, N., *Which socialism – Marxism, Socialism and Democracy* (intro. and ed. by Bellamy, R., London, Polity Press, 1987).

Bocca, G., *Storia dell'Italia partigiana* (Bari, Laterza, 1977).

Bova, S. and Rochat, G., 'Le forze armati in Italia', pp. 463–486 in Farneti, P. (ed.), *Il sistema politico italiano* (Bologna, Il Mulino, 1973).

Brunetta, R., *Spesa pubblica e conflitto* (Bologna, Il Mulino, 1987).

Brusco, S., 'The Emilian model; productive decentralisation and social integration', *Cambridge Journal of Economics*. vol.6 no.2 1982.

Burke, E., *On government, politics and society* (ed. B.W.Hill, London, Fontana, 1975).

Caciagli, M., *Democrazia Cristiana e potere nel Mezzogiorno: il sistema democristiano a Catania* (Firenze, Guaraldi, 1977).

Cafagna, L., 'Italy 1830–1914', pp. 279–328 in Cipolla, C.M. (ed.), *The Fontana Economic History of Europe* vol.3 pt.1, *The emergence of industrial societies* (Glasgow, Fontana/Collins, 1973).

Calamandrei, P., 'L'ostruzionismo di maggioranza,' pp.129–136, 274–281, 433–150 in *Il Ponte*, April May and June 1953.

Calandra, P., *Storia dell'Amministrazione Pubblica in Italia* (Bologna, Il Mulino, 1978).

Camera dei Deputati – Senato della Repubblica, *Relazione della Commissione Parlamentare per le riforme istituzionali* (2 vols. Roma, 29 gennaio 1985).

Candeloro, G., *Il movimento cattolico in Italia* (Roma, Editori Riuniti, 1974, 3rd edn.).

Cappelletti, M., Merryman, J.H. and Perillo, J.M., *The Italian legal system* (Stanford, Calif., Stanford University Press, 1967).

Caracciolo, A., *Il Parlamento nella formazione del Regno d'Italia* (Milano, Giuffrè, 1960).

Caracciolo, A. (ed.), *La formazione dell'Italia industriale* (Bari, Laterza, 1969).

Carli, G., *Pensieri di un ex governatore* (Pordenone, Edizioni Studio Tesi, 1988).

Carocci, G., *Il Parlamento nella storia d'Italia* (Bari, Laterza, 1964).

Cassese, S., 'Special problems of budgetary decision-making in Italy', pp.254–267 in Coombes, D.(ed.), *The power of the purse* (London, Allen and Unwin, 1976).

Cassese, S., *Questione amministrativa e questione meridionale* (Milano, Giuffrè, 1977).

Cassese, S., *Burocrazia ed economia pubblica – cronache degli anni '70* (Bologna, Il Mulino, 1978).

Cassese, S., *Il sistèma amministrativo italiano* (Bologna, Il Mulino, 1983).

Cassese, S., 'The higher civil service in Italy', pp.35–71 in Suleiman, E. (ed.), *Bureaucrats and policymaking – a comparative overview* (London, Holmes and Maier, 1984).

Castronovo, V., 'Il potere economico e il fascismo', pp.47–88 in Quazza, G.(ed.), *Fascismo e società Italiana* (Torino, Einaudi, 1973).

Catti De Gasperi, M.R., *De Gasperi, uomo solo* (Milano, Mondadori, 1965).

Cavazza, F. and Graubard, S., *Il caso italiano* (Milano, Garzanti, 1974).

Cavazzuti, F., *Debito pubblico ricchezza privata* (Bologna, Il Mulino, 1986).

Cendalli Pignatelli, A., 'Italy: the development of a late developing state', pp. 163–199 in Rose, R. (ed.), *Public employment in Western Europe* (Cambridge, Cambridge U.P., 1985).

Cheli, E. (ed.) *Costituzione e sviluppo delle istituzione in Italia* (Bologna, Il Mulino, 1978).

Chiarante, G., 'A proposito della questione democristiana: democrazia, valori cristiani, società borghese', pp.27–42 in *Critica Marxista* vol.15 1975.

Chubb, J., *Patronage, power and poverty in southern Italy* (Cambridge, Cambridge U. P., 1982).

Clark, M., *Modern Italy 1870–1980* (London, Longman, 1984).

Clarke, M., *Corruption – causes, consequences and control* (London, Frances Pinter, 1983).

Collin, R., 'The police in Italy', in Roach, J. and Thomaneck, J. (eds), *The police and public order in Western Europe* (London, Croom Helm, 1985).

Collin, R., *The De Lorenzo gambit – the Italian coup manquè of 1964* (London , Sage, 1976).

Consiglio dello Stato, *La Riforma della Pubblica Amministrazione – stato di attuazione del Rapporto Giannini* vol.1, 21 febbraio 1984 (Roma, Servizio Studi del Consiglio dello Stato, 1984).

*Constitution of the Republic of Italy – Rules of the Chamber of Deputies and of the Senate of the Republic* (Rome, Research Services of the Chamber of Deputies and of the Senate of the Republic, 1979).

Contini, B., 'The irregular economy of Italy – a survey of contributions', pp.237–250 in Feize, E. (ed.), *The underground economies – tax evasion and information distortion* (Cambridge, Cambridge University Press, 1989).

Cornwell, R., *God's Banker – an account of the life and death of Roberto Calvi* (London, Gollancz, 1983).

Cotta, M., *Classe politica e parlamento in Italia* (Bologna, Il Mulino, 1979).

Croce, B., *A History of Italy 1871–1915* (Oxford, Clarendon Press, 1929).

Daalder, H., 'The Italian party system in transition: the end of polarised pluralism,' pp.216–236 in *West European Politics*, vol.6 no.3 July 1983.

Dal Co, M., and Perulli, P., 'The trilateral agreement of 1983: social pact or political truce?', pp. 157–170 in Jacobi, O. *et al.* (eds), *Economic crisis, trade unions and the state* (London, Croom Helm, 1986).

Davis, J., *Conflict and control – law and order in nineteenth-century Italy* (London, Methuen, 1988).

De Felice, R., *Interpretations of Fascism* (Cambridge, Mass., Harvard University Press, 1977).

De Felice, R., *Fascism – an informal introduction to its theory and practice* (Ann Arbor, Mich., University of Michigan, 1976).

De Gasperi, A., 'Il programma della DC per la nuova costituente', pp.23–24 in *Atti e documenti della Democrazia Cristiana 1943–1967* (Roma, Edizioni Cinque Lune, 1968).

De Rosa, G., *Il Movimento Cattolico in Italia, dalla restaurazione all'età giolittiana* (Bari, Laterza, 1972).

De Tocqueville, A., *Democracy in America* (New York, Harper and Row, 1966).

Del Monte, A., 'The impact of Italian industrial policy 1960–1980', pp.128–164 in Scase, R., *The State in Western Europe* (London, Croom Helm, 1980).

Della Sala, V., 'Government by decree: the Craxi government and the use of decree legislation in the Italian Parliament', pp.8–24 in Nanetti *et al.* 1988.

Delzell, C., 'The Italian anti-fascist resistance in retrospect: three decades of historiography', pp.66–96 in *Journal of Modern History*, vol.47 no.1 March 1975.

Demofilo (pseudonym of A. de Gasperi), 'Idee ricostruttive della DC, luglio 1943', pp.1–8 in *Atti e documenti della Democrazia Cristiana 1943–1967* (Rome, Edizioni Cinque Lune, 1968).

Dente, B., 'Centre–local relations in Italy: the impact of the legal and political structures', pp.125–148 in Meny, Y. and Wright, V. (eds), *Centre – periphery relations in Western Europe* (London, Allen and Unwin,1985).

Di Nolfo, E., 'The United States and Italian Communism 1942–1946: World War Two to the Cold War', pp.74–94 in *Journal of Italian History*, vol.1 no.1 Spring 1978.

Di Palma, G., *Surviving without governing – the Italian parties in Parliament* (Berkeley, Calif., University of California Press, 1977).

Douglas, M., *How institutions think* (London, Routledge, 1987) .

Dowse, R.E., 'A functionalist's logic', pp.607–622 in *World Politics*, vol.18 1965–66.

Dunleavy, P., *Democracy, bureaucracy and public choice* (London, Harvester/ Wheatsheaf, 1991). .

Dunleavy, P., and O'Leary B., *Theories of the state* (London, Macmillan, 1987).

Easton, D., *Varieties of political theory* (Englewood Cliffs, NJ, Prentice Hall, 1966).

Eisenhammer, J., 'The politics of the state steel industry', pp.39–61 in Quartermaine, L. (ed.) *Italy today - patterns of life and politics* (Exeter, Exeter University Press,1987, 2nd edition).

Elia, L., 'La forma di governo nell'Italia odierna,' pp. 26–31 in *Quaderni Costituzionali*, vol.11 no.1 aprile 1991.

Ellwood, D., *Italy 1943–1945* (Leicester, Leicester U.P., 1985).

Elster, J., *Logic and society* (Chichester, Wiley, 1978).

Falconi, C., *La chiesa e le organizzazioni cattoliche in Italia 1945–1955* (Torino, Einaudi, 1956).

Fargion, V., 'L'Assistenza Publica in Italia dall'unità al fascismo', pp.25–70 in *Rivista Trimestrale di Scienza dell'Amministrazione*, vol.2, 1983.

Farneti, P., *Il sistema politico italiano* (Bologna, Il Mulino, 1973).

Farneti, P., *The Italian party system 1945–1980* (intro. and ed. Finer, S., London, Frances Pinter, 1985).

Feit, S., *The armed bureaucrats* (Boston, Houghton Mifflin, 1978).

Feiwel, G.R., *The intellectual capital of Michal Kalecki* (Knoxville, University of Tennessee Press, 1975).

Ferraresi, F., *Burocrazia e politica in Italia* (Bologna, Il Mulino, 1980).

Ferrera, M., *Il Welfare State in Italia* (Bologna, Il Mulino, 1984) pp. 27–37.

Ferrera, M., *Reforming the Reform – the Italian Servizio Sanitario Nazionale in the 1980s*, Centro de Estudios Avanzados en Ciencias Sociales, Instituto no.13, Juan March Madrid, Working Papers January 1991.

Flora, P., and Heidenheimer, A.J., *The development of welfare states in Europe and America* (London, Transaction Books, 1981).

Flora, P. (ed.) *Growth to limits – the Western European welfare states since World War II* (5 vols, Berlin, Walter de Gruyter, 1986).

Friedman, A., *Agnelli and the network of power* (London, Harrap, 1988).

Furlong, P.F., 'State, finance and industry in Italy', pp. 142–171 in Cox, A.W.(ed.), *The state, finance and industry* (Brighton, Harvester Press, 1986).

Furlong, P.F., *The Italian Christian Democrats – from Catholic movement to conservative party* (Hull Papers in Politics no. 25, Hull 1983).

Furlong, P.F., 'The constitutional court in Italian Politics' pp.7–23 in *West European Politics* vol.11 no.3, July 1988.

Furlong, P.F., 'The constitution, the constitutional court and political freedom in Italy', unpublished paper delivered to the Conference on Constitutions and political freedom, University of Warwick, September 1989.

Furlong, P.F., 'Parliament in Italian politics' pp.52–66 in *West European Politics*, vol.13 no.3, July 1990.

Furlong, P.F.,'The Vatican in Italian politics', pp.63–79 in Quartermaine L. (ed.) *Italy today – patterns of life and politics* (Exeter, Exeter University Press, 1987, 2nd edition).

Furlong, P.F., 'Authority, change and conflict in Italian Catholicism' pp.116–132 in Gannon, T., (ed.) *World Catholicism in Transition* (London, Macmillan, 1988).

Furlong, P.F., 'Political terrorism in Italy – responses reactions and immobilism', pp.57–90 in Lodge, J.(ed.) *Terrorism – a challenge to the state* (Oxford, Martin Robertson, 1981).

Furlong, P.F., 'The last Congress of the PCI', pp.267–273 in *Government and Opposition*, vol.26 no.2, Spring 1991 .

Furlong, P.F., 'Economic recession and political underdevelopment in Italy', pp.142–171 in Cox, A.W.(ed.) *State responses to the recession in Europe* (London, Macmillan, 1985).

Fusaro, C., 'La legge sulla presidenza del Consiglio, primi adempimenti a otto mesi dall'entrata in vigore', pp.349–373 in *Quaderni Costituzionali* a.IX n.2 agosto 1989.

Galli, G., *L'Italia sotterranea: storia, politica e scandali* (Bari, Laterza, 1983).

Galli, G. (ed.), *Il comportamento elettorale degli italiani* (Bologna, Il Mulino, 1968).

Galli, G., *Fanfani* (Milano, Feltrinelli, 1976).

Galli, G., *I Partiti Politici* (Torino, UTET, 1974).

Galli G. and Prandi, A., *Patterns of political participation in Italy* (New Haven, Conn., Yale U.P., 1970).

Gambale, S., *Struttura e ruolo del bilancio dello stato in Italia* (Bologna, Il Mulino, 1980).

Gerschenkron, A., 'Notes on the rate of industrial growth in Italy', pp.360–375 in *Journal of Economic History*, vol.15 1955.

Gerschenkron, A., *Economic backwardness in historical perspective* (Cambridge, Mass., Harvard University Press, 1962).

Giannini, M.S., *Rapporto sui principali problemi dell'amministrazione dello stato*, in Atti Parlamentari, Senato della Repubblica 11 July 1980.

Ginsborg, P., *A history of contemporary Italy – society and politics 1943–1988*, (London, Penguin, 1990).

Ginsborg, P., 'The communist party and the agrarian question in southern Italy 1943–1948', pp.81–101 in *History Workshop Journal*, no.17 1984.

Golden, M., *Labor divided – austerity and working class politics in contemporary Italy* (London, Cornell U.P., 1988).

Goodman, J.E., 'Monetary policy in France Italy and Germany', pp.171–201 in Guernieri, P. and Padoan, P. (eds), *The political economy of European integration* (London, Harvester/Wheatsheaf, 1989).

Gramsci, A. *Selections from the Prison Notebooks* (Hoare, Q. and Nowell Smith, G. (eds), London, Lawrence and Wishart, 1971).

Gramsci, A., *Quaderni del Carcere* (Edizione critica dell'Istituto Gramsci, a cura di Valentino Gerratana, Torino, Giulio Einaudi Editore, 4 volumes, 1975).

Gramsci, A., *La quistione meridionale* (Roma, Editori Riuniti, 1974, 3rd edn).

Gramsci, A., *Political writings 1921–1926* (London, Lawrence and Wishart, 1976).

Graziano, L., 'Patron–Client relations in southern Italy', pp.3–34 in *European Journal of Political Research* vol.1, 1973 .

Graziano, L., 'Vecchia e nuova scienza politica in Italia', pp. 109–137 in Graziano, L., Easton, D., and Gunnell, J. (eds), *Fra scienza e professione – saggi sullo sviluppo della scienza politica* (Milano, Franco Angeli, 1991).

Graziano, L., 'The development and institutionalisation of political science in Italy', pp.41–57 in *International Political Science Review*, vol.8 no.1 1987.

Graziano, A., 'The Mezzogiorno in the Italian economy', *Cambridge Journal of Economics*, 1978.

Gregor, A.J., *Italian fascism and developmental dictatorship* (Princeton, NJ, Princeton University Press, 1979).

Harper, J.L., *America and the reconstruction of Italy, 1945–1948* (Cambridge, Cambridge U.P., 1986).

Harries-Jenkins, G., 'Armed forces in European society', pp. 286–314 in Archer, M. and Giner, S., *Contemporary Europe* (London, Routledge, 1978).

Hayek, F., *Individualism and economic order* (Chicago, University of Chicago Press, 1948).

Hayek, F., *The constitution of liberty* (London, Routledge, 1960).

Heidenheimer, A.J., Heclo, H., and Adams, C.T., *Comparative public policy – the politics of social choice in Europe and America* (London, Macmillan, 1983, 2nd edn).

Hildebrande, G., *Growth and structure in the economy of modern Italy* (Cambridge, Mass., Harvard U.P.,1965).

Hirschman, A.O., *Exit voice and loyalty* (Cambridge, Mass., Harvard U.P., 1979).

Hoare, Q. and Nowell Smith, G., (eds), *Selections from the Prison Notebooks* (London, Lawrence and Wishart, 1971).

Hobsbawm, E.J., *Primitive rebels* (Manchester, Manchester University Press, 1974).

Hobsbawm, E., *The Italian road to socialism – an interview with Giorgio Napoletano*, (Westport, Conn., Hill Press, 1977).

Holland, S., *The state as entrepreneur* (London, Weidenfeld and Nicolson, 1972).

Homans, G.C., *Social behavior: its elementary forms* (New York, Harcourt Brace, 1961).

Huntington, S., *The soldier and the state* (Cambridge, Mass., Bellknap Press, 1957).

*I programmi dei governi repubblicani* (Roma, Centro Romano Editoriale,1978) pp.91–178.

Irving, R.E.M., *The Christian Democratic parties of Western Europe* (London, RIIA/Allen and Unwin, 1979).

Jacobi, O., Jessop, B., Kastendiek, H. and Regini, M. (eds) *Economic crisis, trade unions and the state* (London, Croom Helm, 1986).

Jemolo, A.C., *Chiesa e stato in Italia dall'unificazione a Giovanni XXIII* (Torino, Einaudi Editore, 1974).

Kalecki, M., 'Political aspects of full employment,' *Political Quarterly*, vol.14, 1943.

Katz, R., *The fall of the House of Savoy* (New York, Macmillan, 1971).

Kertzer, D., *Comrades and Christians* (Cambridge U.P., 1980).

Kindleberger, C.P., 'Banking and industry between the two wars,' pp.7–28 in *Journal of European Economic History*, vol.13 no.2, Fall 1984.

Kitchen, M., *Fascism* (London, Macmillan, 1976).

Kogan, N., *The politics of Italian foreign policy* (London, Pall Mall Press, 1963).

La Malfa, U., *Intervista sul non-governo* (Bari, Laterza, 1977).

La Palombara, J., *Democracy, Italian style* (New Haven, Conn., Yale U.P., 1987).

La Palombara, J., *The Italian Labour movement – problems and prospects* (Ithaca, NY, Cornell UP, 1957).

La Palombara, J., *Interest groups in Italian politics* (Princeton, NJ, Princeton U.P., 1964).

Lane, D., 'How FIAT managed to get out of a corner by putting the foot down', p. 27 in *The Guardian*, 8 April 1987.

Lange, P., and Tarrow, S.G. (eds), *Italy in transition: conflict and consensus* (London, Frank Cass, 1980).

Lange, P., Ross., G. and Vannicelli, M., *Unions – change and crisis* (London, Allen and Unwin, 1982).

Lange, P. and Regini, M. (eds), *Stato e regolazione sociale* (Bologna, Il Mulino, 1987).

Lange, P. and Regini, M., 'Regolazione sociale e politiche pubbliche: schemi analitici per lo studio del caso italiano', pp. 97–121 in *Stato e Mercato*, no.19, April 1987.

Leonardi, R. and Wertman, D.A., *Italian Christian democracy: the politics of dominance* (London, Macmillan, 1989).

Leonardi, R., Nanetti, R.Y. and Putnam, R.D., 'Italy – territorial politics in the postwar years: the case of regional reform', pp.88–107 in *West European Politics*, special edition on Tensions in the territorial politics of Western Europe, vol.10 no. 4 1987.

Lijphart, A., *The politics of accommodation* (Berkeley, University of California Press, 1975, 2nd edition).

Lindblom, C., 'The science of muddling through', pp.79–88 in *Public Administration Review*, vol.19 1958.

Lipset, S.M., *Political man – the social bases of political action* (New York, Doubleday 1960).

Lo Cicero, M., 'Development finance: market and planning', in *Mezzogiorno d'Europa*, no.1, January/March 1984.

Locatelli, G., *Irpiniagate – Ciriaco De Mita da Nusco a palazzo Chigi* (Rome, Newton Compton Editore, 1989).

Locke, J., *The second treatise on government* (Oxford, Basil Blackwell, 1966).

Lutz, V., *Italy – a study in economic development* (London, Allen and Unwin, 1962).

Luzzatto Fegis, *Il volto sconosciuto degli italiani* (Milano, Giuffrè, various years).

Lyttelton, A., *Italian Fascisms from Pareto to Gentile* (London, Jonathan Cape, 1973).

Mack Smith, D., *Italy – a Modern History* (Ann Arbor, University of Michigan Press 1969).

Mack Smith, D., *Cavour* (London, Methuen, 1985).

Mack Smith, D., *Mussolini* (London, Weidenfeld and Nicholson, 1981).

Mafai, M., *L'uomo che sognava la lotta armata* (Milano, Feltrinelli, 1984).

*Mafia e Potere Politico* – relazione di minoranza e proposte unitarie della commissione parlamentare d'inchiesta sulla mafia (Roma, Editori Riuniti, 1976).

Magister, S., *La politica vaticana e l'Italia 1943–1978* (Roma, Editori Riuniti, 1979).

Malintoppi, A., 'Italy: Universities adrift', pp. 103–124 in Daalder, H., and Shils, E. (eds), *Universities, politicians and bureaucrats – Europe and the United States* (Cambridge, Cambridge U.P., 1982).

Mannheimer, R., *Il mercato elettorale, identikit dell'elettore italiano* (Bologna, Il Mulino, 1987).

Mannheimer, R. and Allum, P.A., 'Italy', in Crewe, I. and Denver, D., *Electoral change in Western democracies* (London, Croom Helm, 1985).

Manzella, A., *Il Parlamento* (Bologna, Il Mulino, 1977);.

Marchi, A. and Marchionetti, E., *Montedison 1966–1989* (Milano, Franco Angeli, 1992).

Martinelli, F., 'Public policy and industrial development in southern Italy: anatomy of a dependent industry' in *International Journal of Urban and Regional Research.*, vol.9, pp. 47–81.

Mason, T., 'Italy and modernisation' pp.127–147 in *History Workshop Journal*, vol.25, Spring 1986.

Meade, R.C., *Red Brigade – the story of Italian terrorism* (London, Macmillan, 1990).

Meisel, J.H., *The myth of the ruling class* (Ann Arbor, Michigan, University of Michigan Press, 1962).

Merloni, F. and Ronzani, S., 'The local implementation of the national strategy – the case of steel in the 1970s', paper presented at the ECPR workshop 'The local management of national industrial problems' ECPR Joint workshop sessions 1984.

Merton, R., *Social theory and social structure* (New York, Free Press, 1968).

Meynaud, J., *Rapport sur la classe dirigeante italienne* (Lausanne, Etudes de Science Politique, 1964) (ed.).

Miglio, G.F. (ed.) *Verso una nuova costituzione* (2 vols, Milano, Giuffre, 1983).

Mignella Calvosa, F., 'Stato e burocrazia in Italia: un'analisi storico-sociale (1923–1975)' pp.158–197 in *Revue Internationale de Sociologie*, 1978.

Miliband, R., *The state in capitalist society* (New York, Basic Books, 1969).

Mill, J.S., *Utilitarianism, liberty and representative government* (London, Dent, 1910).

Momigliano, F. (ed.) *Le Leggi della Politica Industriale in Italia* (Bologna, Il Mulino, 1986).

Montesquieu, *The spirit of the laws* (trans. Cohler, A. *et al.*, Cambridge, Cambridge University Press, 1989).

Morisi, M., *Parlamento e politiche pubbliche* (Roma, Edizioni Lavoro, 1988).

Mosca, G., *The ruling class* (ed. A. Livingston, New York, McGraw-Hill, 1939).

Myrdal, G., *Asian Drama – an enquiry into the poverty of nations* (London, Penguin, 1968).

Nanetti, R., Leonardi, R. and Corbetta, P. (eds) *Italian politics: a review*, Vol. 2 (London, Pinter, 1988).

Negri, G., 'La Camera dei Deputati dallo Statuto Albertino alla Costituente Repubblicana', pp.119–135 in *Bollettino di informazioni costituzionali e parlamentari*, settembre 1983.

Neufeld, M.F., *Italy – a school for awakening countries* (Ithaca, NY., Cornell U.P., 1961).

Niskanen, W.A., *Bureaucracy and representative government* (Chicago, Aldine Press, 1971).

O'Connor, J., *The fiscal crisis of the state* (New York, St. Martin's Press, 1973).

Offe, C., *Contradictions of the welfare state* (Cambridge, Mass., MIT Press, 1984).

Olson, M., *The logic of collective action* (Cambridge, Mass., Harvard U.P., 1971).

Onida, V., 'The historical and constitutional foundations of the budgetary system in Italy' pp.215–236 in Coombes, D. (ed.), *The power of the purse* (London, Allen and Unwin, 1976).

Orfei, R., *L'occupazione dello stato – democristiani e potere 1945–1975* (Milano, Longanesi, 1976).

Orfei, R., *Andreotti* (Milano, Feltrinelli, 1975).

Panerai, P. and De Luca, M., *Il Crack – Sindona, La DC, il Vaticano e gli altri amici* (Milano, Mondadori, 1975).

Parisi, A. and Pasquino, G., 'Changes in Italian electoral behaviour: the relationships between parties and voters', pp.6–30 *West European Politics*, vol.2 no.3 October 1979 .

Pasquino, G., *Degenerazioni dei partiti e riforme istituzionali* (Bari, Laterza, 1982).

Pasquino, G., 'The debate on institutional reform', pp.117–133 in Leonardi, R. and Nanetti, R., *Italian politics: a review*, vol I (London, Frances Pinter, 1986).

Pasquino, G., 'That obscure object of desire: a new electoral law for Italy', pp.280–294 in *West European Politics*, vol.12 no.3, July 1989.

Pennock, R. and Chapman, J. (eds), *Nomos X – Representation* (New York, Atherton Press, 1968).

Perez, R., *Le procedure finanziarie dello stato* (Milano, Franco Angeli, 1980).

Peruzzi, C., *Il caso Ferruzzi* (Milano, Il Sole – 24 Ore, 1987).

Petroni, G., 'La Pubblica Amministrazione: analisi delle disfunzioni e indirizzi di riforma', pp.749–824 in Miglio, G.F. (ed.), *Verso una nuova costituzione* (2 vols, Milano, Giuffrè, 1983).

Pinto, D. (ed.), *Contemporary Italian sociology – a reader* (Cambridge, Cambridge U.P., 1981).

Pitkin, H.F., *The concept of representation* (Berkeley, University of California Press, 1967).

Pizzorno, A., *I soggetti del pluralismo* (Bologna, Il Mulino, 1980).

Pizzorno, A., 'I ceti medi nei meccanismi di consenso', pp. 315–338 in Cavazza, F. and Graubard, S., *Il caso italiano* (Milano, Garzanti, 1974).

Poggi, G., 'The church in Italian politics 1945–1950', pp.133–155 in Woolf, S.J., *The rebirth of Italy* (London, Longman, 1972).

Poulantzas, N., *Political power and social classes* (London, New Left Books, 1973).

Powell, J.D., 'Peasant society and clientelist politics,' pp. 411 ff. in *American Political Science Review*, vol.64, 1970.

Predieri, A., *Il processo legislativo nel Parlamento italiano* (Milano, Giuffrè, 1974).

Pressman, J.L. and Wildavsky, A.B., *Implementation* (Berkeley, Calif., University of California Press, 1973).

Procacci, G., *History of the Italian people* (Harmondsworth, Penguin, 1968).

Putnam, R., 'The political attitudes of senior civil servants in Britain, Germany and Italy', pp. 86–126 in Dogan, M., *The Mandarins of Western Europe* (New York, Sage, 1975).

Putnam, R.D., *The comparative study of political elites* (Englewood Cliffs, NJ, Prentice Hall, 1976).

Quazza, G., *Resistenza e storia d'Italia* (Milano, Feltrinelli, 1976).

Regini, M., 'Social pacts in Italy', in Scholten, I. (ed.), *Political stability and neo-corporatism* (London, Sage, 1987).

Regini, M., 'The crisis of representation in class-oriented unions' in Clegg, S., Dow, G. and Boreham, P. (eds), *The state, class and the recession* (London, Croom Helm, 1983).

Revelli, M., 'Defeat at FIAT', pp. 96–109 in *Capital and Class*, no.16, Spring 1982.

Rhodes, R.A.W., *Power dependence, policy communities and intergovernmental networks*, Essex Papers in Politics and Government no. 35, September 1985.

Rhodes, R.A.W., *The national world of local government* (London, Allen and Unwin, 1986);.

Richardson, J. and Jordan, G., *Governing under pressure – the policy process in a post-parliamentary democracy* (Oxford, Martin Robertson, 1979).

Romeo, R., *Breve storia della grande industria in Italia* (Milano, La Nuova/Cappelli, 1961).

Rose, R., *Ministers and ministries – a functional analysis* (Oxford, Clarendon Press, 1987).

Rossi-Doria, M., *Dieci anni di politica agraria nel Mezzogiorno* (Bari, Laterza, 1972).

Ruffolo, G., 'The Italian educational crisis', pp. 24–74 in *Review of Economic Conditions in Italy*, January 1975.

Ruffolo, G., *Rapporto sulla programmazione* (Bari, Laterza, 1973).

Ruffolo, G., 'Project for Socialist planning', pp.69–84 in Holland, S., *Beyond capitalist planning* (Oxford, Basil Blackwell, 1978).

Ruggeri, G., 'Come fatica lo Stato ad investire – parla il Ragioniere dello Stato', pp.1–2 in *Il Messagero*, 14 febbraio 1985.

Salomone, A.W., *Italy in the giolittian era – Italian democracy in the making 1900–1914* (Philadelphia, University of Pennsylvania Press, 1960).

Salvadori, M., *Il mito del buongoverno* (Torino, Einaudi, 1960).

Salvati, M., 'The impasse of Italian capitalism' pp.3–33 in *New Left Review*, November 1972, n.76.

Salvemini, G., *Stato e chiesa in Italia* (Opere II, vol. III, Conti E. (ed.), Milano, Feltrinelli Editore, 1969).

Sani, G., 'Political culture in Italy: continuity and change' in Almond, G.A. and Verba, S., *The Civic Culture Revisited* (Boston, Little Brown, 1980).

Sartori, G., *Teoria dei partiti e caso italiano* (Milano, Sugarco Edizioni, 1982).

Sartori, G. 'European political parties – the case of polarised pluralism', pp.137–176 in La Palombara, J. and Weiner, M., *Political parties and political development* (Princeton, NJ, Princeton U.P., 1966).

Sartori, G., 'Il caso italiano – salvare il pluralismo e superare la polarizzazione', pp.675–678 in *Rivista Italiana di Scienza Politica*, a.IV n.3, dicembre 1974.

Sartori, G., 'Rivisitando il pluralismo polarizzato', pp.196–223 in Cavazza, F. and Graubard, S., *Il caso italiano* (Milano, Garzanti, 1974).

Sartori, G., *Parties and party systems* (Cambridge, Cambridge U.P., 1976).

Sassoon, D., *The strategy of the Italian Communist Party, from the resistance to the historic compromise* (London, Frances Pinter, 1981).

Sassoon, D. (ed.) *The Italian communists speak for themselves* (London, Spokesman Press, 1978).

Sawyer, M., *The economics of Michal Kalecki* (London, Macmillan, 1985).

Scalfari, E. and Turani, S., *Razza Padrona – storia della borghesia di stato* (Milano, Feltrinelli, 1974).

Schmitter P. and Lehmbruch, G., *Trends towards corporatist intermediation* (London, Sage, 1979).

Schumpeter, J., *Capitalism, Socialism and Democracy* (London, Allen and Unwin, 1943).

Scoppola, P., *La proposta politica di De Gasperi* (Bologna, Il Mulino, 1977).

Sereni, E., *Il mezzogiorno all'opposizione* (Torino, Einaudi, 1948).

Seton Watson, C., *Italy from liberalism to fascism* (London, Methuen, 1967).

Settembrini, D., *La chiesa nella politica italiana* (Milano, Rizzoli, 1977).

Spotts, F. and Weiser, T., *Italy – a difficult democracy* (Cambridge, Cambridge University Press, 1986).

Spriano, P., *Storia del Partito Comunista Italiano* (5 vols, Torino, Einaudi Editore, 1975).

Spriano, P., *Le passioni di un decennio* (Milano, Garzanti, 1988).

Stuart Hughes, H., *Consciousness and society* (New York, Knopf Press, 1958).

Sylos-Labini, P., 'L'evasione fiscale autorizzata', pp.9–11 in *Mondoperaio*, no.12, 1984.

Tamburrano, G., *L'Iceberg democristiano* (Milano, Sugarco edizioni, 1975).

Tarrow, S.G., *Peasant Communism in Southern Italy* (New Haven, Conn., Yale U.P., 1967).

Tarrow, S.G., *Between centre and periphery: grassroots politicians in France and Italy* (New Haven, Conn., Yale U.P., 1977) p.64.

The Economist, *Survey, the Italian economy*, 27 February 1989.

Titmus, R., *The gift relationship* (Harmondsworth, Penguin, 1970).

Togliatti, P., *On Gramsci and other writings* (London, Lawrence and Wishart, 1979).

Tosato, E., 'Sugli aspetti fondamentali dello stato', pp.1783–1816 in *Studi in memoria di Carlo Esposito* (Padova, Cedam, 1972).

Tozzi, S., *Pressioni e Veicoli* (Milano, Giuffrè, 1975).

Treves, G., 'The public corporation in Italy' in Friedmann W. and Garner, J.F. (eds), *Government enterprise, a comparative study* (London, Stevens, 1970).

Truman, D., *The governmental process* (New York, Alfred Knopf, 1951).

Turani, G., 'Nuova mappa del capitalismo', pp. 164–169 in *L'Espresso*, 30 June 1985.

Valiani, R., 'What solutions are there to Italy's public debt?' pp.75–95 in *Review of Economic Conditions in Italy*, May–August 1989.

Venditti, R., *Il Manuale Cencelli* (Roma, Editori Riuniti, 1981).

Walston, J., *The mafia and clientelism* (London, Routledge, 1988).

Webster, R.A., *The Cross and the Fasces: Christian Democracy and Fascism in Italy* (Stanford, California, Stanford U.P., 1960).

Weingrod, A., 'Patrons patronage and political parties', pp.377–401 in *Contemporary Studies in Society and History*, July 1968.

Weiss, L., *Creating capitalism – the state and small business since 1945* (Oxford, Basil Blackwell, 1988).

Wertman, D., 'The Catholic church and Italian politics: the impact of secularisation', pp.87–107 in *West European Politics*, vol.5 no.2, April 1982.

White, C., *Patrons and partisans* (Cambridge, Cambridge U.P., 1988).

Whittam, J., *The politics of the Italian army* (London, Croom Helm, 1977).

Wildavsky, A., *Budgeting – a comparative theory of budgetary processes* (Boston, Little, Brown and Co., 1975).

Wilks, S., and Wright, M., *Comparative government–industry relations* (Oxford, Clarendon Press, 1987).

Wyles, J., 'Ringmasters in control', *Financial Times* Survey – Italian Banking Finance and Investment, 22 November 1989.

Zariski, R., *Italy – the politics of uneven development* (Hinsdale, Illinois, Dryden Press, 1972).

Zuckerman, A., *The politics of faction – Christian Democrat rule in Italy* (New Haven, Conn., Yale U.P., 1979).

# Index